GOOD OWNERS GREAT DOGS

BRIAN KILCOMMONS

WITH
SARAH WILSON

WARNER BOOKS

A Time Warner Company

Warner Books, Inc., 1271 Avenue of the Americas, New York, NY 10020

 A Time Warner Company

Printed in the United States of America

First Printing: August 1992

10 9 8 7 6 5 4 3

Book design by H Roberts Design

Library of Congress Cataloging in Publication Data

Kilcommons, Brian.
    Good owners, great dogs / Brian Kilcommons, with Sarah Wilson.
        p.   cm.
    Includes index.
    ISBN 0-446-51675-9
    1. Dogs--Training.   I. Wilson, Sarah.   II. Title.
    SF431.K54 1992   91-58016
    636.7'0887--dc20   CIP

Contents

Part 1
Required Reading

Part 2
Puppyhood

Part 3   95
Caring for and Training Your Adult Dog

Part 4   183
Understanding and Solving Canine Problems

Index

Acknowledgments

Life and accomplishment are a sum total of your experience. The people that have influenced my career and my life are many. Without their love, guidance, lessons and support this book would never have been written. Space limitations make it impossible to list everyone or to fully explain my gratitude to the people I can mention, but my thanks and love to you all.

I would like to thank

Mrs. Joseph Thomas for her support and kindness to me through the years;
Roger and Jill Caras for their friendship, caring, guidance and humor;
Mrs. Muriel Freeman for selling me Beau, a dog of a lifetime;
Mrs. Edith McBeene Newberry for her friendship and generosity to the cause of animals;
Charles and Helen Ingher for their friendship and unending source of information about breeding dogs;
Dr. John Kullberg for his friendship and support;
The veterinarians I've had the pleasure of working with and learning from, especially Dr. Bill Kay, Dr. Howard Kessler, Dr. Phil Freedman, Dr. Louis Berman, Dr. Lawrence Zola, Dr. Jonathan Greenfield, Dr. John Higgins, Dr. Mike Marder, Dr. Michael McGuill, Dr. Thomas DeVincentis and many others;

The staff and students of Tufts University School of Veterinary Medicine, especially Dr. Frank Loew, Dr. Andrew Rowan, Dr. Nick Dodman and Ms. Chris Merck for their ongoing commitment to excellence and the development of new behavioral programs and studies;

A special thanks to Jane and Walter Turken for being who they are;

Mr. Jim Kalett, for lending us his expertise with the camera, his understanding of dogs and his good humor in all things;

Mrs. Margaret Klein Wilson, Ms. Vicki Croke and Mrs. Margaret Gibbs—each of whom went above and beyond in donating their time and expertise, always on a tight schedule—for their guidance, input and help in making this book a reality;

Mr. Mitch Douglas at ICM for his confidence in this project and in us;

Ms. Maureen Mahon Egen, Ms. Anne Milburn, Ms. Anne Hamilton, and the staff at Warner Books for patience, encouragement and fine senses of humor under duress;

Mr. Marc Street, our training director, who went above and beyond in helping us get this book done.

Preface

Franklin M. Loew, D.V.M., Ph.D.
Dean
Tufts University School of Veterinary Medicine
Boston and N. Grafton, MA

Groucho Marx is said to have observed, "Outside of a dog, a book is man's best friend. Inside of a dog, it's too dark to read." Aside from the play on words, whatever humor these statements have depends on an American social milieu in which dogs serve as our very own "Sacred Cows." Think about it: they often (alas) roam our streets, we certainly don't eat them for food, and there are organizations and individuals who care far more about them than about people.

Americans own more than 50 million dogs; together with our 60 million cats, there are more companion animals in the United States than there are people in any member country of the European Economic Community. And we spend more than twice as much each year on pet food as on baby food.

Companion animals? Dogs have been mankind's companions for much of our evolution. Certainly they helped us hunt, and certainly they helped to alert or protect us—even as they do today. More than that, however, they comforted us, warmed us, gave us their adulation and friendship. Rarely have they bitten the hands that fed them.

Yet dog ownership/companionship in late twentieth-century America is mainly an urban phenomenon, quite unlike the setting in which dogs and people evolved. When dogs bark or defend "their" territory, they are only doing what comes naturally.

And it is just these natural "behaviors" that can ruin your relationship with your dog, your relationship with your neighbors, and your dog's relationships with both people and other dogs. Biting, growling, marking territory, dominating, submitting, mating, begging—all of these activities need to be understood by any modern, humane companion to a dog.

This marvelous book is the best guide to understanding and therefore living happily with dogs and their attendant behavior patterns that I have read. Brian Kilcommons and Sarah Wilson are knowledgeable, witty guides to the ways and whys of canine behavior. *Good Owners, Great Dogs* could have had other titles: *Well-behaved dogs and Well-behaved owners are happier than ill-behaved ones*, or, *Dogs are cared for better by owners who understand their behavior*, but somehow these seem too cumbersome! But the statements are true.

You are about to read the best book around if you cherish your dog and the very special relationship that is possible between the two of you, and between your dog and your whole family.

Introduction

A snarl, then a flash of teeth—the movement is swift. I pull my seven-year-old hand away from Lady. I've hugged this cream-colored mix a thousand times, thrown balls for her an equal number. Baffled, I stand with arms folded tightly to my chest, leaning against the wall in a small bathroom, watching her.

Although Lady is owned by my neighbors, she and I are devoted to each other. Now Lady is pacing in the bathroom—lying down, getting up. Something is wrong.

When Lady's owners return home, I tell them Lady tried to bite me. I also tell them she is going to have puppies. They ask what I had done to provoke the dog. They laugh about her having puppies.

Lady has 13 pups that night.

Lady taught me the importance of reading the dog. They will tell you what you need to know if you pay attention. Dogs cannot lie, but they cannot speak up for themselves either. It is our job, our obligation, as owners to see what the dog is trying to tell us.

I am 13 and assisting at a veterinary hospital. The Beagle lying on the table has been run over. I am carefully removing the dead tissue and imbedded dirt from his crushed leg, trying not to touch the sharp ends of the two broken bones that protrude from his leg. He lies quietly, licking my face.

I am amazed to this day by this dog's trust and pain tolerance. Dogs are born with the capacity for utter faith in us. This gift of absolute acceptance and unconditional love can easily be lost. Do not betray it with impatience, anger, inconsistency or force. It is difficult, sometimes impossible, to get back.

At 17, while assisting a professional handler at a dog show, the prizewinning red Doberman bitch, who is my responsibility, jumps out of the exercise pen and takes off at a dead run. I am frantic! I run after her, yelling "Come." She increases her speed, running large circles around the busy parking lot. I am sure she is going to be hit by a car or get lost. I run faster, yelling louder.

A woman with short blond hair shouts at me to stop. She squats down, coos in a high-pitched enthusiastic voice, telling the red streak what a good girl she is. The bitch runs to her, sits and places her head against her neck. Calmly and still cooing, the woman puts a collar on her and brings her to me. "Never chase a dog like that," she says, then smiles and walks away.

Besides blessing the ground she walks on to this day, I learned an important

lesson from this woman. Reaction is not as effective as direction when training a dog. I reacted to the situation by running and screaming—two things bound to excite an excitable dog. The Doberman thought I was playing with her, not trying to get her. The woman directed the dog by showing her what was wanted in a way the dog could understand. By squatting down she made herself less threatening. By using a high-pitched tone, a tone the dog associated with happy things, she invited the dog to come to her. By continuing to praise and remaining relaxed, she calmed the dog. I never chased a dog again and you shouldn't either.

I take the two male Dobermans back to the van. With one on each side of me, the show collars high up on the neck, the leads tight, I give a swift jerk when one of them even thinks about looking at the other dog. I make it back to the van and get them crated. I am told to never try this again. These two males hate each other, fighting at any opportunity.

I made that journey safely because I acted confidently and never gave them the opportunity to misbehave. I corrected the dogs *just as* the thoughts crossed their minds; I did not wait for a problem to develop. You will find this theme throughout the book. Anticipate problems. It is easier to stop a train of thought than it is to stop a 70-pound dog once he is launched into action.

Pay close attention. Learn to read your dog's body language so you can anticipate what he is going to do and redirect him before he is in full swing, whether he is jumping, pulling, grabbing trash on the street, stealing food or rushing out the door.

During the time when I am apprenticing with a professional trainer at age 22, all the trainees are assigned dogs to train. After two months, we are tested. Working with the dogs on a daily basis is a must. Some of us have, others haven't. One particular handler is trying to make up for not practicing by using harsh corrections for the slightest infraction. The dog is confused. He has no understanding of what is wanted. No foundation of understanding was laid. After a few minutes of this treatment, he distrusts the handler. He is being attacked by this man for no reason that he can determine. He becomes increasingly aggressive. The head trainer takes the dog and corrects even harder. He ends up hanging the dog by its collar.

I tell the head trainer that the treatment of the dog is unnecessary and abusive. It wasn't the dog's fault he didn't know what was going on; he was never taught. I am told to mind my own business.

Good training is fun, fair, firm. What I witnessed that day was none of that. Just because we have the physical ability to control these animals does not give us the right to abuse our power. This incident crystallized in my mind how lack of practice, unrealistic expectations and force can cause aggression in an otherwise friendly and stable animal. I call this type of handling "hurt 'em till they stop" dog training. It has been practiced for generations. Unfortunately, it sometimes gets some results, which perpetuates its use, but once you've seen a dog working happily, eyes glued to the owner, tail wagging, practically dancing with joy, you can never think of using, or allowing the use of, such "methods" again.

Since you are reading this book, you are thinking about or are sharing your life with a dog, taking responsibility for an animal that is totally dependent on you. This is not always an easy task. Dogs don't come with instructions attached. Until we learn better, we naturally apply to our dogs our human habits of communicating and behaving. This does not work. I would love to be able to tell you I've never made any mistakes with my dogs, but I have. I've learned from those mistakes, and in this book I try to save you from making the same ones.

A good trainer gives a piece of himself to the dog. Canines do not suffer fools gladly nor do they respond to the empty gesture. To communicate with them effectively, you will have to find in yourself joy, enthusiasm, pride, decisiveness and patience. Teaching is difficult enough. Teaching a different species that may not have any understanding of what we are attempting to do takes understanding, empathy and common sense. We are like Annie Sullivan spilling water into Helen Keller's hand over and over again until she understood. Some dogs catch on quickly, some less so. Neither is better.

Training is teaching with you as the teacher. To be effective, you will have to practice, study the subject matter and control yourself. You will need to learn new vocabulary, new movements and new ways to communicate. You will need to be decisive with what you want and when. It will be necessary to view your dog's behavior and actions from his psychological standpoint and not your own.

All teaching has three distinct phases: Teach It, Use It, Expect It. These roughly correlate to the blackboard work, homework and pop quizzes of elementary school.

Teach It is the step-by-step process of showing the dog what you want. This is done on lead. You give the command, you place the dog in position, you praise him for doing it. Then you do it again and again and again. Remember all those endless "work sheets" in elementary school? They were the "Teach It" phase of your learning.

Use It is when the student starts doing it on his or her own but still under the close supervision of the teacher. With the dog still on lead, you begin setting up the situations in which you need the dog to obey you. You ring the doorbell, then tell him "Sit." You toss down a biscuit and tell him "Leave it." You, the teacher, are still very much in control although you allow the student to work things out on his own. You're doing homework with your dog.

Expect It allows you to use the command when you need it. A guest unexpectedly arrives, you command "Sit" as you open the door. If he does, praise. If he doesn't, guess what—more homework is needed. It doesn't do any good for you the teacher to feel like your pupil should know it by now. If he doesn't, he doesn't. If he fails a "pop quiz," then you know that either you have not done enough homework or he doesn't understand what you are teaching him. If you feel you are making a good effort but are unhappy with the results, call in a professional trainer or behaviorist. They can evaluate what you are doing and give suggestions on how to improve your communication and your dog's behavior.

Teaching has few shortcuts. The only way to speed up the process is to use methods that are effective and to practice.

Is it worth it? Yes! It is hard to describe the love, acceptance and devotion a dog brings into your life: How the constant communication of affection, needs and care enriches your life. How job problems, relationship changes and just the surprises of life are softened by the dog at your side. How the dog gives a sense of safety when you walk out your door with him or when you are at home alone. How a dog makes you and others smile and laugh. How warm you feel knowing that you could stand in a crowd of people and your dog would use all his senses to find you, because you are what matters to him. Simply put, life is easier with a good dog at your side.

Having a good dog is what this book is about—selecting, raising and training a wonderful dog who will increase the quality of your life. It is not without cost; nothing worth anything is. You will invest yourself, your time, your energy and your heart; your dog will reward you tenfold. May you find the love, joy and challenge I have with man's best friend.

The Woodhouse Touch

Barbara Woodhouse was the most brilliant dog trainer I have ever seen or had the privilege of working with. The years I spent with her were invaluable. She could take any dog and have it focused on her every word, wagging its tail and looking like Rin Tin Tin in under five minutes. With the dogs she was the epitome of her "fun, fair, firm" motto. With people she had less patience.

Barbara had no tolerance for seeing a dog mishandled. Owners who were not following instructions were immediately and firmly corrected. It was this quality that made her training shows on the BBC so popular. "You're doing it wrong," she would say as she took the leash. "I said a quick jerk. Do it this way." Brusque and to the point, Barbara changed her beliefs for no man.

One television producer did not realize this. He decided to change plans at the last moment, and to have Barbara do something I knew she would not do. The conversation went something like this:

"She won't do that," I said.

"Oh, yes she will," he replied.

"She won't do it. Take my word for it," I tried again.

"It's live, what can she do?" the producer replied.

"She'll leave," I said.

He smiled. "It's live. No one walks off a live show," he said over his shoulder as he went to explain his plan to her.

I watched from a distance. I made out the word "Rubbish" as Barbara turned on her heels and left the studio, the producer standing slack-jawed. Panic in a producer's life is having a 10-minute live segment to fill in less than five minutes. It all worked out. Barbara did her original segment and all was well.

That "do it my way or no way" attitude was

what she used with the dogs, with considerably more praise and enthusiasm, I may add. Her calm, no-nonsense demeanor, her lightning fast, fairly placed corrections combined with a generous share of effective praise won dogs' hearts in minutes.

She also believed in telepathy between human and canine. By picturing in her mind's eye a dog happily doing exactly what she wanted, she believed she was showing the dog what she literally "had in mind."

I do not know whether such things are possible. It certainly worked for Barbara. Regardless of whether it was telepathy, clarity, skill or instinct, it was obvious that she had the gift.

It was in Chicago that I came to understand. The dogs would work for me, but they were not mesmerized; they lacked that happy focus that Barbara achieved so easily. I was working with an unneutered male Samoyed. Barbara took him from me, as usual. "Do it like this," she said. She took a few steps; the dog looked off to the left; she turned and corrected, then praised immediately, and I understood. The immediate timing of correction and praise, the feeling of connectedness down the lead, the love for the animal all clicked into place. When I got that dog back, I had him.

Barbara noticed, but as with most things human, she did not gush. "Good," she said, and she stopped taking the dogs away from me.

Barbara died a few years back. A great loss for the training world. A great loss to her friends. A great loss to the dogs.

There are few people who have had such a positive global impact on teaching man and dog.

"What a good dog" was her belief. May it become yours.

PART 1

Required Reading

Why a Dog?

Dogs give and receive love unconditionally. They never say "I need my space" or "I'm not ready for a commitment." It is a nonjudgmental, completely accepting relationship. Here you are loved for who you are, not how much weight you've gained or lost, the current status of your bank account, or your popularity.

Dogs do not grow up and move out. They are with you until the end of their lives. Waking with you each morning and lying nearby at night, they offer a sense of security and warmth for child and adult alike.

The soft head that nudges your hand when life is too depressing, a happy bark that suggests a quick game outside, the warm tongue that licks your face when you cry—dogs soothe our souls and enrich our lives. Science is now confirming what pet lovers have known for years: pets make us feel better. We live longer and better with them by our sides. When we touch them, our heartbeat slows, our body relaxes: we are happy.

You are the most special person in your dog's life; his world revolves around you. If you have never owned a dog before, the experience will change your life. You will have, ready at all times, a playmate and companion, guardian and friend. With your dog you can be yourself in complete safety, knowing that this animal adores you without reservation or opinion, thinking you the best in the whole world.

And for all this dogs ask little in return. They require basic physical care that they cannot do for themselves. Grooming, medical attention, a good diet and shelter. But you can give all this and still not give what the dog needs most—your love, attention and understanding. That is what this book is all about—teaching you how to understand and communicate with this wonderful species so that the life you share with your dog is as positive, fun and tension-free as possible. Whether you are selecting a companion, raising your pup, training your dog or looking for a solution to a behavior problem, we will cover it all in simple, commonsense and effective ways.

With their unquestioning devotion comes obligation. Caring for a dog is a commitment, one of the first many of us make in our lives. Often the training ground for parenthood, dogs allow us to practice the skills of caring for another living being before a child arrives. The emotions of puppy owners and new parents are not so very different—protection, concern, confusion, frustration, all wrapped in an overwhelming love. And like an infant, animals too are innocent and trusting. We owe them our highest selves, not our upset, anger or impatience.

Why a dog? In short, to love and be loved.

Play, affection, aggression are all normal canine behaviors.

The apartment is stunning. Antiques and old tapestries line the hall. The living room is full of fresh flowers. Everything is perfect, except the pale blue rug that is covered with urine stains. Mrs. H., tall, coiffed and perfectly dressed, sits to my right. The beautifully groomed Maltese hops from the couch to her lap and back.

"I've tried everything," Mrs. H. begins. "I've scolded him, shown it to him, tied him near it—nothing works. Someone told me to clean it up with white vinegar and then rub the vinegar on his nose. Now he runs away from me if I try to catch him. He's so sweet. I just adore him, but he's being so spiteful." Her voice trails off.

"It's not a matter of spite," I explain. "He does not know what you want."

"Oh, yes, he does. He's so guilty when I find a spot. He runs under the couch and won't come out."

"It's not guilt," I explain. "He knows you're angry, but that does not mean he knows what he did wrong.

It's a matter of teaching. Scolding him, punishing him after the fact, isolating or hitting him does not tell him anything about what he should have done. Just because you tell him you hate urine on the rug does not mean he understands that when he has the urge to pee, he should run back to his papers. Those are two completely different thoughts. It's time we taught him what you want him to do."

Our two species, dogs and humans, have adored each other for centuries. Yet miscommunication between us is common. Dogs do not arrive in your home with instructions. As for us, I believe we are a mystery to them. To live together happily, I suggest you learn the basics of how *Canis familiaris* thinks.

First of all, dogs are social. In the wild they live in tight-knit groups called packs. They hunt, live and raise their young cooperatively. When living with people, they transfer that sociability to us. This transfer leads to the communication we value so highly.

what your dog will be like

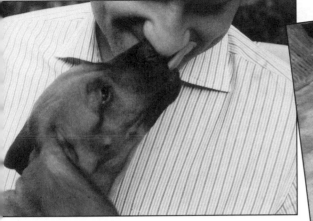

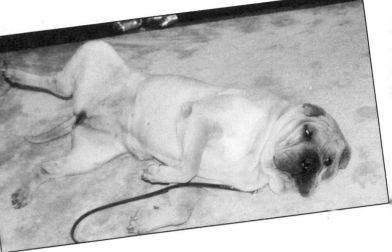

"He reads my mind." "He's my best friend." It's because he adopts us into his world as much as we adopt him into ours.

Dogs are truly a genetic miracle, the most varied species on the planet. Regardless of whether they are 2 pounds or 200, they all have the same motivations, instincts and needs.

There is no democracy in dogdom. Your dog is either being dominant ("I'm in charge and you follow") or submissive ("You're in charge and I follow"). They fit every interaction into one of these two psychological categories. When your dog comes up, drops a toy on your lap and barks at you, he is being dominant. He is commanding you, nicely, to throw it. When you do, you are following his order, which makes you submissive in his eyes. If, instead, you give him a command like "Sit" and then, after he obeys, toss the toy, you are leading. The more you lead, the more obedient your dog will be.

Dogs do not understand English.

If your kindergarten teacher had pointed to an apple while saying "grape," you might well think that the correct word for apple was *grape*. The situation is the same for your dog. If you say "Come" when he is playing but don't make him respond, then he grows up thinking "come" means "play." When teaching a command, you must carefully link the word with the action desired.

For the dog to learn, you have to link word with action within seconds because there is no way to explain to him later. When you come home at five and scold him for chewing the couch at three, he does not understand why you are upset. We call him "spiteful," "stupid" or just plain "bad" when he is actually confused or upset. A dog does not enjoy being in trouble with his owner. Your approval and acceptance are the most important things in your dog's life.

Understanding how a dog thinks will make everything you do with your dog, from selection to training, easier.

Understanding a dog makes living with one more fun for everyone.

Canine Communication

Human beings are a verbal group—specific words define our world. Dogs are nonverbal. They communicate through body signals, eye contact and a variety of sounds Our language encompasses everything from complex ideas to cooking trout. Their communication is limited to defining their social interactions and reacting to their environment.

Dog Talk

BODY POSITION

Dogs communicate through body position, facial expression and sound. In general, the larger the dog is trying to appear, the more confident he feels. When a dog approaches with tail straight up, ears erect, standing tall and making direct eye contact, he is full of himself. A confident dog that is threatening will stand tense, head held high and forward, neck arched, eyes locked on what he is looking at. If you've ever seen a tough kid watch you walk down "his" street, you know the look. The reverse is also true: the smaller he is trying to appear, the more insecure or frightened he feels. See a dog that is cowering, ears folded back, tail tucked, head down, averting his eyes, and you know that dog is frightened.

FACIAL EXPRESSION

Dogs can smile, look depressed, angry, thrilled or bored. These expressions are similar to our own, with the addition of mobile ears. A happy dog's ears are usually relaxed or half-back; the mouth is relaxed and probably open; the eyes tension-free. A worried dog's ears are held to the side, the brow is furrowed; his eyes anxious. A fearful dog's ears are back, head down, eyes averted. A confident or aggressive dog's ears are erect, mouth closed, eyes alert, maintaining direct eye contact with whatever has his attention.

SOUNDS

There are the happy growls of a friendly dog playing and the serious growls of an aggressive dog warning, high-pitched barks meaning "That squirrel is back again," and deep resonant barks telling you "Someone is here." Although it is not always obvious what dog sounds mean, they tend to break down as follows: High-pitched yips, squeals and whines mean excitement. When the dog is in the middle range, he is usually calm and unthreatened. Low-end sounds, like serious growls, are threats and warnings not to be dismissed.

Get to know what your dog's sounds mean over time by watching his body language and facial expression. Two happy dogs playing may growl, but they are both moving, bodies relaxed. Two dogs growling at each other, eyes locked, bodies stiff, moving slowly if at all, is a fight about to happen. Understanding what your dog is telling you is critical if you are going to work together as a successful team.

Here is the face of a completely happy dog. Mouth relaxed, eyes bright, Lacy the Irish Wolfhound would be laughing if she could.

My puppy rolls over on his back and puts his belly in the air all the time. What does this mean?

By exposing his belly, he is saying that he feels submissive. In dog language this is like saying "Uncle! You win. I surrender." It can also signal that the pup feels relaxed and happy. A pup will flop on his back for a belly rub just because he's a happy and submissive dog.

My dog refuses to roll on his back. Does this matter?

It can. Very dominant pups do not like to be in a vulnerable position. If your young pup refuses to be rolled over, seek professional advice.

My female dog mounts other females in the park. Is she confused or what?

She is not confused at all. In the dog world mounting means dominance more often than it means sex. Puppies of either sex will mount each other from all sorts of angles to make a point. They are saying "I am in charge of you." If your puppy mounts other dogs nonstop or doesn't respect an older dog's warnings, he is cruising for a fight. If you find an older dog who'll put him in his place, great. Visit as often as you can. The sooner your young one learns that he is not sole owner of the planet, the better. Puppies that mount humans are sending the same message. Correct this behavior immediately with an "Off." Do lots of "Downs" with him and make him work for every bit of attention he gets. This pup needs an attitude adjustment. Some people will think a mounting puppy is cute. It is not. It is trouble in the making. Treat

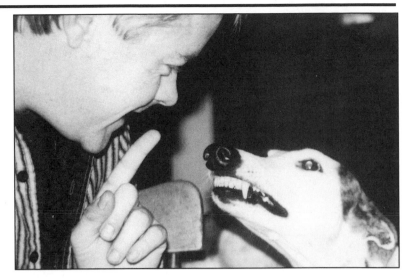

it as such and you will be nipping future problems in the bud.

My puppy plays by putting his paws on the shoulders of other dogs. Sometimes they growl. Should I stop letting him play?

By attempting to stand on the older dogs, your pup is challenging them. They are being restrained when they only growl at him. Your pup should play with nice older dogs frequently. Ones that will put him in his place and then go about their business. If your pup doesn't learn some manners now, you'll have dogfights on your hands in a few months. Let them growl at or pin him for his rudeness. It is rare that a well-socialized adult will hurt a pup.

Sirius, a retired racing Greyhound, is flashing a submissive grin at me. This canine version of a smile saved his life. The vet that was euthanizing all the animals that could no longer race could not bring himself to kill a dog that kept smiling at him.

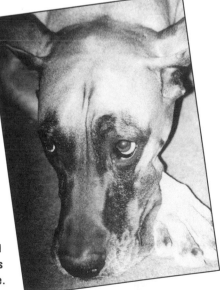

The Great Dane bitch is worried. She does not like Sarah's camera pointed at her pups. Her furrowed brow, half-mast ears and anxious eyes are hard to mistake.

Adult dogs usually give puppies behavioral carte blanche until they begin to mature sexually. Dogs that showed patience with your young pup will begin serious growling and snapping at your adolescent when he's around six to nine months of age. Young adults will go out of their way to bully your adolescent. Since they are closest to your dog in the ranks, they are particularly interested in maintaining their status. It is the way of dogs.

Here is Blackie, an 8-year-old Jack Russell Terrier, showing you the full range of canine body language. At the top of the page he is submissive—on his back, ears back, head down. In the middle he is relaxed—mouth open, ears alert, tail relaxed. At the bottom he is aggressive, with tail up, body leaning forward, mouth closed.

How Human Communication Confuses Dogs

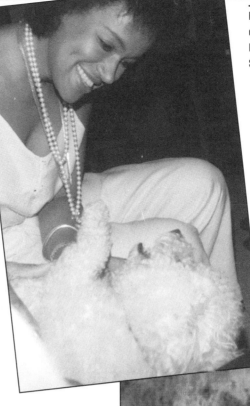

Muffy has learned to accept direct eye contact from Denise. In fact, she loves it. She trusts Denise.

EYE CONTACT

When we communicate with each other, eye contact is considered polite. When dogs interact, eye contact is a matter of dominance. Whoever looks longest is in charge. Because of this, submissive dogs can become frightened by our attempts to look them in the eye. They may withdraw in an effort to be polite. Dominant dogs can interpret the eye contact as a challenge, becoming aggressive as you stare at them. Dogs learn over time that eye contact from humans is often not intended as a threat. But if you're dealing with an unknown dog, do not stare him in the eye.

BODY LANGUAGE

Because our species is two legged and dogs are four legged, we naturally stand above them. Standing over is a key way of establishing and maintaining dominance among dogs. Many dog bites occur when a human bends over and reaches toward a dog. We are trying to be friendly; the dog cannot help but see it as dominant. A fearful or aggressive dog may resent you being so "rude" and snap at you to back you off. Shy dogs may be overwhelmed, immediately flinging themselves on their backs or submissively urinating. Make interaction easier on the dog by turning sideways, squatting down and allowing the dog to approach you. This is polite and unthreatening in dog language.

Even though Toni is standing over Deacon, he is completely relaxed. He understands that she is not challenging him. Both are at ease with each other. Such mutual understanding comes with hard work and training.

What Kind of Dog Do I Want?

WHAT IS THE AKC?

The American Kennel Club, the AKC, is one of the largest pure-breed registries in the world. Their job is to keep track of the family tree of any pure-breed dogs listed with them.

It is not their job to regulate or check for genetic disorders or temperament problems.

If someone implies that AKC papers prove what wonderful quality dogs they have, you are being misled. AKC papers are registration forms only. The fact that a pup is AKC registered does not mean it will be good with the kids, healthy, long-lived or win in the show ring.

The American Kennel Club (AKC) recognizes over 140 breeds and varieties of dog. Add to this the infinite numbers of possible mixed breeds and you have a lot of choices. How do you begin to select a dog?

First, you need to understand a little about the different types of dogs. The main categories are sporting, hound, terrier, toy, working and herding. Every group, in fact every breed, has pros and cons. Let me give brief and generalized classifications:

• Sporting breeds were bred to hunt with man. They are trainable, active and happy. If untrained they may chew, run and can be as sensitive as a brick.

• Hounds use their eyes and nose to pursue game animals. They do not work with man; man runs after them as they run after the game. These active, friendly and comical dogs can be chewers, howlers and hard to housebreak if not directed.

• Terriers, created to hunt down and kill vermin, should all be sold with their own leather jackets. They are often feisty, lively, self-assured. You live with terriers, you do not own them. Out of control they can be aggressive, barky and disobedient.

• Toys dogs were bred to be companions. Sweet, smart and devoted, these little treasures can become snappy and hard to housebreak if untrained.

• Working dogs are intelligent, trainable and territorial. With direction, experience and activity, they make first-rate companions. Otherwise, they can be aggressive and disobedient.

• Herding breeds are similar to working dogs, only with a tendency toward shyness and nipping at heels if left without direction.

There are excellent resource books that will help you to choose the breed that will fit your needs. These books can also help you predict your mixed-breed dog's behavior. Read the relevant sections and combine the breed information and you'll get a fairly clear picture of the behavior you

can expect from your mixed breed.

Next, consider the amount of time available to you. If you have time, a puppy is a viable choice. If your schedule is less flexible, then an adult dog is a better selection. If you're gone more than 10 hours a day, have little time in the mornings to spend with a dog and are too tired in the evening to exercise the animal, then you shouldn't get a dog.

Do you want a male or a female? Generally, males tend to be more assertive, independent and protective than females. Both make wonderful pets, watchdogs and companions when neutered. Neutered pets make better pets. This covered, what are your next considerations?

Are you athletic? All dogs need daily exercise, but if your idea of a workout is walking twice around the block, a toy or giant breed might be a good selection. Do not plan on changing your activity level for the dog—that doesn't work.

Do you have children or plan to in the next 10 years? That scrappy little terrier mix or toy that is perfect for you and your spouse may not be the best choice for a toddler.

Are you a physical person, enjoying a lot of body contact? Then one of the retrievers might be

right. Most believe life should be a contact sport.

Would you rather shake hands than hug? Greyhounds and Whippets have a sweet, quiet dignity when they are not doing laps around your backyard.

What about hair? Dalmatians, Pugs, Akitas and German Shepherds are notable in their ability to drop hair. If you can't picture hair in your bed, then don't get a heavy shedder.

Experience is a critical factor. If you have trained dogs before (not just owned but trained), then one of the more assertive breeds may work well. First-time owners should stay away from the tough, territorial breeds. These are fine animals in the right hands, just as a racing car is great for an experienced driver but dangerous with a newcomer behind the wheel. If this is your first dog, start with an easygoing, less assertive breed.

Looks should be one of your last considerations. The dog that fits your life is a beautiful dog. Many have selected their dog on its "look" and paid the price. With dogs, you definitely can't tell a book by its cover.

Q&A

SHOULD I CHOOSE A PUPPY OR AN ADULT DOG?

Adult dogs are the best-kept secret of dog ownership. If you are fortunate enough to find a healthy, well-tempered adult, you have found a gem. Most adult dogs bond quickly to their new homes, some with an almost desperate intensity. Adult dogs can arrive in your home with other people's mistakes in place—housebreaking problems, separation anxiety— usually nothing that can't be dealt with. Pups are a lot of fun, if you have the schedule and patience it takes to raise and train one.

All dogs demand your time and energy at first. That comes with pet ownership. Adult dogs tend to settle in faster because they are more mature. Pups need no sales pitch. They will always sell themselves.

Where Do I Find My Dog?

Check Out . . .

Finding a dog, your dog, should be a fun experience. Good dogs can be found in any of the places listed; it's just that in the places I recommend, your chances of doing so are much higher than in the places I suggest you avoid.

SHELTERS

Most towns have at least one animal shelter. These hardworking places care for literally millions of animals a year. You will find everything there—big, small, mixed, pure. Dogs adopted from shelters are often grateful for the second chance and attach themselves to you almost immediately.

Shelters are a wonderful source of pets who desperately need homes. Shelter dogs are often understandably tense about being left alone at first; that comes from being abandoned. A good crate, a steady routine, and happy, upbeat training are your adopted dog's best friends next to you. Read the selection section, learn what to look for and how to look, decide ahead of time what kind of temperament you want to live with, then go take a look. You may have to go back several times before you find your dog. Don't despair. He or she will turn up, tail wagging, happy to be adopted into your family.

Shelters have the unfortunate job of having to kill millions of dogs created by uncontrolled breeding. Only we pet owners can stop this misery. Please, spay and neuter your dogs.

RESCUE GROUPS

Most breed clubs have rescue groups. These are people, dedicated to their breed, who house and care for unwanted pups and dogs until they can find a good home. I've had excellent luck working through these groups. Locate rescue groups through the national clubs. Call the AKC (919-233-9767) for the address of any national breed club.

There are also hundreds of dedicated private organizations that rescue and place dogs of all ages and backgrounds. Your local shelter, vet or groomer can help locate these people.

REPUTABLE BREEDERS

Reputable breeders breed their dogs because they love them and want to improve the breed. Typically, they show their dogs and win frequently enough to have a few ribbons and trophies around. They are happy to talk to you about the pros and cons of their breed. If they do not think this breed will work for you, they will tell you so. Unfortunately, many believe themselves to be bettering the breed, and believe that they are reputable. How can you, the buyer, know if they are?

One tip is to ask open-ended questions. If you say what you want right off, disreputable breeders will say, "Oh, I have one of those." Ask and listen. "What do you breed for?" "What are the pros and cons of your breed?" Then pay attention to their answers.

You should like the person you select. They'll be a resource of information for years to come. If you don't like him or her, keep looking. Here are some of the ways you'll know a "good" breeder when you find one:

• They have more questions to ask you than you have to ask them.

• They breed five litters or fewer a year.

• They require spay and neuter contracts on their pet-quality dogs. This means that you won't get your papers until your dog's been neutered.

- They'll want to meet your whole family before selling you a pup.

- They check thoroughly for genetic diseases and speak openly about breed problems.

- You'll meet one or more parents, aunts, uncles and other relatives of your pup.

- The facility is clean.

- When asked what they breed for, "temperament" is one of their answers.

- They want the puppy back if you can't keep her anymore.

- They keep some or all the dogs in the house at least part of the day.

- They work their dogs. This depends on the breed, but look for pet therapy, obedience, lure coursing or agility.

Few people will satisfy all of these criteria, but the good ones will meet half or more. A good breeder will be a friend for the life of your dog and beyond, so take some time and look carefully.

Avoid . . .

Let's first say that wonderful pets have come from every imaginable source. My job here is to steer you away from the places where your chances of finding a healthy, happy puppy are poor.

PET STORES
Although a few pet stores are mak-ing an effort to improve conditions, it is overall a horrendous, heart-wrenching business. No reputable breeder <u>ever</u> sells pups to a puppy store. They would never allow strangers to purchase their dogs.

If your credit card is good, a pet store will sell you a pup: no questions asked. Pets stores also have to make a profit. In order to make that profit, they have to buy cheaply from some place that does not care what happens to its puppies. These places are called puppy mills. A puppy mill often pro-duces puppies like any other live-stock—housed in small cages with wire mesh flooring so the urine and feces will fall through. Mating pairs are kept together and have litter after litter with no rest until the number of puppies in each litter gets small. Then the female is killed. It's economics— no love, no kind words.

Pups from these places sell cheaply, usually between $50 and $200 a pup—to be resold to you for $500 to $2,000. Pet stores are often more expensive than a good breeder, and the puppy you'll get there is poorly bred, of unknown heritage and stressed beyond belief. Many are sick.

You'll spend more money getting them well, if they get well. Skip the trauma. If you are softhearted, don't even go in. Saving one puppy will not make any difference in a millions-of-puppies-a-year business. Every time a loving person buys one of those pup-pies, that terrible, inhumane industry is being encouraged. Walk on by. Don't be part of it.

BACKYARD BREEDERS
These well-intentioned souls are breeding their beloved Bessie

SHOULD I PICK A PURE-BRED OR RANDOM-BRED DOG?

A dog is a dog is a dog. Under the fancy fur, behind the long pedigree and beneath the funny floppy ears beats the heart of a *Canis familiaris*.

"Mixed breed" or "pure" makes no dif-ference to the dog; he hasn't heard the news that pure-bred dogs are "better." They aren't. They're more predictable. Buy a Collie and you know about what size, shape and coat you'll be dealing with. Buy an adorable little mixed breed and you won't know for a bit exactly what size and shape your beloved pet will be. Surprises can be nice. As far as other differences go, both pure or random bred can be neurotic or stable, healthy or sickly.

By learning about sources of dogs, tem-perament testing and general health issues discussed in this chap-ter, you have an excel-lent chance of choos-ing a happy, healthy, wonderful pet.

GAMES PUPPY MILLS PLAY

In order to boost sales and profits, puppy mills play games with the animals and the clients. One favorite is breeding mixed-breed dogs. Small breeds like Maltese have tiny litters of three or fewer pups and frequently need medical care when whelping. This is too much cost for too little a payoff. So they take a Maltese male and breed to a Bichon Frise female (a slightly larger white breed). The litters are larger, medical costs fewer and profits higher. You just end up with a really big, cottony-coated "Maltese." Another favorite is to sell "extra small" toy breeds for extra money. In reality these are just young pups being sold as older. You'll know it happened to you if your Teacup Yorkie doesn't start to teethe till at about "five months." The reverse is done with big breeds. Your "huge" Dobie puppy may have all its teeth by "four months" of age. BUYER BEWARE!

because she is such a good dog. The father is usually a friend or neighbor's dog who is also a "really nice dog." They figure two nice dogs will make nice pups.

If that were true, then breeders would only breed stable, well-tempered champions, and none of us would have to worry about where to get dogs.

The horror stories we hear about this type of breeding are endless. The lovely couple who bred their Yorkie only to have two of the three puppies die due to liver problems. The family that bred their Dalmatian and came up with six out of the eight puppies deaf. Genetics are complex. The genetic problems that lie hidden in every dog are hard to avoid unless you are well versed in the lines and traits of the breed. Even then it is a hard task to breed healthy, beautiful, sweet dogs.

DELIVERED TO YOUR HOME

A whole new marketing scam in the dog world has developed of late. People who "bring your puppy to your door." You call these people, place an "order," and your pup arrives. Remember, a reputable breeder would never allow one of their precious pups to be sold to parties unknown. These are puppy-mill pups being sold directly by the middlemen for higher profits at their end. Stay clear. The small convenience of home delivery will soon be outweighed by possible veterinary costs, genetic problems and temperament disasters.

These three Labrador Retrievers were bred and raised by a wonderful breeder in a loving home. Here you could meet both the parents, see the litter mates, and choose the puppy in a relaxed, loving atmosphere. Such a beginning does not guarantee success, but it's a terrific start.

Puppy Selection: More Than Just a Pretty Face

Selecting a pup is a combination of knowledge, common sense and emotion. Attempt to stick to knowledge and common sense for as long as you can.

Neutered dogs of either gender make terrific pets. Intact males tend to be more assertive, aggressive and harder to handle. Pick a pup of either sex and plan to neuter it.

A seven-week-old puppy already is who he is. Training and environment can influence temperament, but starting with a calm, easygoing, responsive puppy makes everything easier. Don't choose the most assertive, mouthy pup, because he will grow into a pushy, active adult. Skip the pup sitting off by himself; you want a dog that is attracted to people. The pup that stays awake long after the other pups in the litter have fallen asleep may be an overly active adult. Choose the pup that has the type of personality you want right from the start.

Whether you are looking in a shelter or at a breeder's, test a few puppies to give you an idea of the range of responses. Puppy testing helps you choose the best individual puppy for your personality. One of the most important characteristics a dog can have is the ability to calm himself once stressed. Dogs that cannot calm themselves often have chronic behavior problems. The cradle test is your best method to use to judge this (see page 32 for full details). Choose the pup that either struggles and then calms himself, or stays calm and relaxed the whole time.

You can also use these tests to evaluate the puppy you already own. They indicate areas that need work in your dog's temperament. If he has a hard time calming down when stressed, you'll need to teach him how to do that through handling exercises and basic obedience. Such a dog needs a calm leader, as shouting and anger will make him more upset. On the other hand, the hesitant pup needs to be exposed to the sights and sounds of the world and given obedience training to raise his confidence. The aloof pup benefits from food reward, lots of structure and a strong crating schedule that makes you the main event of his day.

Puppy selection is an art, not a science. Individual pups will react differently one day to the next. Still, testing is a valuable tool to help you eliminate the very assertive and the very shy. In most litters there will be more than one puppy that fits your needs. If that's the case, then you can indulge your sense of aesthetics and pick the one that looks good to you.

Here are a few Labrador Retriever puppies in action. An active seven-week-old pup is likely to be an active adult. A stable, friendly pup will probably stay that way if you raise him correctly. Choose the pup with the personality you want to live with for the next decade or so.

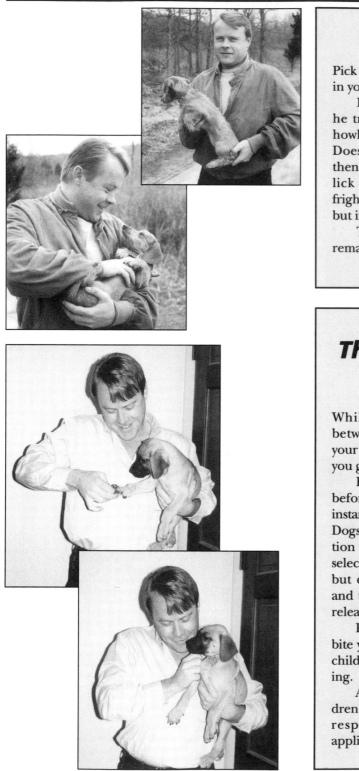

The Cradle Test

Pick up a pup and, supporting it well, cradle it in your arms as shown. How does it respond?

Does he struggle and never give up? Does he try to mouth or bite you? Does he whine, howl or panic? None of these are good signs. Does he struggle or whine for a minute and then settle down? Immediately relax? Or try to lick you? Excellent. Does he seem stiff and frightened? If he relaxes in a few seconds, fine, but if he stays rigid, pass him by.

The best companions are the pups that remain relaxed in this stressful situation.

The Touch-Sensitivity Test

While holding the pup, take the webbing between his toes and squeeze it (do not use your fingernails). Release the paw the moment you get a response.

Pups that can take a fair amount of pressure before pulling away their paw but forgive you instantly are both the norm and what you want. Dogs differ in pain tolerance and vary in reaction when physically uncomfortable. The best selection is a pup that shows signs of discomfort but does not scream or aggressively mouth— and that forgives instantly when the pressure is released.

Pups that yelp at the slightest pressure or bite your hand are not good choices if you have children or if they will require a lot of grooming.

A potentially good choice for active children are the physically tough pups that show no response until a good deal of pressure is applied.

The Sound-Sensitivity Test

While the pup is just walking around, drop a ring of keys nearby. Does he ignore it, or startle but then investigate? Good responses. If he runs away or is too spooked to come up and take a look, don't choose that one.

Pups that startle and can't recover from their fear may grow into nervous animals that fear loud noises. Thunderstorms, vacuum cleaners and traffic may all leave such dogs in a state of panic.

A good response to this test is critical for the city pet that will have to cope with noises and distractions on a daily basis. Natural sensitivity to sound is a difficult thing to successfully eliminate later on.

The Attraction Test

Some pups are interested in human beings, some are not. People-oriented pups make the easiest, most responsive pets.

Set the puppy down in a quiet room, squat down, clap your hands and say nothing. Pups that wander off and don't look back are likely to do the same as adults. Pups that seem frightened should be skipped over too. You want the puppy that comes over to you with a happy, confident attitude. If the pup is being tested in a completely new environment, he may be hesitant. That's okay as long as he would rather come to you than wander off on his own.

Observe the pups as a group if you can. Sit on the floor. Which comes over? Which stays with you? Which is off by himself? Let them get interested in something, then call them excitedly. Which pups are the first to come to you? Do this a few times. Will one or two consistently arrive first? That's a good sign.

Training Takes TEAMwork

CONSISTENCY— THE CORNERSTONE OF DOG TRAINING

To train your dog effectively, you have to be consistent. If you say the same command in the same order in the same way all the time, your dog will learn quickly. If you say "Murphy, sit" in the morning and "Sit down, Murphy" in the afternoon, he will be confused and learning will be slowed.

Consistency extends to your actions as well. If you correct him for mouthing you one minute and are playing wrestlemania the next, how is he supposed to know what you want?

Training also requires family consistency. The more you all pull together—giving the same commands and demanding the same results— the faster your puppy will learn. Basically, the more consistent you are, the more consistent your puppy's response will be.

Tone, Emotion, Attitude and Movement (TEAM) are what training is all about. Working together, you and your dog can easily learn the basics.

To be an effective teacher, you have to be fair, enthusiastic, patient, decisive, consistent and fun. As an attentive follower, he has to learn to pay attention and to trust you enough to try. There is a lot for both of you to learn.

You must learn how he thinks. Then you have to adjust your methods so they are comprehensible to him.

He has to figure out what "Sit" means. Simplistic to us, but learning that a human sound means that he should assume a specific body position is a completely foreign concept to him.

To appreciate the position your dog's in, imagine waking up one morning and finding yourself in a strange country where you don't understand the language or the culture. Someone enters your room and says "Rutshid." You stare at him blankly. "Rutshid, Rutshid," he repeats earnestly. You are still clueless. He glares at you. "Rutshid!" he shouts. Nervous, you back away. "This one is stubborn," he says, "or maybe just stupid."

Were you being stubborn or stupid? No. You just did not know what to do. So it is for your dog. You have the tools necessary to be a good teacher; all you need to do is learn how to use them effectively.

Tone. By using your voice in three clear ways that imitate canine communication, you'll make it much easier for your dog to learn.

Emotion. By controlling your emotion and showing the dog your genuine pleasure in his accomplishments, you will build his trust and enthusiasm, motivating your dog to learn.

Attitude. By cultivating a nonnegotiable, decisive, "we will learn this" attitude, you make it inevitable that your dog will learn.

Movement. By learning the movements required to teach the basic behaviors, you make it possible for your dog to learn. Since he cannot understand our language, we must show him what to do through movement.

TEAMwork is fun. There is little in life as gratifying as the bond you will develop with your dog through positive training.

Your job is to be a good teacher. His job is to be an attentive, obedient student. Your job is the harder one.

Tone

Dogs understand the tone of our voice more quickly than the meaning of our words. Their communication fits into three basic categories—whine, bark and growl. Higher-pitched whinelike sounds generally mean excitement to your dog. Praising in a higher tone will easily be recognized as pleasure. Neutral, matter-of-fact tones—the range of the bark—are the right tones for commands. Lowering your voice to sound more growllike is unmistakably corrective for your dog.

This does not mean that men have to hit high notes when they praise or that women have to go on hormones to sound corrective. It just means you have to use tones higher or lower than your normal range.

People have multiple uses for tone. We soften harsh meaning with a gently inflected tone. When we ask someone to do something, we use a questioning tone: "Would you mind moving out of my way?" Seldom do we say "Move." If we did, we would be considered rude. If we are annoyed or angry, we switch to an ordering type voice "Move!"

People use the same inflection with pets. We "ask" them: "Muffy, Sit?" We think we're being clear. The dog, hearing the soft voice and the questioning tone, thinks, "Oh, this sounds like praise. I guess I'll just wag my tail." We get frustrated—why isn't the dog listening? We either repeat it or flip into our frustrated tone: "Muffy, SIT!"

Muffy is confused—why are you so angry? Maybe she sits with a lowered head or freezes in place because she is not sure what to do. First you "praised"

her, then you yelled at her, and all she did was wag her tail.

Another area of miscommunication between dog and human is mouthing. Your puppy walks up to you and, full of puppy love, chomps on your hand with her sharp puppy teeth. In pain, you squeal "No! Stop it!" in a high-pitched tone, pulling your hand away fast. The pup thinks, "Wow, my person sounds like a large squeaky toy. She's really excited! She must enjoy this! Let me chase her hand!" and leaps at you for another round. And so it goes.

It is critical to use a tone of voice that your dog can understand in training. Notice how happily these dogs are responding to their praise. Find the tone of voice that makes your dog look equally as happy when you praise him.

In order to be effective TEAM players, we have to use the sounds the dog understands best: praise/whine, command/bark, correction/growl.

PRAISE

Effective praise makes your dog wag his tail, look at you adoringly and move closer to you. By being enthusiastic, warm and sincere, you motivate your dog to respond. Poor praise is ignored and too much praise sends some dogs into uncontrollable spasms of delight. Avoid getting into praise ruts. "Good dog, good dog, good dog," people say as the dog yawns, looking for something interesting to do. Remember it is not what you say but how you say it. A game I have my clients play is to say words like "bad dog" but make them sound like praise. Since the words are now "negative" people become more aware of their tone. Dogs thrive on sincerity; tell them what you really think in a warm loving voice and you'll see spectacular results.

COMMANDS

Your tone should be calm, no-nonsense, confident, decisive. Authority is a state of mind and a tone of voice. It is the tone you use when you give someone directions: "Go down three blocks and turn right." It is the voice of the best substitute teacher you ever had. Good substitute teachers know about establishing authority quickly and with little fuss. An inexperienced sub would say "Everyone? Sit down?" in an insecure voice, hoping all would comply. A good sub says "Everyone, sit down" with absolute calm and confidence, and the children respond.

CORRECTIONS

Speak in a deeper tone than normal; be serious, calm. Leave anger and volume out; use intensity to get results. As the pup reaches for your dinner on the table, a brisk, deep "Leave it" will work better than a loud "NO!!" The problem with "no" is that it means too many things: NO! don't jump on the guest; NO! don't steal food off my plate; NO! don't chase the cat; NO! don't eat out of the garbage, etc. "No" does not tell the dog what he is supposed to be doing, nor does it give him a way to get praise. Teaching him specific commands—such as "Leave It," "Off," "No bite"—allows you to instruct the dog as to what you want him to be doing. It also gives the dog an immediate way to get your approval and praise.

Emotion

Emotion is a big plus in praise and a real problem during correction. Pour out your heart when your dog pleases you, but hold back the anger when he does something wrong. Anger may momentarily stop the unwanted behavior, but the dog will go back to it later. Temporary fear does not produce long-term understanding. Once a dog is frightened, he is not thinking about what he's done. He's thinking about how to get out of this situation. To control a dog, you need to control yourself.

One commonly held belief is "He knows he did wrong." We promise you he does not. Picture this. You are a physically small person who waits at home all day for your much-beloved partner to come home. Every once in a while your partner comes home and with an "Uh-oh" starts combing the house for some mistake you have made. You have no idea what you did wrong, but he always finds something. When he does, he screams, threatens and perhaps hits you. Soon, whenever he comes in with an "Uh-oh," you start to panic. "See, you know you did something," he says. "You're acting guilty."

So it is for your dog. He has no idea what he did to get you so upset. The last thing he wants is to be in trouble with you. Chances are his chewing, barking or housebreaking mistakes are partially, if not wholly, caused by anxiety. Anger only makes him MORE anxious, so he chews more and you come home and get angry, and tomorrow when you leave he's nervous and he chews and you come home. . . . How many times do you dial the wrong number before you stop? If a correction does not work in a few tries, then do something else—don't keep dialing.

On the other end of the spectrum is the overly protective owner. Anyone can be a coddler, but it is most common among small-dog owners. It can be hard to remember that a small dog is just that—small but still very much a dog. Mentally, they perceive themselves as equal to a larger dog (except for Yorkies, who consider themselves better).

It can be difficult to separate our emotional needs from the needs of the dog, but, as hard as it is, small-dog owners need to tuck their parental instincts away, set their pups down and say, "You are a dog and I'm going to treat you like one." Otherwise, as the old saying goes . . .

Treat a dog like a human and he'll treat you like a dog.

Tom Blumenfeld, Linda Rosa and Lawrence, their Ibizian Hound, are having a wonderful time. Everyone is relaxed and happy.

Attitude

Training is all about attitude—yours and your dog's. As a teacher, you set the tone for learning. Your attitude needs to be a patient, positive one. Learning takes as long as it takes. One dog may learn to sit in a day, another in two weeks—both are fine. If you keep working, your dog will learn. You'll also need to be decisive. You decide what behavior you'll accept, not the dog. One couple had a dog that was out of control, but he never

jumped on the bed. They thought this was a miracle. I pointed out that it was good training. Both owners had decided not to allow the dog up on the bed. Their attitude was "Sorry, but we just won't allow this." Once they expanded this decisive attitude to the rest of their interactions, the dog's behavior improved.

Three words that Barbara Woodhouse, the well-known British trainer, used to describe the proper attitude for dog training were FUN, FAIR, FIRM.

FUN

Making learning fun makes your dog want to learn. Show him in every way

possible that he is the best dog in the world when he listens to you. If you're not having a good time, he won't be. Praise, play, surprise him with a toy or treat, give him a hug, romp—anything that you both enjoy—and you'll see his learning speed up. While a dog is trying to learn something new, always praise the smallest response to your direction.

FAIR

You're the teacher. It's your job to make things clear to the dog. You can't yell at the dog for jumping on your guests if you pet him for jumping on you. To be fair, you have to use the same commands every day—not "Come" on Monday and "Come over here" on Tuesday. Fairness means not blaming your dog for a mistake you made. If you feed your pup, then fall asleep in front of the TV, don't blame him when you wake up to a mess. Blame yourself.

FIRM

You say it, he does it—that's the deal. For his own safety you need him to respond immediately. What if a door is left open or his collar breaks? You may only have time for one command before your dog is in the street.

Firmness does not mean yelling or being angry; it means deciding what behavior you want and not fluctuating from it.

The proper attitude about the training process makes all the difference between you and your dog working together and you and your dog being at odds. "He's a bad dog" is the wrong attitude. "He doesn't understand what I want" is the attitude that will start you on your way and get you to your goal fastest.

Terry is taking no guff from Jesse. Jesse knows the "Down" command well and has hesitated to respond. Terry corrects her fairly and effectively. Nice forward body movement, horizontal correction and timing. Well done. P.S.: Jesse downed immediately and got lots of praise.

Movement

Dogs, being predators, survive in the wild through understanding and predicting the movement of their prey. Their social interaction is based on reading the body language of other dogs. In training, using movement well means the difference between your dog learning quickly and your dog being confused. Dogs read body language better than we do.

Forward movement toward the dog is seen as assertion or threat. If you move forward when you give a command, your dog will understand that you intend to follow through with this and he will respond more quickly. If you grab at your dog when he makes an error, this will be seen as an attack, leading to jumping away, cowering or possibly aggression.

Standing still can be seen as an act of indecision. Backing away and bending over are definitely submissive. A common mistake people make is backing up or bending over when giving commands. The only time bending over or backing up is called for is when you are working with a shy animal who needs to see you as less threatening. In such a case backing up will almost always encourage the dog to come to you.

You will also have to learn how to use the training equipment properly. This takes time and practice but can be learned by all those who apply themselves to doing so.

Dogs respond to what you say with your body and your tone more than to your words. When teaching your dog make sure that your body language, tone and attitude all match your words.

The Role of Timing

With the proper timing of praise and correction, a dog can learn almost instantly. Praise and correction should come at the moment your dog acts. Your dog thinks about doing it right—praise! Your dog considers doing it wrong—correct. Commands are to be obeyed—right away.

Part of timing is direction. Try to catch the dog before he misbehaves and direct him to do something positive rather than waiting and reacting to unwanted behavior. Tell your dog to sit before he jumps up. That way you are teaching him what you want him to do rather than spending your time in the more difficult task of trying to stop him midjump.

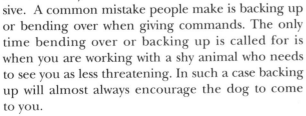

Jane's timing is excellent. Just as she is coming to a stop, she gives the verbal command and the hand signal. Note the loose lead, the dog in the correct position on her left side, attentive and relaxed. What a great pair!

Throughout the book, I will recommend pieces of equipment and training tools to you. The purpose and use of these tools are outlined here. Although there are numerous different collars, leads, and toys on the market, I have found the ones listed here to work the best for the largest number of dogs. Once you have learned how to use them properly, I'm sure they will be as helpful to you as they have been for me.

Sterilized Bone

Purchased at the pet supply store, these thick, hollow bones are hard for any dog to break. By putting a piece of cheese down inside the bone, you create a puppy pacifier. Choose a bone appropriate for your pup. Avoid bones that are too small and can be swallowed.

Odor Neutralizer

This is the only thing to clean up housebreaking mistakes with. Buy at your pet store or veterinarian's. There are many excellent brands. Your pup can smell 1 part urine in 1 million parts water, so don't compromise. Vinegar, club soda or ordinary rug cleaners will not do the trick. Even if you're picking up a stool and there doesn't seem to be any on the rug, wipe it down with an odor neutralizer.

Flat Collar

Your puppy's first collar should be a flat, nylon or leather collar that buckles like a belt. There are now adjustable collars that can be buckled at any length. These are best. Also, get the widest collar possible, especially for small dogs. Wider is gentler on the neck.

Four-Foot Leather Lead

I like these leads because they are easy on the hands (nylon burns if your dog's a puller), a convenient length (six feet leaves too much slack) and long lasting. Choose one with a small buckle. Big buckles can inadvertently smack the dog in the face when you correct him. This will lead to lagging and swinging wide to avoid this uncomfortable situation.

Training Collar

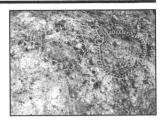

My favorite type of training collar is the Woodhouse Collar. When used properly, its wide links makes it gentle while its noisiness makes it effective. A regular chain collar (right hand side of the photo) can also be an effective tool if fitted properly. If you're unsure, ask your local pet supply store person to show you how to select the right size for your dog.

Antichew Products

There are many antichew products on the market. These are two of the most readily available. There are three types that I recommend: The spray I use on leads, electrical wires and washable woodwork. Because it is alcohol based, use it with care on fine finishes. The furniture cream lasts longer but is messy. The leaf and plant protector is, obviously, for plants.

Shake Can

Make this by putting 15 pennies in an empty, rinsed soda can. Not a coffee can, juice can or anything but an aluminum beverage can. With a quick shake the noise the shake can makes can startle a dog, making him stop what he's doing. Used correctly from behind your back or at your side, this tool will not terrify. Do not use this to intimidate your dog. Tape thread to one or more then tie the thread to an object that your dog steals or chews. Put the object in plain view but set the cans above it on a table or counter top. You've made a shake can booby trap. When he steals the object the cans will fall then chase him. Very effective!

Long Line

This 15 to 30 foot line can be purchased at the pet store or through a mail-order dog supply firm or made from clothesline and a clip from the hardware store. It is used to get distance control on your dog when teaching come and stay, both indoors and out.

Chew Toys

Every dog needs toys to chew on that last. These three do. Rawhides are terrific if your dog gnaws on them. If he is the type to chew the whole thing and swallow big chunks, don't give it to him. Avoid the pressed rawhides made out of tiny bits, often brightly colored and shaped like bones or candy canes. They may be cute but give some dogs loose stool.

Selecting and Using a Crate

Crates are the cribs and playpens of dog training. I would not try to raise a puppy or train a dog without one. It helps prevent chewing, barking or dirtying in the house. It calms anxious dogs and teaches hyperactive dogs to sleep when you are away. It becomes a home away from home wherever you go.

Buy the crate to fit your adult dog, not your fast-growing puppy.

Both solid plastic airline type crates and wire mesh crates work well. If you get the wire mesh variety, invest a few more dollars to get the folding kind. This makes them easy to store and to travel with when the training period is over. NEVER leave a collar on your dog in the crate. If it gets caught—and it can—the dog can strangle itself.

If the crate is used correctly, your dog will regard it as a "room of his own." It's a safe, clean, comfortable place to leave your friend when you can't watch over him. Most dogs try not to urinate or defecate in the crate if they can help it. You will use this instinct to your advantage when you housebreak your dog.

Introducing the crate is easy—it just takes time. If you use the crate when the pup is young, he will adjust to it readily.

Step 1—Introducing the Crate

• Puppies should not be crated for more hours than they are months old plus one. Meaning a three-month-old pup should not be crated for more than four hours; a four-month-old pup for five hours. The self-control of puppies varies; let your puppy guide you. The adult dog can be left for eight to nine hours in the crate, but it is mentally and physically difficult. Large amounts of exercise before or after such stints in the crate are a must. You try not going to the bathroom for eight hours.

• Puppies can usually hold it overnight by four months of age if a consistent feeding and watering schedule is followed.

• Never put papers in the crate. You're trying to teach him NOT to go in there.

• If your dog dirties his bedding, don't put any in with him.

• Don't expect a puppy to get muscle control until four months of age.

• Put a towel UNDER the crate, between the crate and the floor. This will keep it from rattling when the pup steps into it.

• Store all toys and a few treats in the open crate. Allow the dog to get things as he wishes.

• Feed your companion in the crate. Leave the door open, let him come and go as he pleases. If he is hesitant, put the bowl close to the door of the crate so he can easily reach in and get his meal.

Step 2—Closing the Door

Once a pup goes in and out of the crate without fear, it is time to close the door.

• Put your pup in when he is tired and ready for a nap.

• To keep him occupied, give him a sterilized bone with cheese in it. Remember, chewing stimulates defecation, so he may need to go earlier than usual if he really enjoys the bone.

• When you put the pup in or take him out, you want a minimum of fuss. Set a positive tone.

• Leave him in for a few minutes, then let him out. Do NOT let him out if he is barking or whining, as this rewards him for being noisy.

• Close door when he is eating; take him outside the minute he finishes.

• Introduce the closed door during the day at first so if there is a fuss, it won't keep you or your neighbors awake.

Step 3—What to Do About the Noisy Puppy

• Try ignoring it. Some pups will settle after 10 minutes or so.

• A hot-water bottle wrapped in a towel calms some pups. Warmth induces sleep.

• If he doesn't quiet down, come up silently from out of sight and slap the wall. This sudden, surprising noise will usually silence him. You may have to repeat this a few times until he links the sudden noise with his barking or whining and stays quiet.

• If it continues, use a shake can out of sight. A quick shake of the can will quiet most puppies.

• If after three to four shakes the puppy is not quieting down, toss a shake can from out of sight near to the crate. Do not say anything; you want the dog to think this has nothing to do with you—it just happens when he barks.

Tri is, as ever, our willing volunteer for any food-related training demonstration. Here I show him his dinner; then while I tell him excitedly how good it will be, I put it in the crate. In he hops without hesitation. Granted, he is used to the crate. But this is exactly what we did when he was learning, and you can see the results.

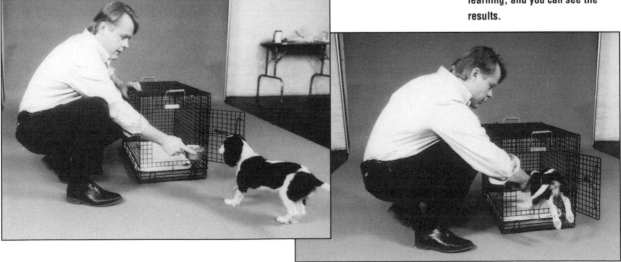

PART 2

Puppyhood

What to Expect the First Year

We have a new puppy in the house. So far today I have cleaned up two puddles (both my fault), taken an electrical cord out of her mouth, stopped her from eating the fringe on the rug, retrieved a sneaker and a pair of slippers from her curious mouth, been out to the backyard with her more times than I'd like to think, quieted her howling four times, had my nose nipped, my face licked, been awakened at 3:00 A.M. and 6:15 A.M. and fallen further in love. It doesn't matter who you are or how many times you've done it before, there is no shortcut through puppyhood. Nor, may I add, would I want there to be.

The advantage that I have is that I have faith that everything will come in time. She will get housebroken because most do. She will learn not to eat everything in sight because the training works. I can relax and enjoy it more. I hope to give you that gift. To lessen your anxiety while giving you insight into how the precious thing lying at your feet operates.

During the first six months, your puppy learns about her world. Few things in life are as heartwarming as a puppy romping with a toy or recognizing his name the first time. However, as with raising any living thing, puppy care is not 100 percent fun. The sweet moment with the warm puppy sleeping on your lap will be balanced by the warm puddles you step in.

Raising a puppy takes time—one way or another. Either you exercise your pup or he works out on your woodwork; you can supervise him closely or you clean up the mess. He will teach you. What I can teach you is how to prevent the common problems and develop the good behavior all in less time with less effort.

Puppies are predictable. They jump, chew, bark, nip and mess all over until taught otherwise. Proper training enriches the communication between the two of you and lays the foundation for your shared life together. This part of the book gives you effective and commonsense techniques that will be easy for you to use and for both of you to understand.

Here is a list of long-wearing toys that most dogs love to play with:

Kong. Also known as Bouncing Billie, this tough rubber toy looks like soft ice cream and lasts forever. It bounces in funny directions when thrown. Dogs love it. Do not throw any hard toy at your dog to catch. That can chip their teeth.

Rope Toy. Hard wearing and machine washable, it is available in a variety of sizes to suit every dog. Pups love to shake it back and forth.

Gumabone. More popular with dogs than the harder Nylabone, Gumabone lasts well, giving hours of chewing fun for your pet. It comes in sizes to suit every pet.

Boomer Ball. Tough as nails, and too big to pick up, many dogs love to play canine soccer with it. Use only in fenced areas, as dogs get very focused on this toy.

Setting Up Your Puppy's New Home

Kitchens and bathrooms are usually the best place for a pup. These rooms are easy to puppy-proof, clean and visit. Isolated areas such as the basement or backyard are no place for a puppy.

Remove items that you don't want chewed or dirtied and anything dangerous. If you store cleaners under the sink, secure the cabinet—some pups can open doors. Coat electrical wires that the pup can reach with Bitter Apple furniture cream. Throw rugs will be chewed. Remove all so your pup won't learn the joys of unraveling carpeting.

Here is a bathroom set up for a puppy. Towels put away, soap and shampoo out of reach, shower curtain over the rod, plungers and chemicals stored in a safe place—now it's ready for a puppy.

You will need to set up a confinement area for your pup if you work, if the pup is too young to take out, or anytime you are forced to leave it for longer than it can comfortably stay in its crate. Start by getting a wire mesh baby gate for the doorway. Insist on wire as pups make short work of plastic or wooden mesh. Always use a gate, as a closed door can lead to puppy frustration, causing barking, scratching and chewing at the door. If you think your pup might try to climb the gate, rest two or three shake cans along the top edge. They'll fall and startle him if he tries to get over the gate.

Place papers in the rear of the area so that he will not have to traipse through his mess coming to say hello.

Put his crate, bowls and toys up front near the gate since that is where he will be spending most of his time. There should be no more than four to five feet between the two areas. You may have to use a bathroom if you have a big kitchen. Too much space leads to mistakes.

Now patrol the rest of your home. Put away breakables. Store chemicals of any kind in safe places. Pups get interested in the most unpredictable things. One distraught owner called us in a panic because her tiny pup had somehow gotten up on her bedside table and eaten two laxative tablets! The results were predictable.

Don't worry about what you think they might like to chew—worry about what they can chew. Some of the favorite items that dogs chew and swallow are steel wool pads (especially if used to clean a roasting pan) razor blades, remote controls, the padding under rugs, pencils, glasses, underwear and pantyhose.

Anything that has touched your body is of interest to your pup. Pups appear to be "out to get you" when they eat your favorite things, but they are simply drawn to things that smell like you. For a pup, carrying around your sock is like having a snapshot of you.

Common Household Dangers

HOUSEPLANTS

Many are toxic to pups, causing vomiting and diarrhea. Put them out of reach or spray the leaves with Bitter Apple leaf protector. If your pup likes to excavate your big plants try large amounts of ground black pepper over the soil.

ELECTRICAL WIRES

Chewing on these has started fires and killed pets. Remove what you can, secure the rest and coat with an antichew product.

BONES

Any bone your dog can crunch should be kept away from your pet. Tiny fragments can cut its insides. Use sterilized bones from the pet store or large beef leg bones. Chicken, pork and fish bones are always bad.

ANTIFREEZE

Bright green, sweet and fatal; it is in many garages and under parked cars in the city. This is a life-and-death emergency if you think your dog might have drunk some.

OPEN WINDOWS

Dogs can and have jumped out of open windows that were many floors up, and from moving cars. One dog we know hates the neighbor's dog so intensely that it jumps out a second-story window to get at him. Get grills for your windows or open them from the top. When driving, keep windows open only a safe width and don't allow your dog to ride with his head out.

STRING, YARN, PANTYHOSE

I know of a Bernese Mountain Dog that was tragically lost to a skein of yarn. It got tangled in her intestines and killed her. Dogs will eat rope, string, pantyhose and the like. If they do, call your vet. If you see some appearing at the other end of your dog, DON'T PULL IT OUT. You could hurt your dog. Immediately go to your vet.

CHOCOLATE

Toxic to dogs. Keep chocolate out of reach.

Bringing Your Puppy Home

THE FAMILY EFFECT

Missy is going home. This happy, distractable little golden bitch is on the hyper side. We've been working hard to calm her down, and as she sits quietly in the elevator next to me, I am pleased with her progress. The elevator opens onto a hallway of sound. "Missy Missy Missy," the three children scream as they all try to touch her. Missy explodes into a whirl of jumping, mouthing energy. The parents join the group, everyone laughing and petting her as she leaps at them with snapping jaws. I try to tell her off, I try to stop the family and explain—I am but a whisper in the bellow of this family. No one is listening to anyone.

Preparing for the puppy before he comes home will make your lives considerably easier. You need to purchase or borrow a crate, a wire baby gate, two metal bowls, toys, a flat buckle collar, lead and whatever food he is used to. Make an appointment at your veterinarian's within the first two days of your pup's arrival.

Choose a name. We suggest something simple, a name that does not rhyme with commands. The shorter the name, the better. Our dogs have been named Irish, Tee, Beau, Nutmeg, Kesl, Sasha, Piper, Fawn, Deacon, Caras, Tri and Rose.

No matter where you get your dog, be sure to find out about diet and feeding schedules, vaccinations, as well as wormings. Has he been going outside or on papers? Has he been crated before? What type of grooming will your breed need? Ask for a list of equipment you will have to purchase.

Discuss the return policy ahead of time. Some pups may just not be right for you, and you should be able to return them with no complaints if that is true. We recently returned a lovely pup because she did not have the temperament we wanted to live with. It happens. If you sign a contract, read the whole thing. Many pet stores won't ever refund your money and will replace the pup only if you bring them the dead body of the first one.

If the dog is pure-bred, get a pedigree from your breeder and inquire about registration. Sometimes it takes a while to get all the paperwork in order, but your breeder should be able to fill you in on the status of the registration and when you might expect it.

Get the names of any local trainers, veterinarians, groomers, dog walkers or boarding kennels that your resource recommends.

Pick your pup up early in the day; that way she has more time to adjust before any of you attempt to sleep. Tell excited friends, neighbors and relatives to stay home. Your pup is a baby; she needs a day or two to settle in before she meets the world.

If you can pick her up on Friday or at the beginning of a vacation, so much the better. The more time you all have together at first the easier the adjustment will be.

Bring a bath towel, a roll of paper towels and some plastic bags for the car ride home. Chances are that you will have an uneventful trip, but with all the excitement your pup may vomit or urinate. It's like an umbrella: if you have this stuff, you'll probably never need it.

The best place for a puppy to ride on the way home is in your lap on the passenger side, so you'll need someone else to drive. Put the pup on a towel in your lap. If the pup is squirmy, put the collar on her for easy holding. You do NOT want a puppy loose in your car.

Many pups fall asleep on the ride home, but some whimper, shake or cry for part, if not all, of the trip home. Others spend their time trying to explore everything nonstop. Those responses are normal, telling you more about your pup's personality. The mellow pup will sleep or play gently. The bold, pushy pup will try repeatedly to get away from you and explore. The sensitives will whimper. If you have a full out, top-of-the-lungs screamer, turn around; this pup will be a pain to live with.

Once home, take her right to her potty area. Let her sniff around for a few minutes. She may go, she may not. After a few minutes take her into the room that will be her area for the next few months. Put her down and let her look around. Everyone should just sit and watch her quietly. She has no way of knowing she's "yours"—give her some time. If she comes over, speak to her sweetly; scratch her gently on the chest. Let her explore at her own speed. I recommend you keep her on an easy-to-clean surface.

The only thing she can't do is develop bad habits. If she starts to chew the wrong thing (which she will), distract her with a clap of your hands and praise her the minute she stops chewing; give her a toy and praise her for playing with that. When she jumps up, gently place her on the floor to pet her. Tell her warmly how good it is for a puppy to have her feet on the floor.

Be careful that the games you play don't teach her bad habits as well. No tug-of-war, wrest-

A big puppy can be a lapful on a long drive home.

If you use his name frequently in conversation—"Bart did the cutest thing today"—or when you talk to the dog but want nothing from him, then your dog will soon learn to ignore his name.

Use your dog's name when you praise him or when you are commanding him. He'll soon pay close attention when he hears it, as it will always mean that you want something from him or he is about to be praised.

In conversation with him or with friends, call him "my dog," the "B-man," anything you want, but save the actual name for important communication between you and him.

ling or rough play that encourages puppy teeth on human flesh. These games teach her to be rough and aggressive.

Keep on the same feeding schedule she's used to. If you don't know the schedule, then three meals a day—morning, noon and late afternoon—is a good program.

Now comes nighttime. We'll do our best, but don't anticipate a lot of sleep. It usually takes three to four days for a puppy to get into a sleep routine in her new home, so be patient.

All this change is hard on your pup. Imagine being a small child from a large family, suddenly scooped up by friendly strangers and taken to a new home all by yourself.

Feed early—no later than 7:00 P.M. No snacks or water after that. Give her a good play session before bed and plenty of time in the bathroom area. If she pants after the playing, give her an ice cube. This will quench her thirst without filling her bladder. All this helps her to be empty before she goes to bed.

Putting a hot-water bottle wrapped in a towel in with her will remind her of her littermates' warmth and is calming for some pups.

A ticking clock helps others. A sterilized bone stuffed with cheese makes others forget their worries. A fake lambskin toy comforts still more. Remember, warmth induces sleep, so keep that puppy warm and dry.

Put the crate next to your bed. It is comforting to the pup if she can see, hear and smell you. It is also easy for you to hear her when she gets restless and needs to go out. You can expect one or two trips a night to the paper or outside the first few weeks. I just sleep in sweatclothes during this period.

Some pups will cry briefly, then settle down. Others will fuss well into the night, tearing at your heartstrings.

One solution is to take the pup into your bed. BUT if you're going to do that, do it from the start. If you let her cry for an hour or so and then take her to bed, the pup learns that if she cries for a long, long period something wonderful will happen. Bad lesson.

If you decide not to give in, don't. Move the pup to an area where she can get to the papers if she needs them. Leaving a radio on may help both of you fall to sleep. Quite a few pups will complain for hours on end. It is a heartbreaking, frustrating and exhausting period. If yours is one of those, practice leaving her for brief periods during the day and use the corrections discussed in the crating section to settle her down. That way, when evening comes, you'll both know what to expect and how to handle it.

After a few nights of crying herself to sleep she'll adjust and bed down quietly.

Regardless of how you make it through the night, the puppy goes out first thing in the A.M. Puppies cannot wait for you to have coffee, shower or shave. When they get up, they have to go RIGHT AWAY. See the section on housebreaking (pages 52–57) for the whole story.

Puppy Behaviors That Nobody Tells You About

Puppies often get the hiccups after they eat. Nothing to worry about. They grow out of it.

Puppies have FRAP (Frenetic Random Activity Periods) two or more times a day. This is when your normally sweet puppy runs like a wild thing through your house jumping up on furniture and people, barking, spinning in circles, charging around and generally having a good time. These usually last five minutes or less. He will also grow out of this.

Puppies lie in the "flying frog" position—back legs straight out behind them, front legs straight out in front. This is extremely cute.

Puppies love to chew on the porcelain cover of the bolt that holds your toilet to the floor. Why? You tell me.

Even famous dog trainers have to get up and take their puppies out. A real-life, 5:30 A.M. snapshot of me doing what has to be done. No one said it was all glamour.

HELPFUL ADVICE

Getting a puppy, like being pregnant, makes you part of the public domain. Everyone who once owned a dog of any breed, age or training level gives you advice. A great deal of that advice is inevitably violent. Hit them with a rolled up newspaper, smack them on the nose if they mouth you, rub their face in their mess if they make a mistake. The list goes on.

These same people will tell you they would never crate a dog; that's cruel. It always confuses me why some people seem to think that hitting is OK but crating is harsh.

Regardless of the exact form of the advice, the intentions are good even if the information is faulty. My advice is thank them very much, give them a big smile and ignore the advice.

Housebreaking

Setting Up a Feeding Schedule

All puppies need to be on a food-and-water schedule during the housebreaking period. If you know when everything goes in, you will be able to predict when it will come out.

• Leave food and water down for 20 minutes. The pup will soon learn to eat when fed. (The exception to this is puppies of tiny breeds who are under five pounds. Very small pups need food available to them at all times. Ask your veterinarian about specifics.)

• Do NOT add yummy extras to the food if your pup doesn't eat. This is the road to picky eating and may upset his stomach. The occasional skipped meal, as long as the puppy is energetic, drinking normally and has normal stools, is usually nothing to worry about.

• Changing foods suddenly can upset his stomach and cause diarrhea. Find one food and stick to it. If you must change, do so over a three-day period, adding in a bit more of the new food every day.

• Feed dry food. It is easier, less expensive and better for the dog's teeth.

• Feed three meals a day before 5 months of age, two meals a day after that, unless your breeder or vet instructs otherwise.

• If your pup is defecating five or more times a day and/or has soft stools, take a stool sample to your vet to be checked for worms. If he does not have worms try cutting back his food by 10 percent. Some greedy pups just eat much more than they can digest, leading to too much soft poop.

• Offer water three to five times a day. Pups need about 1 cup water for every 8 pounds of body weight per day. Offer a 24-pound pup 1 cup of water three times a day. If he always finishes it and looks for more, go to 1½ cups.

• If your pup drinks a lot, he will have to urinate several times in the next few hours. A cup to a 10-pound pup is like 15 cups to a 150-pound man. That man would have to go! Get that puppy outside or to his papers.

• If your pup consistently drinks large amounts or is urinating frequently—10 or more times a day—or urinates tiny amounts all over the place, talk to your vet.

• If your pup is thirsty but it is not time for water, offer him one or two ice cubes, which will quench his thirst without overloading his system.

• Keep toilet seats down, cat food and water bowls up during housebreaking.

• If the weather is hot, offer him free access to water and walk him accordingly.

General Rules for Housebreaking

Routine, prevention, proper cleanup and common sense are the ruling forces of housebreaking and paper training. Housebreaking means teaching your dog only to go to the bathroom outside. Paper training means teaching him only to use papers in the house. You can't do both at once.

• Pup must urinate and defecate first thing in morning and last thing at night.

• He must be taken to his papers or outside anytime he comes out of the crate, after he wakes up, eats, plays hard or chews.

• Out of sight is into trouble. If your pup likes to run out of sight, keep a lead on him in the house. Close supervision is the key.

• Cleaning with an odor neutralizer is a must! NEVER use a product with ammonia in it. Ammonia is in urine and that familiar smell will be an invitation to the pup.

• If you catch the pup making a mistake, make a startling sound by slapping the wall or clapping your hands. This will often stop him midpee. Then scoop him up and take him to the right spot. When he finishes what he started, praise him.

• Do not rub his nose in it, yell, spank or swat him. He is a baby. This is a mistake, not a felony. If you make a big deal over the mistake, you create more problems.

• Put your pup and yourself on a walking schedule.

Here is a sample schedule for a four-month-old puppy.

7:00 A.M. Take him out or to papers. If pup goes to bathroom, enjoy supervised free time while you have breakfast, get dressed, etc. (If pup fails to go, then put him back in crate, give him breakfast, and go out for another walk.)

8:00 A.M. Food and water him in crate.

8:45 A.M. Walk.

12:30 P.M. Walk or take him to papers. (If successful, give him a half-hour of supervised free time. If not, crate him and retry in a half-hour.)

1:00 P.M. or so. Offer food and water.

1:45 P.M. Take him out or to papers. (If successful, free time. If not, as above.)

6:00 P.M. Walk or take him to papers.

7:00 P.M. Feed and water.
No food or water after 7:00 P.M.

7:45 P.M. Take him out or to papers.

11:00 P.M. Take him out or to papers. Puppy must urinate and defecate. Crate overnight.

One of the secrets of cleaning up a wet spot is placing a paper towel over it and then a section of newspaper. Now stand on the spot. After doing this, you won't be able to find the wet spot. The paper towel between the newspaper and the rug protects the carpeting from the newsprint.

• Keep the schedule the same on the weekends. You can sleep in when he's housebroken. Routine, routine, routine. You are teaching the puppy when he can "expect" to go out.

• Take the pup to the same area all the time. This will stimulate him to go quickly. Select a spot that is convenient for you. Some city owners teach their pups to go on the grates in the street. That sure makes for easy cleanup. Regardless of where it is, take him to it every time and he'll soon learn exactly why he's there.

• Don't dawdle. If he's gone, praise him well and then go back in—unless, of course, this is one of his exercise walks. In that case, take him to his spot, wait till he goes, then exercise him. This is another way to reward him for going outside.

• Teach the pup to go on command by saying "Hurry up" as he squats. Praise him calmly until he's done, then make a big deal over him and give him a treat. In a few weeks he'll squat as soon as you say "Hurry up." This is a great command when you're running late or it's cold and rainy outside.

• Once you have had one clean week, then you can add a half-hour to every free period. Pups on this strict type of schedule need plenty of exercise—15 minutes three times a day chasing a ball, playing with another dog or walking fast. If you want to spend some extra time with your pup inside, then put a leash on him and keep him near you after the free period. Be sure he has a toy or rawhide to entertain himself with. This will keep him near you and out of trouble.

• Once the pup has three weeks clean, eliminate the after-meal walks. As the dog matures, slowly shift mid-day walks to later in the day until you are just walking the dog in the morning, when you get home from work and before bed. Usually by eight months, puppies are ready for three walks a day but, as always, let your puppy be the guide.

• Puppies that suddenly leave the room, begin to sniff the floor in circles or pant when they have not been exercising probably need to go. It is better to be safe than sorry. Prevention, not correction, speeds up housebreaking.

• What do you do if you catch them in the act? A sharp "No," scooping the puppy up and running him outside, where you set him down and praise him for completing the task, is good. Yelling, hitting, rubbing his nose in it, etc., will teach the puppy that you get upset when you SEE him going. He will quickly learn to go out of sight. If you do not see him go but discover it later, it is YOUR fault. Yell at yourself if you must, but leave the pup alone.

City House-breaking

Housebreaking a puppy in the city is more difficult than in the suburbs. Because of disease, pups are quarantined indoors until they are 16 weeks old. The only thing to do is to paper-train and then housebreak, unless you are fortunate enough to have access to a garden or a fenced-in, safe rooftop. This double step, paper training then housebreaking, is confusing to many pups. And then there are other problems.

It takes longer for the pup to get the idea because you catch the pup in the act, scoop him up, grab your keys, unlock the three locks, get into the hall, lock the three locks, run to the elevator, ring, wait for its arrival, hop on, ring the ground floor, wait for it to get there, run across the lobby and to the sidewalk. By then even I have forgotten what I went out there for.

Worse yet are the walk-ups. Sarah lost 10 pounds housebreaking her Springer pup, Sasha, from a third-floor walk-up.

And then there are the distractions. One client explained how his puppy would no longer go outside after a fire engine came roaring down the street just as the pup went to squat. Poor little thing thought that his squatting was to blame for this horrible monster.

Here are the rules of city housebreaking:

• Since housebreaking the city dog is a two-step process—paper training and then housebreaking—don't go wild with praise when your pup goes on the paper. Tell him a moderate "Good boy." In a few weeks you'll never want him to go indoors again.

• Carry the pup around with you outside as much as you can. If he is used to the city noises and sights, he will relax faster. Relaxed puppies go to the bathroom. Do not put him down or allow him to visit with other dogs until your vet says it is OK.

• Teach the puppy to "hurry up" on the papers so that when you move to the outside, he'll quickly understand what you mean.

• Pick up after your dog. Whether picking up is required by law or not, it

is disgusting to leave dog feces on the street or in a park. Parks are for everyone—clean up.

Carry a puppy by supporting both the front and rear end (top). Never pick up a pup by the armpits. This can hurt him. Always support both ends when you lift him up.

PAPER-TRAINING GUIDELINES

• Follow same rules as with housebreaking but simply take pup to papers instead of outside.

• Change papers after each use. Put a slightly soiled paper underneath the fresh ones. The scent will encourage the puppy.

• Wipe under papers with an odor neutralizer daily. This keeps the smell off the floor, discouraging the pup from sniffing the edge of the paper but actually going off of it.

• Putting waxed paper or plastic under the papers can save your floor or rug from staining or long-term odor.

• As the pup gets older, take him out of the crate, carry him to different areas of the house, and tell him "Papers." Then walk back to papers with him. This will teach him to run to his papers when he has the urge to go.

Housebreaking 9 to 5

If you work nine to five, you need to make time in the morning for walking, playing with and training your pup. He'll be raring to go after a good night's sleep. It is not fair to expect him to sit in the kitchen all day without a good romp in the morning, and it makes training difficult. Getting a walker in midday to care for the pup is essential for the first eight months, but it is not to replace quality time with you in the morning.

Because the pup is left for long periods, he won't be able to hold it at first. He'll need to use papers for the first few months, so confine him to "his" room. Set it up as instructed on page 46. Someone will have to come home at lunchtime for the first few months. If you can't, hire a walker. Isolating a puppy for 9 to 10 hours straight without any company at all almost always leads to problems.

At about 16 weeks crate him either before or after the midday walk. When he is still older, crate him both before and after the midday walk. Now is also the time to begin to slowly move that midday walk later in the afternoon. The goal is to have the pup at seven months of age holding it for eight hours at a time and walked late in the afternoon. When eight months rolls around, it will be an easy change from walking to waiting until you get home.

Another problem you will no doubt encounter is "working owner guilt." This nagging feeling that you are a bad parent leads to giving the pup nonstop attention whenever you are home. Guilt is a useless emotion. The reality is you have to work and the pup will adjust, given that his basic needs are attended to. Smothering the pup with indiscriminate attention will create confusion and anxiety in your pup. While your pup will love it, it creates an extreme contrast between you being home and you being gone, making it emotionally hard on your pup when you leave. Try to give your guilt a positive direction through training and exercise. After a good romp and a brief training session when you arrive home, allow your pup to be a part of your evening but not the focus of it.

Puppies alone for long hours must be left in a confined area. They will not be able to hold it all day in a crate. If you leave them loose, they can harm themselves, damage your home and develop bad habits. Protect them by putting them in a safe place.

Solving Common Housebreaking Problems

Pup dirties crate.
Either the puppy is crated too long, the crate is too big or there is bedding in the crate. Change all these things. If he still goes in the crate, confine him to a room with papers down and crate door open for two weeks and then try crating again.

Pup eats feces.
Yuck. Sprinkle a product called For-Bid, available from your vet, or Adolph's Meat Tenderizer on his food. This makes the stool unpleasant tasting to some dogs. If this does not work in a few days, stop. Next try spraying the stool with Bitter Apple. Don't let the dog see you spray it; then let him do a taste test. Often it is a chronic problem that only rapid pickup can prevent.

Pup makes mistakes out of sight.
You probably inadvertently taught him this by being harsh when you caught him in the act. The cure is preventing mistakes by keeping him near you either on lead or in the crate for a few months. During this time praise him enthusiastically for going outside. Keep up your end of the deal by sticking to the schedule and not changing his diet. Extra outdoor exercise is needed during this period.

Pup has favorite indoor spot.
Pups often choose out-of-the-way places to mess. He figures, "Hey, no one else is using this spot. I guess it'll make a great bathroom." Likely targets are dining rooms, formal living rooms, the guestroom. First, clean with an odor neutralizer and then spend time there. Read the paper or write a letter in the area with your dog on leash with you. Feed him there. Spending time in this location is not a punishment; it is informing the dog that this area is now a part of his turf. Few dogs want to dirty where they have to spend time.

Pup won't go outside.
This is a common city problem. Take him for a long, brisk walk first thing in the morning; this will often get things moving. If not, on a weekend make a big bowl of warm water mixed with a little wet food first thing in the morning. Let him drink a large amount, then take a good long hike. He'll go. If defecating is the problem, use an infant glycerin suppository to get things moving. It's not glamorous but does the trick. Do not use more than once each day for three days in a row. Teaching the "Hurry up" command will help to tell him exactly what you want. Regardless of how you get him to go, be sure to praise the pup and give a special treat when he does comply.

Pup won't go in the rain.
You're not alone. The best thing to do is wait for a warm rain, don your foul weather gear and go for a nice long walk. Sound happy, sing in the rain, get him used to it. Delicate breeds should wear rain gear of their own. Accept no nonsense about it. If you can stand it, he can.

Pup goes on the way out.
Carry him out if you can. If he is too big, looping a leash or rope under his belly can help keep him from squatting. Do not yell at him, as this will only make matters worse.

Dog goes when he greets me or guests.
This is called submissive urination. Do NOT punish the dog! Any type of scolding, yelling or upset on your part can instill a long-term problem in your dog. See page 197 for details.

Preventing Bad Habits

Your puppy will get his adult teeth between four to six months of age. During that time he will go through periods of increased chewing and discomfort. Get him rawhides, gumabones, rope toys to chew. Choose toys that he can fit in his mouth easily; rawhide sticks often work well. Rope bones can be wet down, wrung out and frozen as a special treat. An ice cube can also help numb the pain and is a favorite for many pups. Other than that, you just have to wait it out. Once this stage is past, some of the mouthing and chewing will stop naturally.

Prevention, easier than correction, is the name of the game when raising a puppy. This section outlines some basic techniques that help to prevent bad habits from developing.

GROOMING

Start grooming immediately, even if there isn't much to brush yet. Handle and rub his feet, look in his ears and eyes. Generally check him over thoroughly. If he struggles to get free, do not release him. This will only train him that struggling wins his freedom. Grasp his collar and give him a quick shake, telling him in a stern voice "Stop it." Immediately praise him when he calms down. Some pups you can just wait out; when he calms down, praise him, then let him go. This will show him that being patient is his quickest route to freedom. If he really gets upset, see instructions on page 212.

COMING WHEN CALLED

One of the worst things you can do to a pup is scold him when he comes to you. A typical scenario is you find something chewed on the floor. "Bosco, come here," you say. And when he arrives, you scold him: "Bad dog! No! What did you do?"

Bosco thinks, "What I did was come to you. What a mistake that was. I sure won't do that again!"

Chasing him also will ruin your recalls. Chase games seem like a great deal of fun, but the pup soon learns that running away gets you to follow him. He'll run away when you try to crate him, get him inside or take something out of his mouth. To teach him how to respond to this command quickly, with a wagging tail, see page 72.

PLAYING

Rough games encourage rough

Puppies chew everything. Close supervision is your only defense. If you can't keep an eye on the pup, put him in his crate or safe area until you have more time to spend watching him.

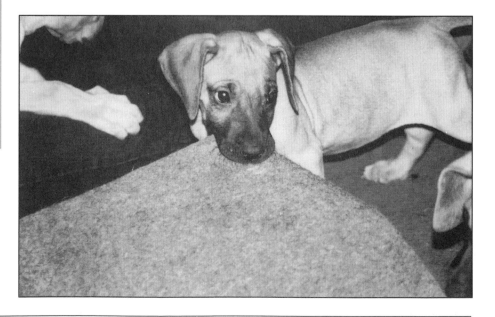

behavior. Tug-of-war, wrestling and other rowdy forms of play develop assertion and aggression. What is cute in a feisty three-month-old pup is scary in a 90-pound adult dog. Skip the problems and play the games taught on page 114.

JUMPING
Petting an eagerly jumping pup is hard to rest but, again, what you teach the pup you are teaching the adult. Don't encourage a puppy to do anything you do not want your adult dog to do. Direction and praise are the keys to success.

CHEWING
Dog toys are the only objects puppies should be given to chew. If you allow him to chew an old shoe, how is he supposed to know which are his and which are yours? Kiss your Reeboks good-bye.

FEEDING
Get your pup used to you touching him while he eats. Stroke him for a few seconds when you put down his bowl, then leave him in peace. For the first month, walk up to him while he eats and toss an extra special treat in. This way he will learn to love it when you approach his bowl. If he tenses up or growls, see the instructions on page 249.

BARKING AND WHINING
Do not pet a barking or whining puppy. This almost automatic human response to soothe the upset youngster is seen as praise by the pup, leading to more of the same later in life. If you can, ignore the noise. When the pup stops, praise him. Soon he will realize that the quickest way to your heart is through silence. If he doesn't stop, barks at you for attention, barks when left alone, or barks in his crate, please see page 43.

HANDLING
Get a puppy used to all kinds of handling early. When you pet your pup, be sure to gently grab his skin, hold his tail for a second, lift up one of his feet. Always be gentle; you do not want to hurt the pup. If you do these things on a regular basis, then when a child enters your home, your dog will take accidental grabbing and pulling in stride. Supervise children and dogs at all times. Children must be taught how to handle a puppy gently.

Giving the puppy the proper article to chew teaches what you want him to do. Replace the wrong articles you find in your puppy's mouth with dog toys and then praise. Soon he'll get the idea.

Your First Trip to the Veterinarian

What Will Happen on the First Visit to the Veterinarian

EXAM

The veterinarian will check your pup's eyes, ears, throat, temperature and skin. He will listen to the heart, palpate the belly and check for swollen glands. This normally takes 5 to 10 minutes and is not painful. This is a good time to ask questions about general care, diet, eating schedules, how to clean the ears, clip the nails or any other health-related issues that you have questions about.

VACCINATIONS

Inoculations are critical for your pet's long-term health and safety. A seven-week-old puppy has usually had one set of vaccinations. These vaccinations are usually given in three- to four-week intervals. If your puppy is due, he will get a shot that protects him from such diseases as parvovirus, an intestinal virus that causes terrible diarrhea and can kill; distemper, another miserable and often fatal illness; canine hepatitis and more. The most common age for completion of vaccinations is 16 weeks, but in some areas it will be as short as 12 or as long as 20. As your puppy's health and life are involved, follow your vet's advice closely.

PARASITE CHECK

It is impossible to housebreak a wormy puppy, so have your pup checked regularly until six months of age. Most pups have roundworms; they can also have hookworms and whipworms. These worms can only be detected and identified under a microscope. Tapeworms' telltale signs are short ricelike segments on the outside of your dog's stool. Although over-the-counter medications exist for these worms, we do not recommend them. Trust your vet to choose the correct type and proper dosage of medication.

Heartworms, another type of internal parasite, can only be detected through a blood test. Transmitted through mosquitoes, these are a more serious type of worm. They are not transmittable to people. You will have to medicate your pup throughout the warm weather as your vet recommends.

If your pup has loose stools, dry skin, dull coat, can't seem to keep weight on or is voraciously hungry all the time, talk to your vet. Worms and other internal parasites can cause these problems.

Dr. Lawrence Zola takes a little extra time introducing himself to a new client.

How to Handle the First Visit

Make your first appointment within two days of coming home. Even if your pup is not due for a vaccination, take him or her in anyway.

If you have to drive to the vet, then set the appointment for a time an hour or more after your pup eats. This will lessen the chances of car sickness. If you are driving alone, put the pup in a crate. If the crate is too large for the car, then tether the pup to a door handle or seat belt so that he can get on and off the seat but not come over and bother you while you're driving. Again, pack paper towels and plastic bags. Anything could happen.

Bring with you the puppy's health record if you have one, a stool sample, and your puppy on leash and collar. Even though you will be carrying the pup the whole time, the leash and collar are a good precaution against a squirming puppy.

The vet will use the stool sample to check for worms microscopically. They need only a small amount to do this. I used to work at a vet's office and saw concerned owners bring in coffee cans filled to the rim. That is way, way too much.

Once you arrive at the office, keep your puppy in your arms. Until your puppy is fully vaccinated, he should not be meeting strange dogs. As clean as all veterinary offices are, sick dogs do come and go, so keep your young one off the floor.

When it is your turn, take your pup in and place him on the table. Talk to your pup in a cheery voice. Be sure that your petting is gentle and relaxed. Often when we get tense, our hands get tense. Holding the pup tightly and petting him quickly or roughly are sure ways to make him nervous about this first visit.

When the vet enters, be friendly with him. The puppy will pick this right up. If you are relaxed and like the vet, your pup will too. Any tension you have about the process can pass right into the pup. The goal is to make this a positive experience.

No matter what the vet does—take the pup's temperature, give him a shot, look in his ears—stay happy, cheerful and relaxed. If you sound upbeat and unconcerned, your puppy will stay more relaxed and happy.

Do NOT reassure, console or comfort him. When you do these things, you will inevitably sound concerned, tense and worried. This in turn will make your pup concerned, tense and worried. Remember, your dog understands your tone of voice better than he does what you say. You have to use your tone to convey the message that all is well. Try to sound more like a cheerleader than a worried friend.

Setting a happy, unconcerned tone will help make your pup's first veterinary experience a positive one.

TiP

MONITORING YOUR PUPPY'S HEALTH

A sudden change in behavior can indicate a problem. If your active pup suddenly doesn't want to get up, or your moderate drinker can't seem to get enough water, or your good eater, turns up his nose at food—call your vet. Vomiting, diarrhea, listlessness, refusing food and/or water, unexplained limping or whimpering, thick discharge from eyes or nose, smelly ears, dragging his hind end across the floor (you'll know exactly what I mean if you see it) all mean a quick trip to your vet.

As active and full of life as your puppy seems, it takes little time for them to dehydrate and get in trouble. Don't delay.

Your Puppy's Developmental Stages

0–7 WEEKS: MOTHER AND SIBLINGS

Puppies learn about social interaction, play and moderating their aggression from their mother and littermates. Pups should stay with their litters until seven weeks of age. As cute as orphaned pups are, avoid picking one as a pet. Without the training from their mother and littermates, they can grow up to be difficult and aggressive.

7–8 WEEKS: TIME TO GO HOME

This is the best time to bring a puppy home. Mentally mature enough to adjust to the change, pups settle in well.

8–16 WEEKS: TIME TO LEARN

Start of Training. Puppy kindergarten can begin. This is the time the puppy learns how to learn, so keep it fun. Make sure the puppy is successful. Her need to be with you is strong and stays strong until four months of age. Now is the time to instill "come."

Socialization. After your vet says it is safe, it's time to see the world. Take the puppy with you. Expose her to as many sounds, sights and smells as possible. Keep her near you as you go about your day. Make sure to let her meet all kinds of people—children, old people, different races. Outside a mall is a wonderful place to relax and let the world come to you. Nothing too scary during this period. Eight to ten weeks old is typically a fear period, a time when the pup is particularly impressionable.

Traumatic experiences can leave lifelong impressions. If your pup seems scared by something, skip it until after eleven weeks of age. Hesitation is normal, panic is not. If she does get spooked, don't baby her. Reassurance can make matters worse. Happily withdraw until she is older, then make a point of getting her used to it.

4–6 MONTHS: KEEP WORKING

Socialization continues. Get into a local puppy class if there is a fun one around. Grab this time while you have it because adolescence will soon be upon you. As the pup gets older, she will become more confident and independent. Keep practicing. Start to add distractions. Practice in strange places. Take the pup everywhere with you. This time is too precious to waste. Teething is during this period also.

6–12 MONTHS: NEUTERING TIME— THE BEGINNING OF ADOLESCENCE

Neuter now. Females do not need one litter. They do not need to go through a heat. Males do not need to "have sex once." Skip it all. Leave breeding to the breeders. Your pet will live a longer, happier life if he or she is neutered. I neuter all my pets that I am not showing and strongly encourage you to do the same.

Soon your puppy will be a dog. Larger breeds tend to mature slower, smaller ones sooner, but they all will have begun to enter adulthood by nine months of age. If your relationship with your dog has not been strong up to now, you may see problems develop during the next six months.

APPLE: A story of wasted youth

Apple runs out of the room when she sees me. Speaking kindly to her and turning away, I offer my hand to the little face peeking around the corner. She ducks out of sight. This is not promising. Asking the couple what her history is, I discover increasingly bad news.

Apple was air-shipped to Mr. and Mrs. T. at 10 weeks of age, right smack in the middle of a fear period. She refused to come out of the crate, huddling in the rear of it, ears pinned back, wide eyed and panicked. She was spooked by everything and in a constant state of anxiety. She ate little, constantly hid for no apparent reason, and was startled by almost every noise.

Apple is frightened of people. She will not approach anyone other than her owners and is even a bit hesitant with the husband. I have them put a lead on her, then hand the leash to me. Apple panics. She bucks, rolls, dives under the chair, rolls some more and tries to bite me. I speak to her calmly, gently bringing her over to me. There she tolerates my stroking with a tense body and low head.

She is terrified of men, children and nonwhite people. Dogs are not racist; they simply learn to accept whoever they are exposed to. This dog had never seen anyone but her adult, white, female breeder. Therefore she is scared of everyone else. Taking a puppy everywhere when it is young and allowing anyone interested to say hello prevents this problem.

Noises spook her, metal on metal in particular. Perhaps a leftover from the flight, her noise sensitivity makes living in the city a trauma. She drags her owners to the curb, goes to the bathroom and then drags them back in.

She urinates on the bed. This is early training, not a socialization problem. The breeder had used bedsheets instead of newspaper for her pups to relieve themselves on. Consequently, they associate sheets, on or off the bed, with going to the bathroom.

If Mr. and Mrs. T. had known the questions to ask they might have avoided this. If they had been able to test the pup, they definitely would have seen trouble ahead of time. Now they are stuck in an uncomfortable position. This is not the dog they wanted or asked for. She may never recover from her early deprivation. What do they do? Do they keep her, living with a terrified, dirty, potentially dangerous dog for the next 10 years? Do they return her to the place that caused this in the first place? Can they possibly place her in another loving home, given her limitations?

This decision is causing them pain. They argue about it frequently. The husband feels strongly one way, the wife equally strongly another.

Owning an animal should never be like this. Buy from a reputable breeder. If you can't physically see the animal, get a video of it. Ask the breeder to do some of the puppy tests on the video.

Prevent these problems by showing your pup the world at the earliest possible opportunity. Learn and pay attention to the critical periods in a pup's development. Try not to do anything too upsetting to the pup during a fear period. If the puppy is traumatized by harsh treatment or an aggressive dog, it can last for the rest of his life. This does not mean to keep him housebound however. Take him out and about, just skip the air travel, visiting that friend with three-year-old boy triplets, and the Fourth of July celebration downtown. Be sensible.

Socialization: Shaping Your Puppy's Attitude to the World

What puppies learn from the age of two to four months of life sticks with them forever. This time period correlates to when wild pups are leaving the safety of the den for the first time. In the wild they must learn everything quickly in order to survive. Whatever is dangerous must be avoided. Wild animals do not have the luxury of making a mistake. A mistake could cost them their life.

Domestic dogs come with that programming still in place. The first few months in your home are some of the most important of all the years you will have together. Time spent now is a sound investment in the sanity of your dog.

If a puppy grows up in a quiet home seeing only adults, as a grown dog he may react with fear or aggression to anything he has never seen, like children, the elderly or other animals. If you want a confident, reliable companion, you need to spend time introducing him to the world when he is a puppy.

Until the pup completes his puppy vaccinations, you restrict how and where you take him. Riding in the car, carrying him around town, taking him to an area where few dogs have been are all good options.

Have the world come to you. Once your pup has settled in, have over friends of all ages. Let the pup follow you around the house so he is exposed to the sights and sounds of modern-day life. The more he sees and hears, the better.

The exception to this is the fear period that happens between 8 and 11 weeks of age. Things that spook the pup during this two-week period can remain ingrained for a long time. During this time avoid frightening experiences. Let the puppy stay at home playing with family and friends.

After this stage is over, your pup should have as many new, fun experiences as possible.

The bold, confident pup will take most things in stride as long as you sound like you're having a good time. His main problem is overenthusiasm. Trying to say hello to everybody and everything. Work on your "Off" and "Leave It" commands, explained on pages 83 and 156–57, respectively. As he gets more exposure, he will settle down.

If your dog is hesitant, don't force him; don't soothe him either. Enthusiasm, not consolation, is what is needed here. Act as you want your pup to act. If you are happy, relaxed and confident, your pup will act more so. You set the tone for the puppy.

The shy or nervous puppy needs extra time. It is critical that you let the pup learn at his own speed. Confidence can be encouraged, nurtured and praised, but it can't be forced. Most fears can be conquered if you are patient, moving forward a step at a time. If your dog becomes frightened of something, here are some things you can do:

FRIGHTENED OF NOISE

Your pup spooks when a truck goes by or during a thunderstorm. Laugh, be happy. Tell him this was the most fun he has had all day. Play a game with him.

When you get home, start to play noise games with your pup. When you make his dinner, mix it up with a metal spoon. Tell him how good this is, how much he will love it, while you rattle away with the spoon. Then set it down and let him eat.

When he is playing, drop a pan in the other room, then laugh and encourage him to come and investigate. If he does, give him a treat. Pet him gently while being verbally enthusiastic! What a brilliant, brave puppy! Over time, as your pup relaxes around noise, you can drop the pan closer to him. Judge the distance by your pup's recovery from the fear. He should be able to recover quickly. If he stays frightened for more than a few seconds, the noise was too loud or too close.

FRIGHTENED OF OBJECTS

Almost every pup is spooked by something at one time or another. Sometimes it is a most peculiar thing like a box or a garbage bag, but it could be anything. You'll see your pup stop dead, stick his head forward, bark and run backward. If he is brave enough to investigate, he'll stretch his nose out in front as far as possible creeping toward the dreaded thing practically on his belly. What can you do to help? Laugh! "What is that? Let's go see!" I tell my dogs "Check it out," and then I go over and squat next to whatever it is. I touch it and pat it, all the while saying what a brave dog I have and what fun we are having. Once the pup takes a few sniffs, he'll often walk right on up—all full of himself for investigating this scary thing.

FRIGHTENED OF PEOPLE

If your dog is frightened of someone, tell that person to ignore the dog. You go stand near a person and act relaxed. Shy dogs are always more comfortable approaching rather than being approached. Chat for a few min-utes and allow the dog to investigate if he wants. If he is hanging way back, try tossing a treat his way. Remember, stay happy and upbeat! When he takes the treat, drop one closer to you, then closer and closer. Ignore the dog. Let him get it if he feels like it.

Instruct the other person to squat down, sideways to the puppy. Direct eye contact will frighten the pup, so have them look at the floor. Be verbally supportive—"What a good dog! Say hello!"—and walk over to the person.

Don't allow the person to reach for the pup. This will set you back. When the pup does come up, have the person reach under his chin and scratch his chest. Reaching over his head will spook him. If he is too frightened to come all the way up, don't press it today, but make arrangements to see this person again.

Exposing your dog to all sorts of sights and sounds will help him to grow up into a stable, confident adult.

TiP

EIGHT EASY STEPS TO RUINING YOUR DOG

1. Isolate him. Make sure he thinks the world is a strange place.

2. Soothe him whenever he is frightened. Tell him it's OK and stroke him gently.

3. Allow him to growl. Tell yourself, "It's OK. He doesn't really mean it."

4. When he struggles to get out of your grasp, let him go. This teaches him that you have no control.

5. Hold the leash tight every time something frightening happens. Even better, say "Uh-oh" as you pull the lead tight.

6. Never let him play with other dogs.

7. Don't neuter him.

8. Leave him with children unsupervised. Allow children to harass him because he is such a "good dog."

Introducing Your Puppy to Your Older Pets

Purchasing a second dog is exciting and nervous making. Will the first one accept the second? Usually, yes. But there are things you can do to make it easier for both pets. Choose the opposite sex from your first dog; this lessens the chance of conflict. Choosing a calm, well-socialized puppy is another thing you can do. A dominant second dog may grow up to challenge the first. A more submissive pup won't.

The bigger the age difference the better. Wait to get a second pet until your first is a year or older. This will lessen tension and ensures the first is well in hand before you add another. Dogs do learn from each other both the good and the bad behaviors.

You want to avoid competition between the two. Start by introducing them off your property. This will be less threatening for the older dog, and you're more likely to have success. Do not force them together; allow them to interact as they wish. If the pup is rude—jumps on or barks at the older dog—expect the dog to growl or correct the puppy. The pup will learn respect and his place.

Do not try to treat them equally. Dogs do not like equality; they see it as ambiguity that must be resolved. They have to know who's in front of whom. Choose the most logical order, normally the older dog as dominant, and support the status quo. Treat your first dog as Number One. Greet him first, feed him first and give him more attention. Treat the newcomer as Number Two. Number Two won't mind. He'd be happy as Number Six, as long as he knew his number.

Some dogs and breeds are more possessive than others. If certain objects create tension, remove them or only give them when the dogs are crated with no possibility of fighting. Rawhides, real bones and food can all cause these types of reactions. Feed them separately, tether them each to a different doorknob during meals. Adult dogs will often protect their food. These simple things go a long way to prevent competition and possible aggression.

If your first pet is a cat, make sure its claws are clipped before you bring the puppy home. Some cats accept the pup immediately; some let the pup know whose house this is immediately; others stay under the bed for a week. Confining the pup for periods during the day will allow the cat to relax and move around. Again, do not force them together; they'll work it out. Put a lead and collar on your puppy and correct him if he chases the cat. (See page 81 for how to give a correction.) This should not be allowed. Be consistent about it and he'll soon stop.

Tri and Caras adored each other from the start, playing almost constantly. Having a nice older dog certainly makes the second puppyhood easier.

Caras does growl if Tri attempts to steal a toy, but that's normal and needed. Tri has to learn his place in the group.

Introducing Pups to . . .

. . . CHILDREN AND . . .

Children and dogs have to be supervised at all times. Children's running and screaming can get any puppy excited. The puppy ends up jumping, nipping or barking at them.

A concerned mother took me outside her home to show me the problem she was having. "Go ahead, John," she said. John, her eight-year-old son, happily complied, throwing himself on the ground and rolling down the hill in front of their home giggling all the way. Their young Springer bounded after, bouncing and barking, trying to mouth the boy as he spun along. "The puppy bites him," said the mother. "How do I stop him from doing that?"

"He's a puppy," I said, "and your son's a child. Put the puppy in the house when your son wants to do this. You can't expect a seven-month-old puppy to have self-control when one of his favorite people is rolling on the ground laughing."

The best games to play are quiet ones—petting, showing the child how to brush the puppy with a soft bristle brush, throwing toys for the pup to chase. Your example is important. If you are calm and relaxed, both the child and the dog will be more so.

Training the puppy around the children and establishing basic rules like no jumping and no mouthing is vital to teach the pup to be gentle with our young.

. . . WELL-MEANING ADULTS

Visiting adults are more difficult. People often think that since they've had dogs, they know exactly what to do with yours. I actually had a woman in New York come up, laugh and play with a pup I was walking, and when the pup went to jump up, she slapped him across the face. I will not share with you here what I said to that person.

In any case, most people mean well. They just get excited to see a pup. Explaining beforehand what you are trying to teach the pup helps prevent misunderstandings. No jumping, tug-of-war or wrestling—you are trying to teach her how to be calm and relaxed around guests, not wound like a top.

If your pup is hesitant, allow her to approach; do not try to force her. Instruct people to scratch her gently on the chest. This will be less intimidating than having someone reach over her head. Be sure that you sound happy and relaxed. Your pup will get courage from you. If the pup has hair over her eyes, trim it or pull it back. Seeing what's going on is critical for a shy puppy.

Food is a great training tool. It is used to teach behaviors; once the dog understands the command, phase out the food but keep up the praise! I use food until the pup begins to respond to the command. Once that happens, I praise him enthusiastically but only give him the treat every other time. When that's going well, I move to food every third or fourth time—always continuing to praise. Gradually I eliminate the food altogether. If your pup knows the command but will only do it for a treat—NO MORE TREATS! Put him on lead, insist that he respond, then praise him for being such a good dog.

Food is a terrific tool for teaching shy, fearful or active dogs. Use it to focus the pup, then phase it out. The problem with food is not in using it but in removing it after the pup has learned the basics. Food should be used like gold stars, a terrific way to motivate youngsters but counterproductive if given out to more advanced students.

Puppy Kindergarten

By the age of seven weeks, your pup is ready to learn the basic commands if taught in a fun, relaxed manner. His attention span is short, so do three- to five-minute sessions a few times a day. These should always be positive and fun for both you and your pup.

Every day your pup lives with you, he learns things. If he mouths you and you squeal, he learns that mouthing you is entertaining. If you call him and he runs under the bed, he is learning that you can be avoided. Since he is learning anyway, why

not teach him to behave well?

Puppy kindergarten sets the foundation upon which your future communication is built. It teaches him early the joy of learning, that you both can communicate clearly, and that you're a lot of fun to listen to. Like all training, puppy kindergarten has three levels:

TEACH IT

The first level, teaching, is the repetition of word followed by action. You command "Sit," guide the dog into a sit, and then praise him as if he spoke his first word. You do this over and over until amazingly one day you say "Sit," and he does.

USE IT

This is the homework stage of dog training. The pup is still on lead, and you set aside time to practice the command. He is doing it on his own, but you are right there to guide him if he forgets or is confused. This is the longest stage of any training and involves practicing in different locations, around different distractions from different positions, but always in control and ready to guide the dog into the correct response.

EXPECT IT

The last level of training is the stage we all want: when the doorbell rings, you tell the dog to sit and he does. It's not a miracle. It's the result of hard work, practice and praise. If you use the command frequently around the house, your dog will develop an almost automatic response to it, and you will come to expect immediate obedience.

Introducing the Collar and Lead

Start training your puppy on a flat nylon or leather buckle collar. Slip or choke collars are unnecessary for most pups. Put the buckle collar on tight enough that it can't slip over his head, but loose enough that you can fit two of your fingers underneath easily.

The first time you put a collar on your pup, it will annoy him. Like a toddler with shoes, a pup will spend most of the time trying to get this new thing off. He may scratch, shake, spin and roll. The collar isn't hurting him; the pup is reacting to a new sensation. After a while, he'll get used to it and relax. When that happens, you're ready to add the lead.

Being on leash will bring about another flurry of confusion in your pup. All of a sudden he can't go where he wants—and has no understanding of why. Now something pulls on his neck every time he tries to walk around. Your pup may freeze in place, start biting the lead, buck around like a wild mustang, or balk for a moment and then accept it—those are normal reactions.

Your job is to help him through this as smoothly and quickly as possible, while teaching him that you are the source of praise and guidance. If your pup freezes in place, do not go over to him. This will only reward him

Rose, Sarah's Australian Shepherd pup, has never worn a collar before. Her reactions are perfectly normal. She'll get used to it quickly.

THE FIFTH-WEEK PLATEAU

About five weeks into teaching your pup anything new, he will wake up one morning with a blank look on his face. You will say "Sit" or "Down" or whatever it is that you have been teaching him, and he will stare at you.

This is a normal part of learning. The thing he did so well for the last week is lost somewhere in his brain. Some say it is moving from short-term memory to long-term memory and while it's in transit, it is unavailable. Whatever the reason is, understanding will return by the next week, stronger than ever.

Have faith. Be patient. Keep at it.

for his immobility. Squat down, praise him, clap your hands, encourage him to come to you. If he does—terrific! Have a party! He has just learned to go to you when unsure—an important lesson. If he refuses to move, fine; just drop the leash and go about your business. He won't stay frozen forever. Once he relaxes and walks around, you can start your training. Some pups need to learn at their own speed.

Allow the puppy to buck and spin at the end of the leash; at that point he can't listen to you anyway—he's busy. The moment he stops, praise him and call him over to you. Praise him enthusiastically for his bravery and give him a treat. This teaches him to come to you if he's upset and scared. Next, stand up and take a few steps while you continue praising. If

he is hesitant, use a treat to lure him to follow. Hold it low so he can see it, then move it forward so he takes a few steps with you. If he follows, great! Praise and give the treat. If he bucks, just stop and wait him out. It won't take long for him to figure out that bucking does not change anything and the fun option is to walk with you.

If your puppy completely loses his mind, bucks for over two minutes straight without stopping or makes a lot of noise, then just let him drag the lead for a few days. While he's doing that, you should be finding a local training class because your pup has a hard time calming himself when he gets upset and may develop other problems without the guidance of a professional. If your pup chews on the lead, spray it with Bitter Apple, then get on with your lesson.

JOE: A story of good intentions and common mistakes

Joe meets me at the door full of joy. This happy nine-month-old Springer Spaniel leaps, tail wagging, spinning around; the owners stand in the rear. "No!" they yell. "No! Bad dog!" Joe springs with increased fury. They both have embarrassed, hopeless, exasperated looks on their faces. "We've tried it all," they say. "None of it works."

I suggest they put on the leash and show me what they can do together. The husband, Pat, runs through their paces. Joe strains on his nylon choke collar, gasping for air as Pat gamely struggles to keep Joe by his side. "Sit . . . Sit . . . Joe, SIT DOWN!" Pat commands angrily. Joe sits slowly. "He's so stubborn," Pat says. "We work hard with him but never seem to get anywhere."

"You are working hard," I say. "But when do you all get to have fun?" Both husband and wife look puzzled.

I take the lead, change the collar to a Woodhouse training collar and begin. "Joe, let's go," I say, as I set off toward the kitchen. Joe, feeling slack on the lead, shoots past me like a canine bullet. I turn swiftly back toward the living room, give him a quick correction and start to praise. "That's a good boy, Joe, what happened? Where'd I go?" Joe gets one more correction, then decides that I am worth watching. I have his attention.

Joe is not stubborn. Joe is a bright, sensitive dog who tries too hard. His owners made several common mistakes that made it impossible for Joe to learn.

1. Confusing use of language—repetition and word changes. By telling Joe "Sit" over and over, then changing to "Sit down," they confused the dog. "Which 'Sit' am I supposed to listen to?" Joe might think. "If they don't know what they want, I won't even try to guess."

2. Too much focus on the bad behavior. They happily told Joe "No" repeatedly, but not once did they tell him "Good." How is Joe supposed to know what to do if they don't tell?

3. Keeping the leash tight. By holding Joe in place, the owners made it hard for him to "ask his questions." When a dog makes a "mistake" during training, it is because he doesn't quite understand. He is asking "What if I pull ahead?" If you answer his question (by correcting him) and then tell him the right answer (by praising him), he'll quickly learn what you want. The more "questions" your dog asks during training, the quicker he'll come to understand exactly what you mean.

4. Anger does not help training. In fact, in many cases anger makes the dog more wild, not less.

5. Not using what they know. Joe should have been on lead when I came to the door. If he had been, the owners might have been able to control him better. One rule of training: if the dog is not responding well on lead then you don't have a chance off lead.

Once the owners understood the basics of how Joe learned, they all improved. Keep in mind, if a dog doesn't understand what you are asking, he can't possibly do it.

Teaching the Puppy to "Come"

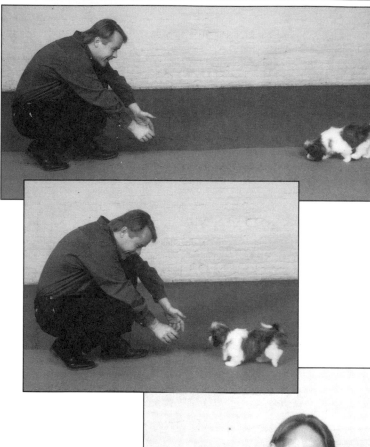

If any command is going to save your dog's life one day, it will be this one. Yet it is one of the most difficult commands to get the dog to respond to reliably. Starting young, when the pup is too unsure to wander far, is the best way to lay a strong foundation for this command.

Start in a quiet room. Squat down, open your arms, say "Come," then praise immediately on the assumption he will obey. Don't wait to see what he will do; set a positive tone.

Try to sound like someone your puppy would want to come to. Most pups hate to miss a good time and come right over to see what all this is about. When he does, do not grab at him. Let him come up to you, then lightly scratch his chest. If your pup is small enough, scoop him up and tell him how wonderful he is.

The whole family can do this together, taking turns calling the pup from different areas of the house. Keep moving to new places when you call. It is more fun for him if he has to hunt for you. Keep up the praise, even if you can't see the pup. Pups need your voice to follow if they are going to find you.

If you have access to a safe field, one that is well away from a road and not frequented by adult dogs, take your puppy there and put him down. Let him explore. When he is not looking, hide. Duck behind a tree or a corner of a building. Then call him enthusiastically. Keep praising! Have faith that he is coming. When he arrives, celebrate! Clap your hands, laugh, have a good time. Play this a few times and your dog will always

I am calling this little Shih Tzu pup from across the room. By squatting down and opening my arms, I am making myself inviting. I keep up the enthusiastic praise even when she gets distracted. Praise is the path you build between you and the puppy. The stronger the praise, the easier the path is for her to follow.

Once she arrives, it's time for a celebration. "What a terrific, smart little dog!" This puppy enjoyed the whole thing. Next time she'll respond even faster.

keep an eye on you when out on a walk.

Another good game is simply to turn and walk in the opposite direction when your pup runs ahead of you. Quietly call him but do not slow down and do not look back. If he is slow to catch up, run! Increase the distance between you and him. Most young pups under 5½ months of age do not want to be left behind. After that age you will have to use more care, and independent pups may wander further away without a backward glance.

If the pup doesn't come, go slowly to him, put on the leash and guide him back to where you called him from, praising him the whole time. This teaches the pup that he has to do it but that you aren't angry. Using a little food reward for uninterested pups can make this more fun for them. Show the food to the pup, tell him to come, then back away, praising him all the time. As he comes to you, squat down and hold the food close to your body. Make him come up to you, and while he is licking it from between your fingers, pet and praise him some more. Soon he'll think this is a fascinating command.

Common Errors People Make When Teaching "Come"

SCOLDING ON RECALL

Many times I've seen someone yelling at their dog to come and then, when the dog finally arrives, scolding it for not coming faster. This will only teach him to avoid you in the future. If you need to do something the dog hates, like give him a bath, don't call him—go and get him, instead. Try not to link unpleasant things with coming to you.

WAITING FOR PUPPY TO RESPOND

Everyone does this at first. You'll call "Mandy, come," then stand there waiting for the pup to respond. The problem is the dog does not know what "Come" means. She'll stop momentarily, look at you, see you're not doing much, figure you didn't want anything, and go about her business. Squat down, clap your hands, sound happy, make your puppy want to come to you!

NOT PRAISING UNTIL DOG STARTS TO COME

"Why should I praise?" my clients say. "He's not doing anything yet." Praise on the assumption he will do it. Praise to make him want to do it.

NOT USING THE COMMAND

Most of the day, our dogs are underfoot. Unlike the "Sit" command, which you use all the time, you may not need to call your dog to you very often. But if your dog does not hear the command, he cannot learn it. Make up reasons to call him, practice with your friends and family. He should hear "Come" at least 10 times a day.

Teaching the Puppy to Sit Using Voice and Hands

"Sit" is the command you will use the most. Whether you are in an elevator, greeting a guest, waiting at the veterinarian or putting down a full food bowl, you will need the dog to sit. You are going to learn two methods of teaching your dog to sit. As always, put your pup on lead before you start training.

The first way is to squat down next to your pup. Put one hand on his chest, place the other on the back of his rear legs. In your command tone tell your pup "Sit." Gently apply pressure rearward with the hand on his chest and press behind his knees with the hand in the rear. This will "scoop" him into a sit.

Once he is sitting, lightly scratch his chest and tell him how bright he is. He can get up if he wants. This is not a "Stay." The important thing is to let him know how pleased you are with him. Enthusiasm and praise get your message across to the young canine mind.

Do this throughout your day with your pup. Petting him? Scoop him into a sit. Throwing a toy? Have him sit. Telling him how wonderful he is? Tell him after he sits. The more he links sitting with the things he enjoys, the more responsive he will be.

Porterhouse is a 4¼-month-old Miniature Bull Terrier. I am teaching him to sit by scooping him into position. Note the position of my hands behind his rear legs. Although it is hard to show in pictures, as I scoop him under in back, I guide him backward using gentle pressure on his chest. A nice method for most dogs.

Inducing the Puppy to Sit Using Voice and Food Reward

This method works for all pups, particularly shy pups who collapse whenever you try to place them and for hyperactive pups who are jumping, spinning, mouthing or flopping around so much that it is hard to place them. Food will focus them.

Take a small piece of cheese between your thumb and index finger, fold the rest of your fingers against your palm. Put the food in front of your pup's nose, no more than a half-inch from it. You should now have his attention. Command "Sit" in your calm, decisive voice.

While the puppy licks and nibbles at the cheese, slowly lift the cheese up and over his head. Hold it there; as he lifts his head up to nibble at the food, his bottom will go down. Praise him warmly and give him the treat.

If he jumps at the food, you are holding it too high. If he backs up, put your other hand on his rump and gently guide him into the sit the first few times—then praise! If he nips your fingers hard, either try a food he likes less, or try just placing him as explained on the previous page.

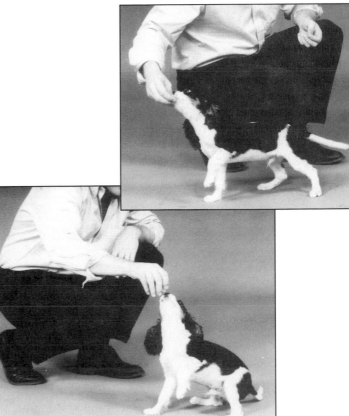

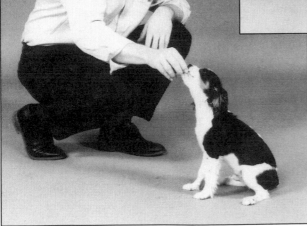

Tri happily volunteered for this assignment. Food is a terrific tool for shy or wild pups. It helps the shy pup be more bold and gives the wild pup something to focus on. Since pups tire easily, using food toward the end of a session can give her renewed interest in learning. Once a pup learns the command, wean her away from the food.

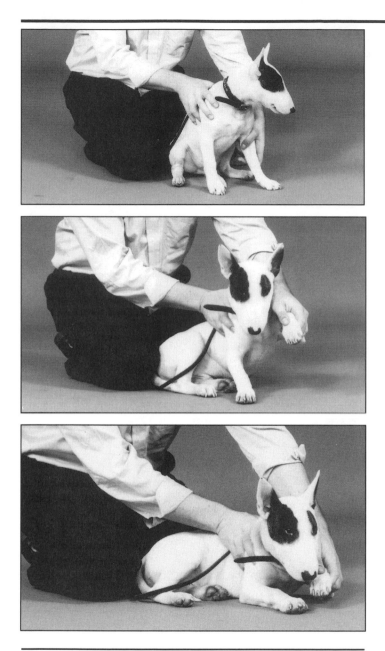

Teaching the "Down" Command Using Hands and Voice

"Down," one of the most useful commands for calming wild puppies and asserting your authority without argument, can be introduced in two different ways. This first method, using hands and voice, is good for most pups. Extremely shy, fearful or playful pups who squirm, freeze or become frightened by the placement initially, are better off starting with the food method.

Start with the puppy sitting, with you behind the pup. Reaching forward, place your right hand on the pup's right shoulder blade (this is on his right side; you'll feel a bony ridge if you're in the right place). With your left hand grasp the pup's left leg. Tell him "Down."

Now lift his left paw up off the ground and gently ease him to the left with your right hand. Read this a few times and study the pictures; it's confusing.

Gently place him (do this on a rug so he does not bang his elbows) and PRAISE! Remember, this is guiding your pup over into position, not forcing.

He fights it? Are you easing him over in the same direction of the paw lifted? A common mistake is to lift the left paw and push to the right.

If pup mouths you, read the "No Bite" section on page 82.

This method works wonderfully once the human component figures it out. By lifting one paw and easing him over in that same direction, "down" is trouble-free for both of you. Look at these pictures carefully before you try it with your dog.

Here's Porterhouse again being delightful. He is completely relaxed while I place him. His owners have done a wonderful job teaching him to accept all kinds of handling. The hard work they have done during his early months will pay off in years of easy care. Nail cutting, medicating, vet visits and routine grooming will all be a pleasure with this dog.

Inducing "Down" Using Voice and Food Reward

Start with the puppy sitting next to you. Take a small piece of food between your fingers and put it in front of his nose. Rest your other hand on the pup's shoulder blades. Tell him "Down."

Now slowly lower the treat straight down between his paws and then slowly pull it away. This movement should look like a capital L. If necessary, gently help guide him with the hand on the shoulders. Do not force him. The pup should be doing the movement, not you.

Once he is down, praise and give him the treat. If he stands up, make sure that you are lowering the food straight down and that you are going slowly. If you pull the food away too fast or at an angle, he will stand up.

He refuses to down? Some pups are just not that motivated by food. Some do not want to assume a submissive posture. Try the placement down, or use a more tempting treat. One puppy worked only for raisins, another only for raw zucchini, so you never know. The more usual hard-to-resist treats are boiled chicken or turkey, small bits of beef or cheese. Soft foods can be eaten quickly, which helps speed training along.

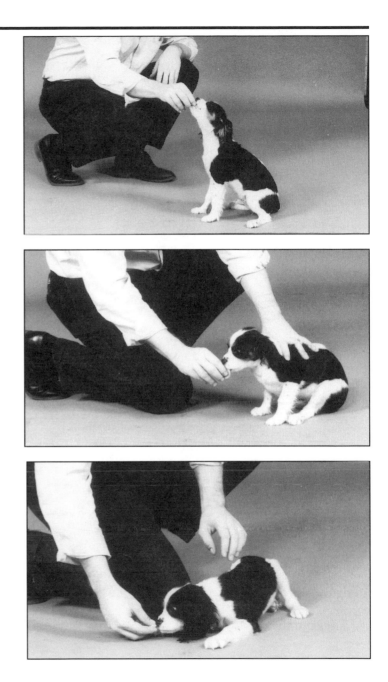

Tri is really enjoying this photo shoot. It is important to bring the food straight down to the floor before you pull it away. My hand on his back is helping to guide him down; even though it looks like I'm pressing down, I'm not. Most pups pick this up in just one or two sessions.

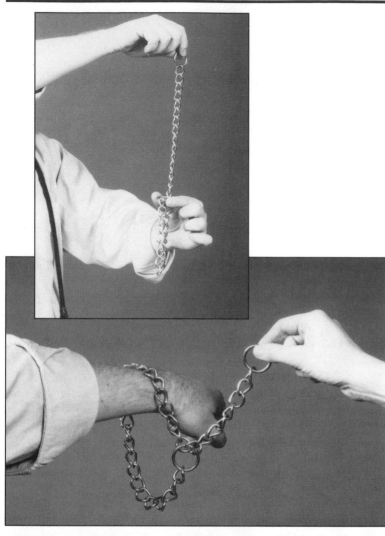

Introducing the Woodhouse Collar

The Woodhouse collar is the most versatile and humane training collar around. Its large links make it gentle on the neck. It is specially designed to make a chinking sound that most dogs respond to well. When buckled back it becomes a nontightening, noise-based collar, wonderful for puppies who don't respond well to a buckle collar but don't need a slip or choke collar. This collar changes as your puppy grows. You can buckle it back when he's a pup, then use it as a slip-type collar when he matures.

To select the proper size, measure around the widest part of the head, usually just in front of the ears. Put the tape measure around his head as if your were putting on a bonnet. Take that measurement and add two inches to it. Since these collars only come in even sizes, round up to the next even number. If the head is 19 inches, adding two inches gives you 21 inches in all. Buy a 22-inch collar.

Putting on any type of training collar can be a mystery. Neither of the big rings fit through each other, so how is it supposed to go on?

Putting on the collar properly is the key to having it work effectively. A training collar can be used only from one side. We are showing you how to set it up so it will work with your dog on the left. Notice how the ring that attaches to the lead comes from over the dog's neck when it is on correctly (middle). When it is on wrong, the part that attaches to the lead comes from under the dog's neck, which means it cannot loosen after a correction (bottom).

1. Hold the collar vertically so that the big end-rings are on the top and the bottom.

2. Drop the chain itself through one of the larger end-rings. It does not matter which end-ring it is.

3. Now hold the collar in front of you so it forms a *P*. In that position, face your dog and slip it over his head. Properly fitted, the tail of the *P* will come up over your dog's neck, not from underneath it, when he is on your left.

4. Next take the large ring from the tail of the *P* and fold it back. You are wrapping the chain around the other large ring. Once the tail of the *P* is folded back, you anchor it in place with the clip of the lead.

5. Check the fit. When done correctly, it is loose enough to fit three fingers underneath but not so loose that it can slip off over his head.

Always check to make sure the collar cannot come off before taking your puppy outside with it on.

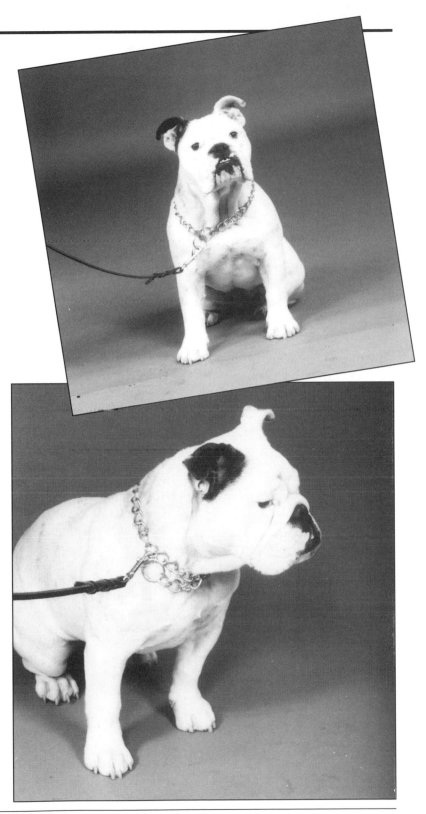

Ruby is modeling the Woodhouse collar for us. In the top picture she is wearing it on the "active" ring, meaning the collar will tighten if a correction is given. In the bottom the Woodhouse collar is buckled back. It cannot tighten, but it will make noise—very effective for puppies and dogs with delicate necks.

Using the Woodhouse Collar Takes Practice

A leash correction is a quick, downward or sideways snap on the lead. When it is done properly, it will break the dog's train of thought, reorienting him to you.

Speed and timing are the main components of the leash correction—not force. A well-timed correction takes little force. An effective leash correction uses the least amount of force necessary to stop the puppy from the unwanted behavior. Because dogs differ in sensitivity, always start with a light correction, gradually increasing the speed and strength of the correction until you discover what works with your particular student.

It is important to remember that it is the dog, not the person, who sets the level of correction needed. It would be wonderful if every dog stopped dead in its tracks and begged your forgiveness at the slightest chink of the training collar, but such is not life. If you find that your dog or puppy requires a strong correction, seek professional guidance. You may need to take a different approach.

Corrections should be consciously placed. Done right, only one or two will be needed in any one training sequence. If you find yourself giving corrections over and over again, something is wrong. Stop and evaluate what is going on. Your dog is not getting the basic idea.

Giving a correction properly, like any skill, takes time to learn. The mother of skill is repetition. Practice *does* make perfect. Giving a good correction takes physical coordination, timing and an understanding of your dog. Don't expect to get it right off the bat.

Here in the photos on the left the pup sees another dog and pulls toward it. Pups are pretty much distracted by everything at first. I step quickly toward the pup. I also reach forward. For a moment, I will have slack in the lead. You must have slack if you are to give an effective correction.

While I have that slack, I snap back quickly. I will always snap slightly sideways or downward. This ensures that the impact of the correction will hit the muscular side or top of the neck. NEVER snap any collar upward, as this impacts the delicate trachea area on the dogs. Damage to the trachea, coughing and choking can all result from upward corrections.

The moment I feel the lead tighten and I hear the collar, I release the pressure by reaching back in toward the dog. Reach in, snap out, reach back in. This takes two seconds or less. Speed is critical to effective corrections.

Please note: The puppy in the picture has not moved. She stopped pulling ahead, but she is in exactly the same place. This is because I released immediately. If the puppy is moved by the snap, you are not letting go fast enough. Be sure to praise the minute your dog looks up at you or stops doing the wrong thing.

How to Give a Correction

• Always begin and end a correction with slack in your lead. In most cases you will have to reach and/or step toward your dog quickly just before giving the correction. It is impossible to give an effective correction with a tight lead.

• Place your correction just as the dog begins to misbehave. Give the correction just as the dog begins to pull, just as he starts to jump, just as he rushes out the door.

• Once you have gotten slack in your lead, snap off to the side. Release the moment you hear the collar *chink* and feel the correction impact on your dog. Improperly done, you will see the dog physically moved by the force, with no chinking.

• Always snap sideways or downward. NEVER pull upward, which applies pressure to the trachea. Pulling upward can lead to coughing and possible injury of your dog.

• Always snap the lead across your body or downward. This is tough, especially for women, because the bicep is the strongest arm muscle and we naturally want to use it. Unfortunately, if you use it, you'll be snapping upward. Upward corrections are harder to do, less effective and more dangerous.

• When you give a correction, grasp the lead halfway down. Do not choke up, grabbing it short near the collar. This will not give you the slack you need for a good snap. You'll just be yanking on the dog. Yanking and choking do not work.

This Dalmatian has just been corrected. Notice that his ears are flapping, but his body has not moved, his head is not forced down. My hands are relaxed; you can see that I used my left for the pop. My right hand did nothing. The leash is loose. All the force was downward.

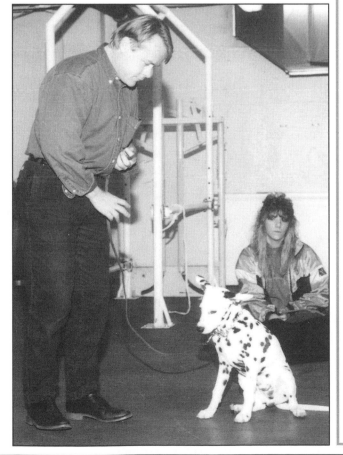

"No Bite"

The best training is the training that happens throughout the day. When you reach to pet him, have him sit. When you put down his food, have him sit. When you throw his ball, have him sit.

The more you link obedience to the things he enjoys, the more responsive he will be.

The other benefit to this type of training is that your puppy learns to listen to you even when he is excited. Learning to control himself when he does not want to is what training is all about. The more self-control you encourage in him, the easier it will be for you to control him as he matures.

MAKE EVERY INTERACTION COUNT.

Puppies use their mouths to explore, play with and test everything (including you). They do not understand how hard those sharp little puppy teeth are on our tender, furless skin. They have to be taught not to ever put their teeth on a human. The command I use is "No bite." If your pup aggressively uses his mouth when you take toys away from him or touch him when he is eating, seek professional advice immediately. This is not normal.

Have your puppy on lead when he is romping around the house. This allows you to control him without grabbing or yelling. When he attempts to mouth, hold the lead about two feet from the collar. Keep your hand or leg or whatever's in his mouth perfectly still. In a deep, calm, serious tone, command "No bite." Lean slightly over and toward the pup as you say this.

If the pup responds, calmly praise him. If petting starts him mouthing again, then don't pet him. Use your voice to let him know how pleased you are.

If he keeps mouthing, reach toward the pup, snap the lead quickly and sharply sideways and then give slack again. If done properly, you'll hear the collar chink, but the puppy won't actually move. He will take his mouth off you in surprise. You'll immediately praise him—calmly.

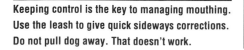
Keeping control is the key to managing mouthing. Use the leash to give quick sideways corrections. Do not pull dog away. That doesn't work.

"Off"

Puppies jump for all kinds of reasons and, because they are so cute, mostly get praised for doing so. Yet jumping adult dogs are obnoxious, painful and, with the elderly or the young, dangerous.

Prevention is best, but if you're looking at this section, it's too late for that. Now it's time to teach the "Off" command. "Off" means the dog voluntarily removes himself from whatever he is on. "Off" does not mean that you push, pull or shove the pup away. You're not supposed to be doing the work, your puppy is.

This method allows the pup to learn at his own speed. It prevents jumping without you having to put much energy into it. Simply leave the lead on the pup. When he looks like he's about to jump, step on the lead. The best place to step is at the point where it hits the floor when the pup is standing. This way, when he jumps up, he will correct himself. Wait for him to stop jumping, tell him to sit, and make sure he does. Now praise him for being so brilliant. If he goes to jump again, keep your foot on the lead and ignore him. He'll soon figure out that jumping gets him nothing but pressure on his neck, whereas sitting gets him love and attention. An easy choice for a dog.

This Airedale puppy is making it hard for his mom to make him his dinner. He is jumping at the counter and at her nonstop. A foot on the lead solves the problems, allows the owner to give him some positive attention, and lets her finish preparing his meal. These photos were taken as it happened. It took the pup about 35 seconds to figure out it was better to sit than jump.

OTHER WAYS TO CONTROL JUMPING

Keep a shake can by the front door or any place your dog tends to jump. When your pup starts to jump, put the can behind your back, command "Off," and then give the can a quick shake. If this works, PRAISE! If it does not, try tossing it down near his back feet. Immediate praise is critical to your success. Be sure to bend down to praise him; if you stay standing he'll jump up again. A set of keys can be tossed near the feet in the same way. The sudden and unseen noise surprises the dog, who hops off to see what's going on. If none of these methods seem effective for your pup, use the leash and collar method taught on pages 152–54.

Using the Lead Correctly

The lead enables you to keep control of your pupil at times when he would rather be doing something else.

The goal of training, however, is to phase out the lead. The idea is for you to be able to invite in guests, open the front door or walk along a beach, with your dog obediently responding to your vocal commands. In order for you to realize this goal, the lead must be used to support your most important tool of training—your voice.

During training the lead should be loose unless you are placing a correction. That means 95 percent of the time there is slack in your lead. The most common mistake is using the lead to hold the dog in place. This seems like a great thing because you say "Let's go" and there the dog is at your side. The problem is that the dog is not learning to control himself; you are controlling him. The minute you give him slack, he is out ahead of you pulling like a sled dog.

Good training teaches the dog to control himself upon your command. The training process allows the dog to make mistakes, shows him why that was the poor choice, and then teaches him what behavior would have worked better, earning him the attention and praise he loves.

Jumping is a common problem that illustrates this point well. I come to the door of a client. The client opens the door; the dog, on leash, is on its hind legs, straining in an effort to reach me. The owner, apologizing

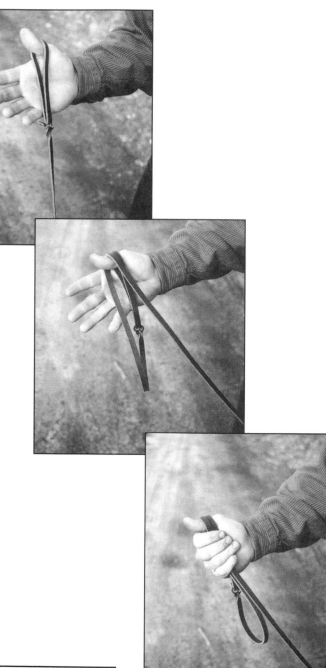

With your right thumb through the loop on the lead, hold the lead with your right hand only, as shown.

percent of the time.

profusely, holds on for dear life. When I tell him to let the dog go, the dog hits me like a ton of bricks, jumping, licking and basically losing her mind. What we teach is for the owner to open the door with the dog on a loose lead. As soon as the dog goes to jump, the owner commands "Off," giving a quick sideways snap on the lead. Immediately the dog is commanded to sit and praised for doing so. The proper leash correction does not pull the dog off the guest; the proper correction makes it unpleasant to jump, so she'll choose not to.

If the dog decides to jump again, the correction is repeated. IT IS UP TO THE DOG HOW MANY TIMES SHE JUMPS. Your job is not to stop her but to correct her every time she jumps and redirect her to the right behavior—sitting. Some dogs jump twice, some five times, but eventually they decide that this jumping business is not working well anymore. At that point the dog has made her own decision. Since she is the one that no longer wants to jump, she will control herself. You won't have to.

Learning how to use the leash takes time. Many of you are so used to restraining the dog that it will feel strange when the lead is loose. I see owners all the time who tighten up the lead even when the dog is in the right place doing the right thing. As with all learning, practice makes perfect.

Too loose.

Too tight.

Just right.

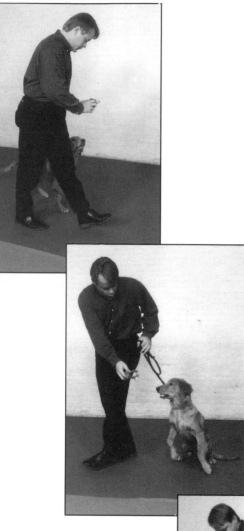

"Let's Go"

Taking a walk with your puppy can be terrific fun or a pain in the neck—depending on how your young one behaves on the lead. "Let's go" means walk on my left side with your head even with my knee on a loose lead. Do not leap, pull, yank, spin or trip me. Pay attention.

Begin teaching this command in a quiet area. To start, hold the lead in your left hand and a toy or a treat in the right. Tell him "Let's go" and step off with confidence. Hold your right arm across your body so the treat or toy is held above and slightly in front of the pup's head. Encourage him to look up at you by teasing him a bit with the toy or treat. Speak excitedly, bob your hand up and down to get and keep his attention. When the pup looks up at you, praise him warmly. If he is distracted, squeak the toy, get his attention, and praise him. Try to get him to pay attention to your voice by being warm and lively.

If he jumps for the toy, give a quick horizontal snap on the lead. Lower your enthusiasm slightly until he is back under control.

After the pup has given you 20 to 30 seconds of attention, give him the toy or treat. Play a bit, relax, then work again. Short, enthusiastic sessions are better than boring drills.

Once the foundation is laid that walking on your left side is fun, it is time to teach him not to pull away. For detailed instruction about this please see pages 136–47 in part 3.

This happy young Golden Retriever has a hard time concentrating. This toy helped her to focus on me and kept me from having to correct her. She's the kind of dog you can correct a lot and not get very far. She behaved like a typical puppy, jumping up, getting tangled, mouthing my hand—all to be expected, given her breed, age and personality.

Common Problems with "Let's Go" and How to Solve Them

REFUSING TO WALK

There are puppies who just put on the brakes. You're walking along and the pup just stops dead, bracing itself against the lead. Some creative pups lie down and refuse to get up. If you stop to discuss this with them, they learn that they can control you by stopping. Soon they'll stop more and more. Do NOT pick up the dog. Everyone loves a free ride. Your dog will stop walking outside completely if you pick him up. Nip this in the bud by simply not stopping. ALWAYS USE A WELL-FITTED FLAT BUCKLE COLLAR OR A BUCKLED-BACK WOODHOUSE—NOT SLIP OR CHOKE COLLARS. Keep walking while praising happily. The dog will drag along for a few steps, realize the parade is not stopping and begin to walk. The minute he does, stop, squat down, and praise him. Message to the dog is "Walking gets me attention, stopping gets me nothing." Do this on a carpeted or grassy area.

DRAGGING AHEAD

If your pup fancies himself a sled dog and you the sled, you'll need to read the "Let's Go" section on pages 136–47 for detailed help. Be sure you practice your "Sits" and "Downs" in the house and work on the "Leave it" both in the house and outside. These basic control commands need to be in place before you can hope to control an excited puppy.

JUMPING UP AND MOUTHING

Happy, exuberant puppies share their joy of life by leaping around nipping at your hands. The instinct is to stop and discuss this with the puppy. This is not the right plan. Keep walking. As the pup jumps up for a nip, sidestep to the right. As you are sidestepping, command "Off," grasp the leash in the middle with your left hand and snap and release to the right across your body. As he pops off, calmly praise him verbally and continue walking.

GETTING TANGLED IN YOUR LEGS

This is a typical puppy thing to do. Resist the temptation to untangle the leash yourself. If you do, she learns it's a great way to stop the parade and get your attention. Instead, keep walking and pull the lead out to your left with your left hand as you walk. If you keep moving the pup will quickly come around to the proper position. Once she's there, praise her.

GETTING TANGLED IN THE LEAD

A few dogs are masters of getting their feet tangled in the leads and then stand, looking forlorn, waiting for you to untangle them. It is another good way of stopping the parade. The best solution is to keep walking; when your puppy realizes you aren't going to undo him, he will undo himself. If he does not after 10 or so feet, reach down, untangle him, and continue as if nothing happened.

Common Owner Errors
During "Let's Go"

HESITATION

Frequently I see owners in class who say "Let's go" to their dog and then stand there waiting to see if the dog is going to start walking. The dog is not in charge of this parade—you are. Once you say "Let's go"—GO! Praise merrily and walk briskly. If you don't seem to know what you're doing or where you're going, how can you expect the dog to follow?

GETTING DISTRACTED WITH THE DOG

You're walking along, and your dog stops in his tracks, peering off down the street. You stop in your tracks and peer off down the street trying to see what it is he is interested in. What important lesson did you just teach your dog? You taught him that stopping dead is a terrific way to control you. Who cares what he is looking at? Unless it's a bus out of control, don't concern yourself. Keep going. Physics being what it is, he'll follow along. After a few experiments he'll walk right along with you, catching his glimpses of the world while still going at your pace.

NOT PRACTICING

All learning takes time, even when you know what is going on. Your dog needs extra time because first he has to understand exactly what you want, and only then can he start learning how to do it properly. Walking next to you on your left side makes no sense to your dog. It is not a natural behavior like sitting or lying down. Dogs do not walk through the wild side by side. You walk down the street and think, "All this dog does is pull me! When he is going to learn not to do this?" Your dog is thinking the same thing: "Boy, we walk down this street every day. Why doesn't my owner stop yanking on me. We're both going in the same direction. When is he going to learn?" Walking next to you on a loose lead is a foreign and complex concept. He'll need lots of time to learn it, so you'll need to spend plenty of time practicing.

MAKING EXCUSES FOR THE DOG

Because we love our dogs, we tend to make excuses for them. When he yanks you to a dog, it's "He's just being friendly." When he pulls you to a squirrel, "He loves to chase squirrels." When he drags you over to a fire hydrant, "He had to go to the bathroom." As long as you're willing to excuse behavior, he'll be willing to do it. There are no excuses for pulling. He pulls, he gets a correction. It's your job to set the standards of behavior.

HOLDING THE LEASH TOO TIGHT

This is the most common and least effective way of dealing with a pulling dog. It's tiring for both of you and teaches your dog nothing. If you've been in the habit, it will take a while to change your ways. Every time you notice it, give him some slack. If you don't allow him to make mistakes, then you're not allowing him to learn.

Frequently Asked Questions

When is the right time to neuter my dog?
After the age of six months is a good time. There is no reason to wait longer. Many old wives' tales exist about letting a female go through her first heat or waiting for a male to mature; they're just myths. Neuter early.

Why won't my puppy go down the stairs?

Puppies don't have very good depth perception. When they look down from the top, it just looks like a cliff to them. Help him get over his fear by putting him on the bottom step and calling him. When he hops off, praise him. When he gets confident about this, jumping off the minute you put him down, put him on the second step up. When he masters that, the third and so on. Soon he'll be bouncing down the steps with ease.

Are group classes a good idea?
Yes! They are wonderful socialization for your pup and good practice for you. Go to a few without your pup to see if you feel comfortable with the teacher. If the dogs and the owners look happy in class, chances are you've found a good one. Try to find someone who limits class size to ten or fewer so you won't get lost in the shuffle.

My pup eats out of the cat box. What can I do?
Dogs love to eat feces of all kinds—sorry. The best solution to the cat box is moving the box to someplace the cat can get to but the dog can't. For small dogs this may be the bathtub, if your cat does not mind. For larger dogs, putting the box in the bathroom, putting a nail in the door molding and taking a loop of rope and putting it around the knob and the nail so that the door only opens far enough for the cat, but not the dog, to scoot in and out is the best solution.

How do I stop my pup from unraveling the toilet paper?
The pup has a wonderful time doing this. To stop this, rest a shake can on the roll; it will tumble down, surprising him, if he pulls on it. Don't worry about the can hitting the pup; it rarely does. The can rattles as it tumbles and the pup jumps back in surprise.

I can't pet my puppy without him mouthing me. I've got marks all over my arms. What can I do?

First of all, leave the leash and collar on him when he is loose in the house so you can correct him without any fuss. Make sure no one is playing tug-of-war or wrestling with the pup. Up the exercise he is getting. Whenever a pup is obnoxious, I up its exercise. And lastly, set up the "No bite" situation and practice with him. Are you praising him warmly when he removes his teeth from your flesh? Don't try to pet him, but praise is required to encourage the teeth-off behavior.

My pup lies down on the sidewalk every time we meet another dog. It's embarrassing. Is this normal?
Perfectly. He is being a polite young thing. He'll probably grow out of it if you don't scold him for it. You can help him through it by allowing him plenty of time to socialize with other nice dogs. Ignore him when he's belly up. Don't wait for him. If you stand there patiently while he does this routine, he'll soon figure out it's a way to stop you. When you are ready to go, tell him "Let's go" in a happy voice and go! Don't wait to see if he is coming or not. He'll get himself up quickly when he realizes you're serious. Always follow this with lots of praise for catching up with you. He'll soon learn that it is best to stay on his feet because you might be leaving at any moment.

Summing Up

You've made it through the first few weeks. The puppy sleeps through the night, most of the time. He goes to the bathroom outside, if you stick to the schedule. He stops mouthing when you tell him to. He comes happily, sits sometimes and downs with guidance. It sounds like you're doing well.

Raising a pup is not about perfection. Maturity takes time. No pup is going to behave with the consistency or focus of an adult dog. Keep the training sessions short and happy. Use commands frequently. Some puppies learn quickly. Some don't. Most can learn if the information is presented in a way that makes sense to them. That's your job. If one method does not work, try another. As long as it is humane and does not make the dog frightened of you, use it. There is no one method that works for all dogs.

PART 3

Caring
for and
Training
Your
Adult
Dog

The Daily Routine

Caring for my animals is one of the rhythms of my day. Other things—work, sleep, waking up, exercise and relaxation—are fit within the framework of their needs. I get up in the morning and let them out. I fill their bowls with food and water, let them back in, then tend to my own morning rituals. As I have my tea and toast, I watch the morning news, occasionally scratching a furry head that comes over for a "good morning" pat. Before I sit down to work on this book, I go for a walk in the woods, my four companions playing at my side. Following trails with their noses, chasing chipmunks, charging around in huge loops for the fun of it, reminding me everywhere of all that I cannot smell, see or feel as well as they can. As I work, they lie at my feet—occasionally playing but more often napping in the sun or chewing a bone. They rise when I rise, following me to the kitchen, the bathroom or wherever I'm off to.

That is dog care in a nutshell—daily routine, seldom thought of but extremely important to the health and well-being of your favorite companion. You get no days off, no breaks, no vacations, and in return your dog takes no time away from his devotion to you. Of course, things do not always go smoothly. Dogs have much to learn before they can fit into our days without a hitch. It takes time, a lot of it, to teach them what they need to know. There are no shortcuts, no miracles. There is only understanding. The more you understand this delightful creature that is dog, the more painless caring and training will be. That is what this section is all about, making dog ownership as pleasant as possible for both you and your dog.

After Puppyhood: "He Never Did That Before!"

Adolescence begins at different ages for different individuals, but the results are the same. As an animal begins to mature sexually, his interests and needs change. Classically, nine months of age is the first serious stage. I get calls all the time from frenzied owners of nine-month-old dogs: "He used to come to me. Now I call him, he just looks at me, then he walks away." "He sniffs everything. It takes fifteen minutes to go down the block." "He's fighting with other dogs. He's always been so good with them." "He knows 'Sit.' We've done it since he was a puppy. Now he won't, he's gotten so stubborn."

What's happening? He's heading for adulthood.

His protection, assertion, aggression and independence levels will all rise. Soon he will be barking at the door, lifting his leg and challenging your leadership. It's all perfectly normal but not always acceptable.

Like most teenagers, he may be moody, distracted, confused, difficult and surprising. He'll be youthful one minute, adult the next. Luckily it is a relatively brief period in a dog's life, normally from 9 to 24 months of age; large breeds may be a little later. Small breeds hit it at 6 to 12 months. You'll know when he's in it because he'll be annoying you in brand new ways.

Boundary testing begins in earnest. This usually presents itself as a strike or a work slowdown. Suddenly your dog looks at you blankly when you give a command. Has he ever heard that word before? Or he obeys, but slowly. It will take him 15 seconds or more to sit. If you move to place him, he'll sit instantly, but until then he stares at you while moving like a snail. Ah, teenagers. Stay relaxed. Insist on compliance. If you hold the line here, other problems will never arise.

All dogs go through it. When Caras, our Australian Shepherd, hit 10 months, he started barking at you when you gave him a command. He'd do it but he'd bark. Kesl, Sarah's Bouvier, decided that if any dog in a group was aggressive, he, Kesl, should pee on the aggressor's owner. It's just typical canine logic: "I pee on the owner. Therefore the owner is mine, and all that is his is mine, including that obnoxious aggressive dog over there." Tri, our Cavalier, simply "forgot" "Come," wandering off with a wagging tail. He seemed afflicted with a sudden case of selective deafness. They all got through it. Yours will too. Be patient, prepared, persistent. Demand obedience. Praise compliance. Do lots of "Downs."

The Stages of Adulthood

The radical physical growth is slowed. He hasn't unraveled the toilet paper for weeks. He actually lies quietly at your feet for hours. What's wrong? Nothing. He's growing up. Canine adulthood, from two years til death, has different stages just as puppyhood does. A dog doesn't simply mature and then stop. He continues to change, influenced by interactions, training, environment, personality and breed.

Adult dogs are concerned with rank. Although they willingly accept you as the leader, they cannot understand a lack of guidance. If you do not give consistent direction or if you stop leading for a while, they will assume that you abdicated the throne. They're not capable of thinking "Oh, my owner is taking a week off" or "My owner loves me so much that she doesn't ask me to do anything." Seeing no one at the helm, they grab the wheel. It's as pressing to them as it would be for you if you went into the cockpit and saw no pilot. Something has to be done and they do it.

You won't notice much at first, maybe a slowing of response time, a reluctance to get off the couch, a wandering farther away for longer. Disobedience creeps up on you, until suddenly, "out of the blue," the dog runs away or growls or steals the chicken off the counter. It was not "out of the blue." It's as predictable as a train coming down the tracks. My job is to point to that train while it is still way off and convince you that it will arrive unless you change its course now.

Aggression develops in slow stages with predictable arrival times. Nine to 12 months is your first round. The next is around 18 months, when late adolescence leads to more assertion, independence and aggression. By 24 to 26 months of age, full adulthood has arrived and what has been building up can now land with surprising force. Many dogs have their first serious bite in these months. Late-maturing breeds will hit another round of changes at three years of age. From my experience most serious dog bites come from unaltered male dogs between the ages of one and three years. Consistent guidance, structure and training can steer you clear of these obstacles.

As dogs mature, they become increasingly interested in "territory." Urinating on objects is the canine way of saying "This is mine!" Any other dog found within a dog's territory is considered an intruder. This leads to dog-to-dog aggression in the city, as 10 or more dogs may consider a single block theirs. Neutering helps to lessen this problem.

Tender Loving Care

That training and caring for a dog is a commitment is not news; that it's an act of two-way communication may be. Dogs do not come with instructions attached. We do our best—we guess, we read, we ask for advice, we get advice we didn't ask for and stumble through. The one we should be listening to is our dog. Care and training is largely about paying attention. Dogs do things for specific reasons. Our job is to figure out what those reasons are. I recently worked with a miniature Dachshund who was suddenly frightened of going into stores. His owner had taken him shopping since he was a pup, and this new fear baffled her. I asked the simple question "Has he been stepped on lately?" and sure enough, during the holidays he had been tripped over more than once in a crowded aisle. End of mystery. Dogs don't make things up. If they steal food, it's because it tastes good. If they don't obey, it's because they do not understand.

There is no real mystery to canine care. All dogs need a good diet, regular health care, thorough grooming, exercise, structure and direction to be happy, healthy, and responsive. The first four needs are physical. The last two, the mental needs, are what change your dog from simply an animal in your house to a beloved companion in your home. Behavior problems often mean that one or more of these basics is being neglected. Unless every one of these needs is taken care of, training will not work. The function of this section is to teach you to "read" your dog effectively. Do that and he'll "tell" you everything you need to know about caring for and training him.

This is one of my favorite photographs. It captures the trust and kindness flowing in both directions at that particular moment in time.

Diet

The five-year-old Miniature Schnauzer was a mystery. She had never been a barker (that in itself makes her unusual for a Mini Schnauzer), but recently she'd been barking nonstop. After questioning the owner closely, I learned that she had run out of the dog's regular food three weeks ago and purchased a new brand. I suggested she change back. The barking stopped almost immediately.

A balanced diet of dog food is the foundation of mental and physical health. A good diet is a brand-name dry food. It can be mixed with canned food or table scraps, but no more than 10 percent of the diet should be these "extras." Dry food is easy, stores well, and is better for their teeth than canned or semimoist foods. The fact that it is usually less expensive should not be held against it.

Dogs do not need variety. Changing foods can cause stomach upset and behavioral changes. When you find a food that works, stick with it. By "works" I mean the dog eats it, his stools are brown and firm, his coat is shiny, and his skin is supple. You will find that everyone has their favorite foods. Don't listen to everyone; choose experienced sources and take their advice.

Dog foods are researched and balanced; they do not need supplements. Unless your vet recommends it, do not add anything to a brand-name food. Vitamins and minerals work together. If you give one without the others, you can create imbal-

A good, balanced food is the foundation of health and good behavior.

ances. The only supplements I use on a regular basis are some of the fatty acids that are good for the coat. I find that many dogs with dry skin benefit from these products.

For treats I use hard dog biscuits, freeze-dried liver or cheese. I avoid the beef jerky–type treats. Go easy on the freeze-dried liver; too much of it can give a dog loose stools.

Feed adult dogs twice a day. Once a day is traditional, but I find the dogs are better off with two meals. This is especially true of large breeds, which can be prone to a problem called bloat. Bloat, a painful and possibly fatal condition, occurs when the stomach fills with gas. It may also twist inside the dog. The causes are not fully known. Please discuss the problem and its prevention with your vet.

The general advice I've heard through the years on avoiding bloat is to feed the dog a few small meals a day instead of one large one. Soak dry food in water before feeding. Don't run the dog hard before or after she eats. Feed her a good-quality food with ingredients she digests easily to avoid the creation of gas. A breeder

friend changed food and her five-year-old bitch, which had never bloated before, bloat four times in a month. She changed the food back and now has no trouble.

If your dog's belly looks distended and tight; if your dog keeps getting up and lying down, trying to get comfortable; if he attempts to vomit and cannot—IT IS AN EMERGENCY. Call your vet and get over there, fast!

Use metal or ceramic bowls. These are easy to clean and hard for the dog to damage. Plastic bowls seem to be responsible for loss of pigment in some dogs' noses. This means that instead of having a brown or black nose, your dog will develop light-colored splotches. Not a medical problem of any kind, it corrects itself after the bowls are changed.

There are many types of bowls: hard-to-tip bowls, bowls made specially for long-eared dogs, tall dogs, small dogs. Short-faced dogs sometimes need shallower, wider bowls so they can get at their meals without getting it all over themselves. Get what you want and what works for you and your dog.

Tall dogs find it easier to eat out of raised dishes such as these. Raised dishes are a great convenience to both you and your dog.

Grooming

Man created dogs in all different sizes and shapes, colors and coat lengths, and in so doing, he made animals that could not care for themselves. They cannot brush their fur, clean their own ears, take care of their teeth, trim their nails or bathe themselves. Nor can they ask for help. We have to attend to these things ourselves on a regular basis.

All dogs need to be brushed. It keeps shedding and doggy odor under control, prevents tangles, and gives the coat a nice sheen. Short-coated dogs like Beagles, Doberman Pinschers and Great Danes should be groomed with a soft bristle brush once a week. Double-coated dogs—Akitas, German Shepherds and Siberian Huskies—are the hard-core shedders of the canine world. They need a brisk brushing with a slicker brush twice a week. During the spring and fall shedding periods, they need daily attention to keep hair around the house to a minimum. A shedding blade is a good tool for these dogs; it pulls out much of the dead hair quickly and easily. Here's a hot tip: use antistatic spray to make hair removal easy from rugs, clothing and furniture.

Long-coated breeds—Afghans, Shih Tzus, Briards, Cocker Spaniels, to name a few—require a great deal of attention. Some of the soft, cottony coats tangle easily and require an hour or more of daily care to avoid matting. You'll need several types of brushes and combs to maintain these coats. The best advice I can give you is hire a professional groomer or your breeder to spend time showing you exactly what equipment you'll need and how to use it. Set up three to four weekly sessions so they can evaluate how you're doing and give you pointers as problems arise. Such dogs, some of the most elegant in the dog world, take long hours of dedication to keep them looking their best.

For ease of control, lie your dog down when you brush him. Leave on his lead and collar so you can correct him if he fusses. For squirmy dogs, kneeling on the lead up near the clip will leave both hands free for brushing.

Gently grasping the beard of a long-coated dog allows you to brush his face without too much of a fuss. Part the hair all the way to the skin when you brush the dog. This way you'll be able to find any mats, tangles, cuts, fleas or ticks.

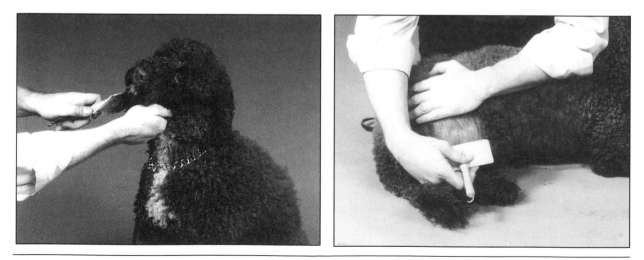

Bathing Your Dog

Most of us have to bathe our dogs at one time or another. One of the keys to successful bathing is to brush the dog thoroughly first. Never bathe a dog with tangles, as it will only make matters worse. Using a detangler spray can make getting the knots out easier for both of you. If your dog is badly tangled, let a professional groomer take care of him this time. Then either have his hair trimmed to a manageable length or keep up with the brushing.

Once he is brushed, you can begin the bath. First, get everything you'll need within easy reach of the tub—towels, shampoo, cotton, a garbage can. Run the water lukewarm. Dogs, like infants, are sensitive to hot water. Now get your dog. (Don't call him to you for this. That will only make him distrust coming to you.) Leave a leash and collar on him if he's likely to attempt escape. Once in the bathroom, close the door. You don't want your soaking-wet, soapy dog careering around your house if he gets out of your grasp. Put him in the tub. Get help if you need it. If the dog's large and unwilling, try lifting the front legs in first and then the back legs separately. Once he is in, wet him down, top, bottom and sides. Don't wet his head. Dogs with dry heads shake less in the tub. A good shake always begins in front. Keeping

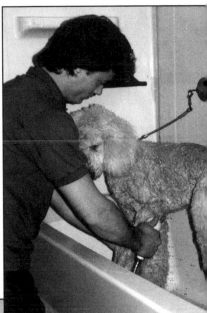

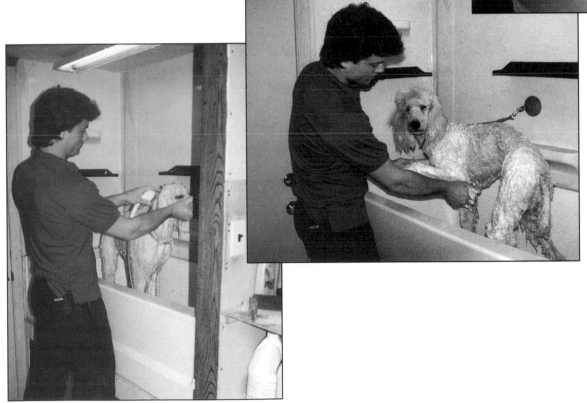

a firm hold of his muzzle or the skin on the back of his neck will prevent him from giving you an unwanted shower.

With any shampoo use only a small amount at a time. Too much may work up a glorious lather but be hard to rinse out. If your dog has long hair, squeeze the shampoo through the coat; don't rub it. Rubbing will form tangles, just what you don't want. Rinse, then relather the dirty areas. Last but not least, do his head. Put cotton in his ears, then carefully wet down his head. Put some shampoo on your fingers and soap up his skull, ears and muzzle. Keep soap away from his eyes.

Rinse, then rinse again. I've rinsed using bowls and buckets, but it is much easier with a hand-held shower fixture. When you're finished, rinse one more time. Soap residue left on the dog can cause skin irritations.

Now grab a towel, hold it in front of you, and let that dog shake. If he stands there like a statue, try blowing a quick burst of air in his ear. That almost always works. Dry the top of his back and head first, then his belly and legs. If your dog has long hair, squeeze the coat rather than rubbing it dry. Again, this will avoid tangles. When you let him out of the tub, don't be surprised if he charges around the house like a wild thing. Something about a bath brings this out in a dog.

Ear Care

Dog ears need routine care. Long-eared dogs like Basset Hounds, Beagles and spaniels of any type need weekly attention. Ask your vet, breeder or groomer to show you what to do. Train your dog early to accept this grooming by making ear handling part of your praise. While you're petting your dog, pick up the ear flap, look inside, put it down and praise some more. Gently rub the inside of the ear (NOT deep; never go farther than you can see). Practice this daily, and when the time comes to clean the ear, you'll have no problems.

Nail Care

Cutting your dog's toenails need not be a wrestling match. The problem is that most of us do not handle our dog's feet and toes except when we plan a pedicure. Daily handling mixed in with belly-rubbing sessions will make almost any dog relaxed about having his feet handled. Go back and forth, rub his belly, hold his paw, scratch his chest, gently grasp his toe, rub his belly some more. By linking something he enjoys (belly rubs) with something he is not too sure about (having his feet handled), you can improve his view of toenail cutting. Do this daily, as part of your normal routine, and he'll lie with his feet happily in the air next pedicure time. When you start to cut his nails, don't try to get them all cut at once. Snip one, belly-rub for a while, snip another. Maybe it will take you two or three sessions to get them all done, but who cares? It was easy and painless for all concerned. Get instructions from your vet or groomer before you try to do this. If you cut the nail too short, it is painful for the dog and can bleed profusely.

Have your vet or groomer show you how to cut your dog's nails before you do it yourself. Only use nail cutters specially made for pets.

CONTROLLING FLEAS

Fleas spend only 10 percent of their time feasting on your dog. The rest of the time they quietly live their lives, laying eggs in your house and yard. The general rule is for every one flea you see on your dog, ten more are in your home. In order to control them, you have to kill them everywhere at once. Flea baths are not much use, having little lasting value. After a thorough bath, your dog can be reinfested in days. Flea collars get mixed reviews. The best flea-control products are powders, dips, or sprays for your dog and flea bombs for your house. NEVER mix different flea products together, like flea bathing your dog and then putting a collar on, unless instructed to do so by your vet. You can poison your animal. Always read and follow directions carefully. The easiest and least toxic way to control fleas is to vacuum your home every few days, vacuuming the dog's favorite areas daily. Put a flea collar in the vacuum cleaner bag to kill anything you suck up. And keep your animal brushed and clean. A flea comb with teeth so close together that fleas get caught is environmentally sound and works.

Health Care
Your Vet's Role

Your vet is your ally in health care. See him twice a year for check-ups, wormings and vaccinations. The more he sees your dog, the better able he will be to tell if something is wrong. Insist on seeing the same doctor, even if there is more than one vet at the practice. That way he or she will become familiar with your particular dog. Knowledge of your pet is an important part of animal health care. Select a doctor both you and your dog like. No question is silly or stupid, and no doctor should make you feel like it is. Pick a professional who takes the time to explain things thoroughly.

Sometimes it seems easiest to delay in taking a pet to the vet. "I thought it would clear up in a few days" is a common statement. Delay can be costly both to your pet's health and to your pocketbook. A problem that would have been minor had you attended to it immediately can become major during the delay period. If something is wrong, nip it in the bud. Get that dog to his vet.

Your Role

You are the most important part of your dog's health-care picture. You know him better than anyone. One client was irate that the vet had not noticed some hair loss on her spaniel's ears during the last visit. I told her: "Why didn't you notice? You're the one who is with the dog every day. If you don't see it, don't expect that the vet will." Watch for and note any changes in your dog's normal behavior. Limping, unusual whining, scratching, increased or decreased appetite, increased or decreased drinking, vomiting, diarrhea, restlessness, lethargy, not wanting to play can all be signs of trouble.

Sarah took her Bouvier des Flandres, Kesl, to the vet immediately when he did not want to play dead, his favorite trick. Normally he would fling himself down, rolling back and forth in "death throes." Suddenly he was responding slowly, going onto his back only with encouragement. It turned out he had Lyme disease, which made him stiff and achy. A dog cannot tell us where it hurts. Some bear discomfort stoically, so if you love him, watch him.

WEEKLY HEALTH CHECK

A weekly health check helps catch many problems early. An animal that is uncomfortable or sick will not behave normally and cannot be expected to learn. More than one aggression problem I have been called in to fix has been caused by a painful ear infection that had gone unnoticed. Choose a time once a week, possibly during a favorite TV show, and do this five-minute health check.

Eyes. Look at your dog's eyes. Do they have any thick discharge? This is not good. Gently pull the eyelid down. Does it look red or irritated?

Teeth. Pull up your dog's lips. Are the gums red? Is there tartar or plaque? It may be time to start brushing his teeth. Smell his breath. It will be doggy but not foul. Bad breath can signal a number of problems.

Skin. Part the hair along your dog's back. Is the skin healthy or is it red? Look for fleas and ticks, strange bumps, dry skin and matted hair. I lost a dog due to advanced skin problems that she had when I adopted her. It was a long, uncomfortable battle for all of us. Prevent this kind of pain by caring for your animal well.

Ears. Pull back the flap of the ear. Look inside. Is the ear a healthy pale color or is it inflamed? If you're not sure, compare it to the other ear. Look for dark, waxy discharge. Smell the ear—it should have little, if any, odor. A strong waxy, musty smell means trouble. Watch your dog for head shaking, ear scratching and rubbing his head along the ground—signs that something is wrong.

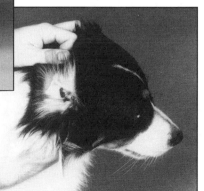

General Nursing

It is hard not to dote on a sick dog, giving it that extra dose of love and attention. Unfortunately, the dog does not understand exactly why it is being showered with all this goodwill and, when it recovers, will not understand why the attention stops. More than one animal who has been seriously ill recovers only to become an anxious, insecure, needy dog. As difficult as it is, treat your sick dog in a caring but not doting manner. No 10-minute pet-a-thons as you console him for how miserable his life is. Do not keep him on your lap constantly, feed him tidbits by hand (unless he medically has to eat and does not want to), or make a big deal over his discomfort. Treat him in a matter-of-fact manner so that when he recovers, he will not be emotionally handicapped by the illness.

Anytime you have to care for a sick or injured dog, it is especially important that you behave as you want the dog to behave. If you're upset, your dog will be, too. Praise the dog happily throughout any medical procedure. This relaxes your dog. Shamelessly use treats to distract him. And lastly, get help ahead of time if you think you'll need it.

TAKING A DOG'S TEMPERATURE

Canine temperatures are taken rectally. This task is made easier if you have a helper hold your dog's head as you handle the other end. If you are doing this alone, putting the dog on lead and tethering him to something immobile can make things easier. One trick I use for medium to large dogs is to squat down next to them and put one knee under their belly. This allows me to control the end in question fairly easily.

You will need a rectal thermometer, Vaseline (or another gentle lubricant), paper towels, rubbing alcohol and a view of a clock. Make sure the thermometer is well shaken down. Lubricate the end with the mercury with Vaseline, lift up your dog's tail if he has one, and insert the thermometer halfway into the rectum and hold on to it. If you let go, the thermometer could conceivably disappear from view, and getting it out is not fun for anyone involved. After two minutes remove, wipe down with a paper towel, and read. Normal for a dog is around 101.5° F, plus or minus 1°. Before you put it away, clean with rubbing alcohol and shake it down. If you are unsure about this procedure, speak to your veterinarian.

GIVING A PILL

Most dogs will readily eat a pill that is imbedded in cream cheese or peanut butter. If they seem suspicious, tempt them a bit with the treat. Show it to them, but don't let them have it; pretend to eat it yourself, making "yummy, yummy" noises—be obnoxious about it. Then offer it. Often dogs will eat it immediately after being tempted this way.

If not, then you will have to make them take it. Have your dog sit. Stand or squat behind the dog so he is sitting between your legs. Reach over the head; grasp the muzzle. Place your forefinger behind the large canine tooth and touch the roof of the mouth. This will open the mouth. Now, insert the pill into the back of the throat as far as you can. Try to push it way back on the tongue. Now, quickly, close the mouth and point his nose skyward. Holding his mouth shut, stroke his throat. This encourages him to swallow. Hold him in this position until you see him lick his lips. Now let him go and watch him carefully to see if he spits it out. Some dogs are masters of avoiding pills. As you can see, trickery is easier.

GIVING LIQUID MEDICINE

Put the dog in the same position as for forceful pilling, but instead of opening the dog's mouth, take his lips on one side and gently pull them out away from the teeth. This forms a pocket into which you pour the medicine—slowly. A helper who can keep the head tilted up while you manage the medicine will ensure more goes down the throat than on the floor. Do it a tablespoon or so at a time, releasing the lips and allowing the dog to swallow in between. Keep that nose pointed upward.

ADMINISTERING EYE OINTMENT

In the same dog-sitting-between-legs position as for pilling, gently pull the eyelid up and, reaching over the head, squeeze a line of medicine along the white part of the eye. What the dog does not see, he will not be afraid of. Having a helper hold a treat for the dog to nibble at while you do this keeps his mind off what you're up to. Keep up that happy babble as well. Always consult your vet if you have any questions.

GIVING EAR MEDICATION

With your dog sitting between your legs, grasp the ear and gently pull the ear flap back and over the dog's head. Insert the bottle or tube into the ear and squeeze out the correct amount. Put the medicine down and massage the ear. If done properly, you will usually hear the medicine squooshing around inside.

TIP

SPAYING AND NEUTERING

Neutered dogs make better pets. They are more relaxed and willing to please. They live longer, healthier lives. Other dogs are less likely to be aggressive toward them and for their part they are less likely to roam. Your pet will be healthier and happier— what possible reason could you have for not neutering?

Here are some of the excuses owners give: "I want her to have one litter." (Her biological clock does not tick. Unspayed females have a higher incidence of mammary tumors, uterine infections and cancer.) "I couldn't do it to him." (He is an animal. He does not lie around thinking about the poodle down the street. He thinks about sex when a female in heat, and that is the only time he thinks about it. The mounting he does at other times is about dominance, not sexuality.) "He'll be a wimp afterwards." (Wrong. Neutered males and females both make terrific watchdogs.) With 13 million dogs being killed every year, there is no excuse for casual breeding. If you love animals, neuter your dog.

Exercise

If one single factor is responsible for problems between dog and owner, it is insufficient exercise. Dogs are active. If you give them an outlet, they will burn off the excess energy running and playing. If you don't, they can make your life miserable. They'll bark, chew, dig or be constantly in motion. Pent-up energy makes anxiety and stress problems worse and adds housebreaking mistakes and whining to the list of optimal ways to spend time.

Not only is exercise good for your pet, but it is fun as well. Dogs are playmates. Who else will take a walk, play a good game of Frisbee, or romp with you at the drop of a hat? The gleeful look of a dog returning to you, stick in mouth, romping through the snow with a canine smile on his face, is enough to brighten the darkest day.

You need to oversee your dog's activity. Putting your dog in the backyard while you have a cup of coffee is not exercise. Large dogs under 18 months of age should not be jogged for long distances or encouraged to jump. These activities stress their still-growing bodies. No dog should be exercised strenuously during hot weather, with the exception of taking them for a good swim. Dogs overheat quickly. In the summer limit your romps to early morning and evening, when it is relatively cool. Owners of short-nosed dogs are well advised to be extra cautious, carrying water and a chemical cool pack (the ones from the drugstore that get cold when you squeeze them) when outside with their pets.

Sasha, (top photo) a Springer Spaniel specially bred for hunting, needed endless amounts of exercise. She would literally run til she dropped. She'd have to be carried back to the car. Fetch is one of the best dog games (bottom photo)—exhausting for the dog, easy for the owner.

How Dogs Play

One of the best exercises for your dog is romping with another dog. Dogs play in ways that can make you nervous until you understand their behavior. Games usually fall into one of two categories: chase type and mock fight type. These two can be combined for the maximum amount of fun. Chase type games involve one or more dogs pursuing the "prey." Equally matched companions can do this for hours—careening around, the frontrunner trying to avoid being caught, the pursuers cutting corners, strategizing ways to get him. When the "prey" is caught, he may be rolled to the ground, grabbed by the neck or simply spin around to start pursuing another of the group. This is all normal behavior. What you have to watch for is overexcitement during this game that can lead to the "hunter" being too rough on the "hunted." Smaller, younger dogs can become frightened, which causes some dogs to become increasingly aggressive. After all, a frightened animal is acting even more like prey. If that starts to happen, simply separate those two animals.

Mock fighting involves lots of wrestling. One dog will pin another, with flashing teeth and play growling, and general fun will be had by all. As long as the dogs are exchanging roles—first one on top, then the other, with both moving around—all is well. Such games can become quite loud without being the least bit dangerous.

There are warning signs to watch out for anytime you allow your dog to play in a group. If one dog is constantly mounting the other animals, trouble is brewing. This undersocialized, dominant dog may appear playful, but if a dog takes offense, and most adult dogs would, a fight will soon develop. The same applies to dogs who try to put their paws on the shoulders and backs of other dogs. This is as playful as someone coming up and pushing you, over and over again. If you see two dogs rearing up on their hind legs pawing at each other, a fight is likely. What they are telling you is that neither is willing to submit. They are both trying to get above the other. Trouble. As long as one dog clearly submits, ears back, head lowered, eyes looking away, all is well.

If a fight does erupt, do not try to grab your dog's collar. This will get you bitten. Instead, grab a rear leg or the base of the tail, lifting up and back. This will stop the attack, yet keep you in a safe position.

These dogs are having a terrific time. Flashing teeth, rolling around, play growls are all normal parts of play. It will take time for you to learn the difference between a friendly wrestling match and a real fight.

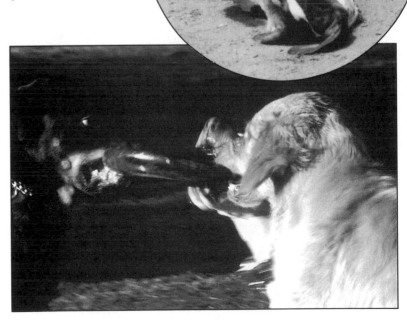

Nine-to-Five Dog

Dogs thrive on routine: walk, play, feed, train, owner leaves for work, hang around the house, owner arrives home, walk, play, feed, train, hang around with owner, walk, sleep, etc. Once they know the routine, they expect it. Changes in routine mean trouble. Anticipation can prevent problems. Dogs who are normally well behaved can fall apart if you go out in the evening after being away all day. You are THE event in their day. On the days you have social plans, come home, give your dog a little extra exercise and training, crate him with a good chew toy, and leave with no fuss. Even if you don't normally crate the dog anymore, crate him when your schedule changes.

The single factor that guarantees you a happier nine-to-five dog with fewer problems is exercise. Both mental and physical exercise are important. Physical exercise comes in the form of active play for 45 minutes or more a day. Romping with another dog, chasing a ball, swimming or fast walking are all good. Regardless of weather, your energy level, schedule or mood, your dog must be exercised in the morning if you expect him to be well behaved during the long day alone.

Hiring a walker for the middle of the day is a kindness to your dog. Reliability is key, as your dog will come to anticipate the walker's arrival; if the walker is hours early or late, it causes stress. A walker does not excuse you from exercising the dog, however. An extra 20-minute stroll is not going to make much of a dent in your pet's energy level.

Mental exercise means work. The more your dog works for and with you, the better-behaved he'll be. Period. No secrets. Give him things to do. Make him stay while you wait for the elevator, or sit as you prepare his food. He can "down" before you toss a toy or come to you so you can pick him up. Fill his days and he will stay out of trouble.

What to Do with Your Dog

Nowadays there are more activities than ever that you can do with your dog. Everything from a fun game of catch to the serious task of searching for lost people. There is something for just about every type of dog and owner.

AGILITY

A popular sport in England, it is new and growing in America. It involves your dog going over an obstacle course off leash. With tunnels, see-saws, ladders and jumps, this is an exciting sport to do and to watch—and very popular with the dogs. Contact the United States Dog Agility Association, Inc. (USDAA), P.O. Box 850955, Richardson, TX 75085-0955.

OBEDIENCE

Most areas have some group that does competition-type obedience. Highly precise, the training for this sport is an art in itself. Most areas have local kennel clubs that hold classes for all levels of dog/owner teams. Contact the American Kennel Club for information on clubs near you.

SEARCH AND RESCUE

Being trained to locate lost people is not a casual pastime. Not only do you have to train your dog in the complex task of locating a missing person, but you have to be in excellent shape, fully versed in first aid, orienteering and outdoor survival. This takes up a lot of time, but people involved cannot imagine doing anything else. A call to your local sheriff's department will usually give you the names of a few people to talk to.

Of course, not everything you can do with your pet involves formal activities. Swimming, hiking, jogging, camping and bicycling are all fun for you and your dog. Always keep safety, both yours and his, uppermost in your mind when you begin an activity. If your dog is young, older, or overweight, give your vet a quick call before you begin any rigorous activity.

Matisse is having a great time playing catch with a rope toy. Having fun doesn't have to be fancy.

DEAR DOG ...

If I could have five minutes to talk to man's best friend, here are a few of the things I would ask:

Why do you always throw up on carpets, regardless of how much linoleum there is?

Is there a reason you want to lick my face after you drink out of the toilet?

Why do you roll in disgusting things or run through a mud puddle moments before I intend to put you in the car?

How is it that you won't eat the $40-a-bag dog food I buy you, but the cat box is haute cuisine?

Is it mandatory that you look at me blankly when I issue a command in front of guests, though you do these things by heart when it is just you and me?

How do you manage to shed all your dark hair on my light-colored clothing and all your light hair on my blue suit?

How come you belch exclusively in my face?

Instructive Play

Some of the most fun games to play with your dog teach them the worst kinds of behavior. Tug-of-war, wrestling, chasing the dog around the house all lead to trouble. Tug-of-war teaches the dog that you enjoy it when he fights with you. It's such fun, he'll start the game on his own with your robe, a bath towel or your pant leg. Wrestling is too rough. A dog that thinks humans like this type of play may knock you over or frighten a child by leaping at them playfully. Chase games are not fun when you are late for work, or it is freezing outside, or when your dog has a dead rat in his mouth.

The best kind of play reinforces desirable qualities in your dog. Three such games are fetch, hide and seek, and beat the clock.

FETCH

Some dogs enjoy this game, some have no idea what you want. If your dog naturally enjoys it, great! It gives your dog an excellent workout while you basically get to do nothing. One of the tricks to getting a dog to bring a toy back is not to focus on the toy. When he comes to you, pet him, praise him, tell him how brilliant he is for at least 10 seconds before you remove the toy. This way he will not develop the "dodge out of my owner's reach" problem so common with this game. If your dog really has a problem with dropping the toy, try bringing three out with you. When he runs and gets one, toss the second in another direction. While he's stampeding after that, go get the third and

toss that one. You can get a good round-robin going this way.

HIDE AND SEEK

This fun, potentially useful, game develops a good recall while exercising your dog. You need two or more people to play this game; kids are particularly good. While you hold the dog, have the child make a big fuss over the dog and then run off to hide in a close, obvious place. You release the dog as you say "Where's Mary? Go find Mary." Encourage him with praise to locate the child. If the dog is really confused, have the hider call him. When he finds the person—celebrate, praise, have a party. Then do it again. As the dog gets the hang of it, have the hider hide in increasingly difficult places. An excellent rainy day game for everyone, and if your child is ever lost, he may be able to help you look. Dogs are fully capable of learning to locate family members by name—even in large families.

BEAT THE CLOCK

A one-on-one game, this is played with the dog on leash. Start to play with your dog; as the dog gets excited, give him a command. Insist that the dog respond immediately. Once he has obeyed, start to play again with great enthusiasm. Throw in another command. One of the keys to this is for you to be happily verbal when he obeys and quiet if he is resisting the command. You want him to learn that he is in control of this game. The quicker he does it, the quicker the game begins again. This teaches your dog to listen even when he is excited or distracted.

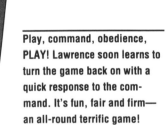

Play, command, obedience, PLAY! Lawrence soon learns to turn the game back on with a quick response to the command. It's fun, fair and firm—an all-round terrific game!

Structure and Direction

A dog who knows his place in the family is a happy dog. Dogs learn their social position through your behavior toward them. A dog can only interpret your actions within the narrow confines of his understanding. This means if he nudges you and you pet him, he doesn't think "Hey, my mom's petting me because she loves me." What he understands is that he commanded you and you obeyed. It is your job to make your leadership position clear in dog terms. With dogs every interaction counts. Therefore, it's vital to act in ways that make sense to the dog, if you want him to take you seriously.

Training happens almost every time you interact with your dog. Either he is training you or you are training him—it's that simple. If you want amazing results in a three-day period, follow these five simple suggestions:

• Before you do anything for your dog, make him do something for you. This canine version of "Please" teaches the dog that all good things come from listening to you. Before you pet, feed, play with, pick up, hug, kiss, throw a toy, open a door or do anything your pet enjoys, give him a command. Calmly enforce it if he does not immediately comply, then reward him with praise and whatever he wanted in the first place. This makes obedience relevant to your dog. Instead of being something you want him to do, it becomes something he wants to do.

• No more than 10 minutes of attention per hour when you are home. If you were training your dog strictly with food you would not feed him 20 meals a day. If you fed him that much, he would always be full and that bit of biscuit you give him for sitting would not be particularly interesting. The same with attention. If you hope to motivate your dog with your praise, don't give him it for free just for being alive. Why should he be thrilled with a "Good dog" if you just spent 15 minutes rubbing his back as you watched TV? Make him a little "hungry" for your praise.

• Say commands once. Your dog is neither deaf nor stupid. Repetition simply encourages him to ignore you. These are commands, not multiple-choice questions.

• Praise him sincerely when he obeys. This is his salary; don't be stingy. Bonuses for work well done are as appreciated in the canine world as they are in the human.

• Keep a leash on him when you are home. Hold on to it as much as you can, let him drag it *under supervision* the rest of the time. Until you get verbal control, you must have physical control. With the lead you can calmly enforce your commands. Without the lead you are stuck grabbing, chasing or yelling at the dog. NEVER leave a lead or tightening collar on your dog if you can't watch him. If he chews the leash, correct him and then spray it with Bitter Apple.

Keeping a leash on your dog when he is around the house gives you the control you need to enforce your commands.

A dog with work to do is a happy dog.

DO YOU HAVE A PUSHY DOG?

Does your dog nudge you when he wants a pat? Does he bark at you for a biscuit? You have a pushy dog. Pushy dogs wind their way into your heart with a wagging tail, soft brown eyes and a will of steel. Some-how, some way, they take charge of your home. Chances are you don't mind much—except when he barks nonstop when you're on the phone, or whines in that high-pitched piti-ful way when you have guests over. Of course, that barreling out the door is get-ting tiresome. And you're worried that he just doesn't come when called.

Unfortunately, dog training is an all-or-nothing venture. You can't expect respect from your dog if you wait on him hand and foot. Why should he obey "Come" outside when he doesn't obey "Sit" inside? If you want him to obey you, I suggest you turn every interaction around. Command him to do things for you before you do things for him.

Common Misconceptions about Dog Training

Training is not natural. He's an animal. He should be free, able to do what he wants.

This is a loving, but completely misinformed, sentiment. *Because* he is a social animal, your dog requires structure, boundaries and direction to be happy. "Freedom" to do what he wants to in your home, when he wants, is unnatural. To him, such freedom means that no one is in charge. This is no more reassuring for him than awakening as a child to find that your parents have left would be for you. "Freedom" will frighten and confuse him, leading to hyperactivity, barking, chewing, overdependence and possibly aggression. Do what is truly natural: be your dog's leader.

I'd like him to listen to me, but I don't want to be mean to him.

Good. I don't want you to be mean. I want you to decide what you want. Asserting your will with your dog can be difficult. The fear is that by being "bossy" you'll lose his devotion and love. Nothing could be further from the truth. Actually, whoever demands the most from your dog will get the lion's share of his attention and devotion.

I took him through obedience class, but he forgot everything.

Training is not a one-shot deal. It is a day-to-day task for the rest of your lives together. Granted, it takes more time and energy in the beginning, but even when your dog fully understands the commands, training will still be a part of your life. This does not mean putting him on lead and marching around the house once a day. This will only teach him to listen when in "school." It is better to integrate your commands by having him sit or down for petting, praise, food and play. If you don't direct his behavior frequently, he will assume you cannot and vote himself in as leader. This gives him the right to decide what his behavior will be. Leaders do not have to listen to underlings. Keep yourself in charge through daily use of commands.

He knows what I want.

If he knew what you wanted, he would do it. Dogs cannot guess what it is you want. You have to teach them thoughtfully, tell them clearly, then practice frequently before you can expect them to respond to you on a consistent basis. Even then, you will have to clearly tell them exactly what you expect. Dogs aren't psychic.

I don't have time to train.

Training takes less time than dealing with an ill-behaved dog. Chasing after him when he runs away, apologizing to guests for paw prints on their clothes, cleaning up one more shredded newspaper all take time. Invest that time in developing good behavior, instead of coping with the bad behavior, and you will be thrilled with the results.

Training is too expensive.

Training can be expensive, but not compared to the camera case, two pairs of shoes, the Oriental rug, the couch cushions or the last pair of glasses he ate. How about replacing the scratched door or cleaning the rugs for the umpteenth time? Compared to the cost of bad behavior, training is a bargain.

Setting Boundaries

In the wild, dogs live in highly structured groups. Every dog knows who's ahead of whom in rank. Although ambitious dogs will always be looking for a chink in the leader's armor, it is nonetheless an orderly society. The rules are well-known. Underlings do not bump into leaders. Leaders eat first. If the top dog wants something—a stick, a bone, whatever—he can have it. If an underling is in the way of the dominant dog, the underling moves. No mystery. No confusion. No time off. The leader works every day to maintain his rank.

Now your dog enters your home. You allow him to bump you at will. In fact, often he is rewarded with praise and petting for bumping you. If he is in your way, you step around him. He sticks his face in your dinner with no real ramifications. The only message your dog is capable of receiving is that he is the boss and you are his follower.

Take back control! One of the best rules for setting boundaries with a dog is that *IF NO ONE ELSE ON THE PLANET CAN DO SOMETHING, YOUR DOG CAN'T EITHER.* Can anyone else stick his face in your dinner? Who can leap on you or jump into your lap without permission? Is there someone who can block your path repeatedly and still have you stepping politely around them? One couple had not slept together for a year because their toy poodle whimpered at the bedroom door if put outside, and kept trying to get between them if allowed in the room. Who else could do such a thing?

Put a lead and collar on your dog and start making yourself clear. He jumps up, you tell him "Off" and make sure he does. Then praise him for doing what you want. Become nonnegotiable. Set up situations so you'll be ready to correct and redirect. He'll be surprised at first, but with your praise and encouragement he'll learn the rules have changed. Once he realizes this, he will be more responsive than he has ever been. Most dogs love their owners, but many don't respect them. Respect is earned, not given. Dogs adore and respect a confident leader who is decisive and fair.

Instead of petting her when she nudges me, I tell her to sit. *After* she does, I give her some attention. This calms her, making her more attentive.

Rewards

Dogs learn through reward and correction. If they do something and get pleasure from it, they will do that thing again. Reward, positive reinforcement, is often thought of as praise, play or a treat. These are useful training tools, but often the most powerful tools are not even considered rewards. Your attention is an incredible reward for your companion. Dogs can tolerate many things, but being ignored is not one of them. Use attention to motivate your dog and training can go along much more quickly.

Tri's response is enthusiastic because I am.

Here's what I mean: You are watching TV when your dog walks in carrying a shoe. You yell "No" and give chase. He leads you around the dining room table twice, behind the couch, and dodges past you in the hall, but you finally corner him under the kitchen table. No matter what you do to him now, he's had a glorious time being chased. The most fun he's had all day, in fact. And when you, huffing and angry, get the shoe and yell at him for being a brat, his only thought is "Boy, the chase was great, but she's a real witch when she catches me. I'll have to make that part more difficult next time."

While pursuing him, you gave him your undivided attention. You are actually rewarding him for stealing a shoe. (For effective solutions to this problem please see page 223). Attention, petting, praise, food, play, toys, being let outside, being let off leash in a safe area, playing with another dog are all rewards. Use these things thoughtfully to develop the behaviors you want in your dog.

Rewards are best given *just as* the dog does something right. He'll enjoy the praise five minutes after the fact but won't necessarily understand what it's for. Reward also supports your dog's obedience as he does it. If your dog is in a "Down"/"Stay," calm praise as he stays there will let him know he is on the right track. When you call him, praise every step he takes in your direction. Use praise freely. It is difficult to praise too much for a job well done. So difficult in fact that you shouldn't worry about it.

Another school of thought asks "Why should I praise him? He knows what he's supposed to do." I find it strange that many people are willing to correct but hesitate to praise as readily. Praise does not cost you a thing, your dog enjoys it, and given half a chance, you'll enjoy it too. Punitive methods are largely ineffective; don't lose control of yourself in an attempt to gain control of your dog. Try reward. You will see the joy on your pet's face, how hard he is trying to understand. The trust that praise fosters between you and your dog will convince you it's worth doing.

Dogs like gentle stroking or scratching best. Stroking the dog from front to back in a relaxed manner is calming and pleasurable to most dogs. Scratching gently behind the ears, on the chest, and on top of the base of the tail are all loved. You'll know you are doing something the dog enjoys if he stands in place or moves closer to you.

It may seem strange that praise can be given incorrectly, but it can.

Rule one is match your praise to your dog. Reading your dog's response to your praise will tell you what he likes and dislikes. Your dog is the one who decides what kind of praise he needs, not you. If your dog needs wildly enthusiastic praise to learn, then you have to give it to him. If your dog likes stroking, then you have to hold back those wild back poundings that you enjoy so much.

Each dog comes equipped with a praise effectiveness gauge: his tail. If it's not wagging, the praise isn't working. For many of us, when our voices become happy, our hands become rougher. "Good boy!" we say, pounding on the dog's side or grabbing his face and squishing it. Although some dogs learn to accept harsher praise, most prefer a lighter touch. Every dog needs something a little different. Your goal is for your dog to be looking at you, wagging his tail, happy and relaxed.

If the dog pulls away, turns his head away or looks away, he isn't enjoying what you are doing. Effective praise literally draws your pet closer to you. Good praise builds the enthusiasm and trust needed to work well as a team.

Corrections

Corrections, negative reinforcements, range from a clean leash correction to something as subtle as simply not praising.

Discussions, negotiation, ignoring the dog for long periods, hitting, arguing, nagging, blaming and becoming angry don't make sense to your dog. Good corrections are short, sweet and to the point. Effective corrections let him know immediately

that he made the wrong choice, without creating any fear or distrust of you. If the dog steals a napkin from the table and that napkin is tied to three shake cans, the cans will noisily chase after him. He'll drop the napkin in surprise, deciding that some napkins are unpredictable. The cans corrected him *just as* he stole it. **Just as** is the key concept when correcting a dog. If you cannot correct *just as* he attempts the unwanted behavior, then don't correct. Set it up again, concen-

This correction is fair. The dog knows this command. You have to teach the command before you can expect obedience.

trating on getting the critical timing needed.

A good correction will not cause your dog to fear you. Hitting, yelling, chasing, and threatening are not good corrections. A good correction for the dog that walks in with your shoe in his mouth may be to ignore him. Many animals will simply drop it when no one chases them. By ignoring him, you corrected him. He wanted your attention, you refused to give it to him. Dogs do things to get things, often starting unwanted behaviors to get your attention. Deny them what they want and they'll often stop doing it.

ACTION VERUS REACTION

It is easy to spend your time reacting to your dog's unwanted behavior—Yelling "No!" *after* he has tipped over the trash; calling "Come here, boy" *after* he sprints out the door; commanding "Off, off, off" *after* the dog's paws are up around your shoulders. *After* is too late. You need to anticipate your dog's behavior and take action accordingly. Your pet is predictable. You know that he will jump on guests, pull you out the door and try to steal the cat food. This is not news. That being the case, why not prepare yourself? Set up the situation, leave the lead on the dog, and give him the command or correction *just as* he thinks about doing the wrong action. As your guest enters, command "Sit." As you reach for the doorknob, tell him "Wait." As he turns his head toward the cat food, issue a no-nonsense "Leave it." Always praise lavishly when he obeys. If he never gets to consider it, he'll never be able to do it.

SMALL DOGS, BIG PROBLEMS

If you own a small dog, you have a curse: your dog is cute. When he barks at other dogs on the street, passers-by laugh good-naturedly. When he mounts your friend's leg, he's brushed off with a "What a little stud!" When he jumps onto your lap and hides when someone enters the room, they coo about what a baby he is. These reactions can lead to problems. Judge all your dog's behaviors by this rule: would I allow this if he were the size of a German Shepherd? What would people say if your German Shepherd snarled at another dog, locked onto their leg or tried to hide in your armpit every time a stranger entered the room? They'd say he had some problems. He would. And so does your little one.

Small dogs do not think of themselves as small. They are simply a dog like any other. Treat them that way and you'll have a sociable, well-balanced, friendly pet.

If your dog is a chewer, then you have to retrieve that shoe. Get up calmly, command your dog to down to put him in a submissive frame of mind and then command "Out." Calmly take the shoe, being sure to praise him for obeying the commands. Once you have it, get an appropriate chew toy and encourage him to play with that. Praise him whenever he is playing with a toy.

You have gotten the shoe, broken the chase cycle, increased his willingness to allow you to take something out of his mouth and shown him what he was supposed to be doing. Good job!

Now you can teach him not to take your things in the first place. Booby-trap the item (see page 223) or leave the dog on lead when you are home so you can correct and control him if he pulls this stunt again.

Whenever possible, let the equipment do the correcting for you. You want to be the source of direction and praise for the dog. Let him think that "bad" things just happen out of the blue when he does certain things—you had nothing to do with it. This makes you the port in the storm as opposed to the storm itself. He will learn to trust you, often running to you when he is upset or unsure.

The most misused and overused correction is "No!" I don't say it, because it is not instructive. "No!" means everything from "Don't eat out of the cat box" to "Don't jump on Aunt Annabelle." Even a brilliant dog will give up trying to understand what you mean by "No!" Teach specific commands such as "Leave it," for "Stop paying attention to that distraction"; "Off," meaning "Four feet on the ground now"; "Out," as in "Spit it out pronto." Use these three commands to direct your dog to do what you want instead of yelling at him to stop some unspecified action.

The Psychology of Training

Training teaches canines self-control. Many things that you want do not make much sense to your animal. Walking at your side, ignoring the food on the table, not rolling on the dead squirrel are all foreign concepts to your dog. Teach him to resist these temptations through clear instruction, positive reinforcement, unemotional correction and repetition. Do your job correctly and your dog will learn to inhibit his whims on command.

Learning this is hard work. Help your dog by making your desires clear and by always giving him something to do to please you. Frequently, I see clients who talk at their dogs but never tell them exactly what to do. The Westie sat in the corner. "Brooksy?" the owner said. "Brooksy what?" I asked. "Oh, I want her to come," he replied. "Well, don't keep it a secret. Tell her what you want." The owner laughed. "Brooksy, come," he called happily. Brooksy trotted over with a wagging tail. Dogs are great but they aren't psychic. They can't obey if you don't tell them exactly what to do.

Once the dog obeys a command, all **must be** forgiven. Whether it's dropping the dead rat, getting off the white bedspread, or coming to you after a 10-minute wind sprint up and down the street, if the dog responds, you *must* praise.

Here, Duncan is awaiting Sarah's next command. He is calm, eager and ready, totally focused on her. He thinks training is great fun.

TRAINING EQUIPMENT THAT I *DON'T* LIKE

Harnesses. These are useless for training. People tell me all the time that their small dogs can't wear a collar, it might hurt them. If they don't pull, it won't hurt them. If you correct horizontally, it won't hurt them. Harnesses cannot give you the precise control you need to train properly.

Nylon Choke Collars. Since there is no noise involved, this collar relies solely on physical force to control your dog. People mistakenly believe that it will be gentler because it is nylon. Not true. You will have to correct harder and more frequently with this collar than any chain collar.

Nylon Leads. These burn your hands if your dog pulls, and seem to inevitably have huge clips on them. Big clips have a tendency to hit the dog in the head or face when corrections are given. The only good use of these leads is for the dog to drag it around when you are home.

THURMAN: No Other Choice

When Thurman's owner called, distraught, she had just been bitten. I was surprised. Thurman had been a lovely puppy: easy to work with, calm, willing. It had been six months since our last session. We set an appointment for the next day. Sitting around the kitchen table, the story unfolded. Thurman had been behaving well. So well, in fact, that Mrs. K. stopped asking much of him. Quiet, loving, sweet, Thurman pretty much did as he pleased all day, every day. One habit that he developed was chewing books. He was quite the connoisseur, eating the bindings of expensive coffee-table books. This upset Mrs. K. She would discover him in the act and explode. "Thurman," she would start, storming over to him. "Bad dog! Shame on you!" Head down, ears back, Thurman would surrender the book. Mrs. K. would continue: "Shame! Bad dog! I've told you. . . ." What is her mistake?

Mrs. K. forgot to praise Thurman for releasing the book. Soon Thurman came to fear her approach, knowing there was no escape. Since submissive signals had only brought him more anger and punishment, he had to try something else. When Mrs. K. came toward him enraged, he snarled. Mrs. K., incensed, came on stronger.

Thurman is now behaviorally backed into a corner. Submission had not worked. There was no escape. Mrs. K. gave Thurman no other option; he snapped at her. A frightened Mrs. K. withdrew, teaching Thurman a dangerous lesson: aggression works.

Soon he snarled when Mrs. K. even looked at him with something in his mouth. He began to test his power. He stole her glove and then would back her off with a snarl and snap. He stole clothing, food off plates, pillows, books, records—anything he could get his mouth on. The bite occurred when they both went for one of Mrs. K.'s gloves at the same time, causing 10 stitches and a phone call to me.

All is well now. Mrs. K. works hard with him. She keeps up the structure, always gives him a clear way to succeed, and does not get angry at the dog. She directs him consistently and constantly, always praising him when he responds well. Thurman, wagging tail and happy face, is back to being his normal, sweet self.

Your Basic Control Commands

"I wish he'd stop pulling me down the street."

"She's constantly pawing me for attention."

"He won't come when I call him, no matter how much I yell."

"She's so stubborn. She knows what I mean, she just won't do it."

All these complaints can be summed up in one statement: "I want more control over my dog." You can get that control, starting with your three basic commands. Obedience to "Sit," "Down," and "Let's go" gives you immediate control of your animal. No dog can be too terrible if it is obeying one of these three commands. Without this foundation advanced work cannot be accomplished.

When you begin to teach your dog, you will feel awkward and frustrated. The words and movements are new. Give yourself time to learn them. Noting success is as important to encouraging yourself as it is to training the dog. Don't be hard on yourself, saying "I botched up that command again." Chances are you did some of it correctly. "I said the command once, and I tried to follow through right away. I need a little more work on handling the leash." Mistakes are a necessary part of all learning. If you knew how to do it, you wouldn't be reading this book, would you? By staying aware of what you did well, you will be more relaxed. When you are at ease, both you and your dog will learn the commands faster.

No matter what level of training you are at, it is important that you practice the commands on a daily basis by integrating them into your interactions with your dog. Your companion has no other way to learn the words. He cannot read this book, watch a TV show about training, or discuss it with his friends. The only time he can learn this material is when you use it with him.

Your first few weeks of training are not just about teaching commands. More importantly, they are about teaching your dog to enjoy learning. Once he learns how to learn, there will be few things you cannot teach him.

COLLARS: WHICH ONE IS RIGHT FOR MY DOG?

Flat Collar. The gentlest of all collars. This one is good for sensitive or fearful dogs.

Buckled-Back Woodhouse. Like the flat collar but with noise. This is a good choice for novices learning to correct. Many dogs don't need a slip collar or react badly to one. **Always check this collar after putting it on to make sure it cannot slip over your dog's head.** You should be able to fit three fingers snugly between the collar and your pet's neck.

Woodhouse Collar. My favorite piece of training equipment. Used correctly, this is an effective and versatile tool, a terrific collar for the majority of dogs.

Regular Training Collar. A solid, readily available training tool. This is the right choice for dogs that are less sensitive to sound and to touch.

High Collar. A regular training collar that you buy to fit snugly behind the ears. (As shown to the left) This gives you extra control on the hard-to-handle, aggressive or large dogs. I use it when the dog is much stronger than the owner.

ENTHUSIASM

When Kesl first learned to climb the ladder so he could slide down the slide (now a favorite activity), he had a difficult time. He climbed halfway up, hesitated, then peeled off the ladder, landing with a thud in the sand. Sarah immediately began to cheer. "What a good effort! Wasn't that fun?" Kesl stood up, looked at her quizzically, shook himself off, and climbed the ladder to the top. He had been confused, unsure how to respond. Sarah's enthusiastic response put him at ease, gave him confidence. Instead of saying "It's OK" with worry and concern, she set a fun, positive and contagious tone. She had fun. Kesl had fun.

Dogs look to you for guidance in new situations. The more enthusiastic you are, the more likely they are to be enthusiastic and happy. Stay upbeat and your dog will think whatever you are doing is fun! Sound bored and your dog's attention will wander. If you're worried, his anxiety will increase. It's up to you. You set the tone for learning.

"Sit"

Without a doubt, "Sit" is the most used and useful command between man and dog. It is easy to use throughout your day to maintain control, support leadership and keep the dog out of trouble. You can use "Sit" to keep your dog away from the door when you open it, give medications, groom, put on the lead and collar, wait for the elevator, and stay put when outside. "Sit" is a terrific positive alternative to the all-encompassing "No."

Dogs intially trained with treats but never weaned off them can reach adulthood with a "What's in it for me?" attitude about obedience. They only respond if they see a treat in your hand. If you have such a dog, end all treats today. Resist feeling guilty when he gives you those big brown eyes; put him on lead and insist that he respond. His reward for obedience is now your enthusiastic praise, so don't hold back on that.

Treats do have a place in training the adult dog to sit. They can be a great first step for shy, fearful or hyperactive dogs that have a tough time focusing and learning in a traditional manner. If you think you may have one of these types, please read the section on food reward and "Sit" on page 75. As soon as your dog responds in a relaxed, happy way, begin to phase treats out. For a few days reward with food every second or third time the dog responds, then use the food less and less until you no longer use it at all. Always maintain happy, enthusiastic praise.

Whether your dog is learning "Sit" for the first time or relearning it without treats, this command is done without force. Positioning is accomplished through gradual directing pressure versus shoving the hind end down. Force creates resistance. If you struggle to shove him into a "Sit," he'll struggle to remain standing. Commands are neither a punishment nor a confrontation. The idea is to show him what to do. When he understands, he will obey.

Teach this command on lead. With your dog on your left-hand side, put your right thumb through the loop of the lead and gather the excess in your right hand so there is a little slack between you and your dog. (See pages 84–85 for full instruction.) As you give the command "Sit," give the hand signal with your left hand. The hand signal starts with your left arm hanging at your side, palm forward. Next, bend your elbow and raise your hand up in a smooth motion, as if you were tossing something over your shoulder. Hand signals are easier for the dog to learn than words, as dogs communicate with their bodies and are naturally attracted to movement. Do not be concerned if the dog does not see it at first. He will learn to look for it as the training progresses. Right now, I am more concerned with training you. When you are doing everything right, your dog will too.

Once the verbal command and hand signal are given in conjunction, bring your right hand, holding the lead, to your right hip bone. The lead should now be across your body with even tension. It should not be tight. If you are holding up your dog's head, if he can't breathe normally or seems to be on tiptoes, loosen up. (Upward pulling works; the dog will sit, but it also becomes part of the command. Poor response off lead is common if you do this.)

With the lead across your hip, reach down with your left hand and place your thumb and forefinger just in front of his hipbones. This requires that you form a "U" with your fingers. With the "U" in place, gently press inward with your fingers as you guide him down and *back* with even guiding pressure. Your dog will scoot away from the "U" pressure right into a "Sit." If you try to force the dog by pushing hard, squeezing hard, moving quickly or roughly, you will create resistance in your animal. Always move in a deliberate, guiding manner. If you place the dog with the same type of movement that you would like used on you, you won't go far wrong.

Once the dog has complied, immediately release all pressures (a clear reward for assuming the "Sit" position), speak warmly to him, and scratch his chest. Gentle chest scratching encourages the dog to sit tall, while head pats may eventually lead to a hangdog look.

Do not be overly concerned if he stands up immediately. You are not teaching "Stay" yet. If he pops up instantaneously, simply command, place, and praise again. Do not scold him. Learning takes time. Repetition, not reaction, is the key here.

Flynn is an easy and eager student. Notice that as I do the hand signal, I bring the lead over to my hip. As I place him, notice the lead is taut but not pulling on him in any way. Also, look at my hand position on his rear. The "U" is placed directly in front of his hipbones. Lots of praise afterward. You can tell by his doggy smile that Flynn enjoys it.

Dog turns and mouths.

If your lead is taut against your right hip, your dog will not be able to turn and mouth. Be sure to use even, guiding pressure. If you are being gentle and he is still touchy, check with your vet to make sure he does not have a physical problem, like hip dysplasia, that is making this command painful for him.

Dog resists placement.

Confused dogs often freeze in place, which is frequently misinterpreted by owners as the dog being stubborn. People unwittingly make the situation worse by becoming more forceful, angry or upset. If your dog locks up, relax. Do not escalate force or emotion, just apply a steady, even pressure. Try quietly praising the dog while you gently rock the hips from side to side a few inches while continuing the gentle pressure down and back. As the dog, relaxes he will allow himself to be placed. Praise every milimeter of progress into the "Sit." This may take 30 seconds, it may take 3 minutes. Don't worry about that now. As he relaxes, he will learn to respond more quickly. Alternatively, use the scoop "Sit" method taught on page 74.

Dog lies down.

Submissive and playful dogs will often collapse onto the ground and roll over when you attempt to place them in to a "Sit." If the lead is properly positioned at your hip, this will be difficult for your dog to do. Also, reaching for the chest swiftly and beginning to scratch will help most dogs to sit up. If he insists on collapsing into a pile, do not correct or scold. This will only make the dog more submissive. Simply ignore it, take a few steps forward, and try again. Verbally praise as the dog sits, but stop the praise immediately if he collapses. In a few minutes he'll get the message. If you continue to have a problem, use food reward or a toy to encourage him to sit properly.

"Down"

When in doubt, "Down" is a sensible code to live by. When your dog assumes this position on command, he is being submissive. I use the "Down" as a behavioral thermometer. The dog's willingness to obey this command or his resistance to it is a direct reflection of his current state of mind. If he responds quickly, he is feeling compliant. If he knows the command but he refuses to obey, he is feeling competitive or overly confident. The moment he complies, he will be put in a more submissive frame of mind. If your dog is running off, thinking about becoming aggressive, jumping all over you, or is otherwise out of control, head right for the "Down" command. The command is "Down," given in a relaxed, firm tone of voice.

Try for a breathy word that comes from your chest. Think of throwing the word down into the ground. Tamar Arnon, one of our talented instructors, came up with the idea of saying it as if it was spelled "Dhown." This keeps it soft.

Common mistakes are issuing a quick, nasal "DOWN!" an endless "Dooowwwnn," a requesting "Down?" and a rapid-fire "Down? Down? Down? Down?" Keep it simple. Say it once and enforce it.

The hand signal is a downward sweep of the arm from the shoulder. Raise your left hand straight up and then swing it forward and downward so it ends up at your side, palm to the rear. Make this an even, deliberate move, not lightning fast but not slow, either. If you allow your voice to follow your arm motion, it will help you get the right intonation. Do not be concerned if the dog does not notice the signal; he will learn to if you use the signal consistently. Eventually you will be able to give the sign from across the room, with no vocal command, and your dog will obey. Impressive.

At this outdoor café, Chester is learning to lie down during meals. With my foot on the lead, he'll correct himself if he tries to stand up. I'll ignore him if he tries to get up, praising him warmly when he lies back down. It won't take him long to figure out what he's supposed to be doing.

This is the "Down" hand signal. It starts with the arm above your head and ends with it extended by your side.

THE PLACEMENT "DOWN"

This is the same technique outlined in the puppy section. It is made more difficult by the size of most adult dogs, so I am outlining the method again with tips on how to handle different-size animals. I like this method because it involves little struggle with the dog when done properly.

With your dog sitting on your left side, reach over his shoulder and put your left hand on his left shoulder. With your right hand grasp his right leg, down by the joint above his paw. Now lift up the right front paw and ease him to the right by pushing his left shoulder in that direction.

The concept is that you are removing his support on one side, then tipping him in that direction. You can do this in either direction, depending on how he is sitting. If he is sitting up straight, you can go either way. If he is slouching on one hip, then it is best to ease him over in the direction he is slouching. Why fight it?

Always take care to do this on a soft surface and to ease him down gently. If he bangs his elbows, he'll resist the placement next time. Who could blame him?

Once he is lying down, make a big fuss. Place him, then spend at least 15 seconds telling him how fabu-

Flynn does not notice the hand signal. That's OK, he'll learn as we go along. He is relaxed and accepts the placement with ease. Keep your dog on lead when you train him.

lous he is. You want him to believe that this is a terrifically fun thing to do. Sometimes owners are so interested in the dog learning that they forget to celebrate each small success.

After you've finished praising, release him with a clear "OK." Encourage him to get up, praise him a bit more, then repeat. Soon he'll be wagging his tail through the whole process.

LARGE BREEDS

Some of the big breeds brace themselves admirably, resisting any form of placement you might do. Try the "Down" using food, as taught on page 77. If that works, great. If not, go straight to the enforced "Down." Take your time. Praise heavily.

DACHSHUNDS

The long and low dogs can be difficult to roll onto one shoulder. Start with the dog sitting next to you; put one hand on the top of his shoulders. With the other hand grasp both front paws, keeping your index finger between them. Lift them up and gently ease him down with pressure on the shoulders. Stay relaxed and talk to the dog throughout.

CAUTION!

Dominant dogs can take great offense to being made to lie down. Some will struggle, some will freeze in place, and others will think about becoming aggressive. For these reasons I chose the methods listed in this section. Techniques that require you to put your face near your dog's while placing him down may be dangerous.

If your dog threatens you, if you feel frightened at any time during training, stop Immediately. Call a professional. Trust your instincts. **NEVER** dismiss a threat or aggression. A growl, grumble, or glare are all serious signals. Your dog is not kidding when he issues them. Do not try to "show him who's boss." Leadership is not established through confrontation. Realize that you have a problem, seek professional guidance, make that dog work for every bit of attention your family gives him, and don't put yourself in a position to get hurt.

THE ENFORCED "DOWN"

Now that your dog allows you to place him in the "Down" position easily, accepts praise in that position and remains relaxed, it is time for the next step. The goal of this stage is to have the dog down on command while you remain standing. It is easier for dogs to down if you bend over first; making the leap to obeying with you fully upright can be a big step.

This technique is done on a non-tightening collar—either a buckled-back Woodhouse collar or a flat collar. Ideally, you start this on a slippery surface such as tile or wood. With your dog sitting at your left-hand side,

give the command and the hand signal. Now place your left foot on the lead by the clip. Keeping the lead taut with your right hand, slowly apply downward pressure with your left foot. This is a guiding pressure, not doggy kung fu. If you are having a hard time staying balanced, then lean against a wall or countertop.

Initially, your dog will not know what is going on. He may resist the downward pressure. His natural reaction will be to pull away. Remain calm. Do NOT try to "help" by pushing him down. With him in a half-push-up position, he'll be down soon. Wait him out. Let him learn. Most dogs resist for one or two minutes the

The lead is nice and loose as I begin the command. The vocal command and the hand signal are given at the same moment. As I place my foot on the lead, I tighten it with my right hand. See how close my foot is to the clip of the lead? Once he is down, I squat and give him praise but keep my foot on the lead until I tell him "OK."

first time, less than one minute the second time, and understand exactly what you want after that.

To help your dog relax, stroke him gently. If he stands up, ease his rear into the "Sit" position but don't tell him to sit. That would only confuse the issue. Just place him and let him be. Have faith. Be patient. This technique works beautifully once they learn that lying down is more comfortable than resisting the pressure on their neck.

When he does comply, squat down and tell him how marvelous he is, brilliant, extraordinary and the best dog in the world. Keeping your foot on the lead, praise him for at least 20 to 30 seconds. Then tell him "OK" and release him. Clap your hands, smile, laugh, then do it again. Never stint on praise, especially when the dog has made a good effort at something new.

I like this method because it takes all the struggle between you and your dog out of the "Down." Your dog learns that resisting you is useless. He also learns that compliance brings pleasure and that you're the source of direction and praise. Your attitude throughout should be supportive, not reassuring. After all, you had nothing to do with the pressure on his neck. Who knows why that happened? You're just pleased he decided to lie down.

TiP

HOW TO GET IMMEDIATE AND CONSISTENT RESPONSE

You dream about your dog running across a field. You call him once. He pivots 180 degrees before the sound leaves the air, and runs back to you at high speed. Or maybe, the doorbell rings. You quietly tell your dog "Down" as you open the door. You accept the UPS package, chat with the driver, and close the door. Your dog has never moved. It can happen. Your dog's abilities are limited largely by your persistence. If you practice often, praise him enthusiastically for obedience, correct him immediately for noncompliance and accept nothing less than a job well done, you can get there. But if all you do is dream, complaining about your dog, practicing inconsistently and rewarding halfheartedly, then all you will have are dreams.

Dog resists enforcement.

First of all, did you spend three or more days doing several sessions of placement "Downs" a day? If not, do that first. That will introduce him to the exercise and set his initial positive feeling about it.

If you have been practicing and he is still resistant, either your foot is not close enough to the buckle, the collar is too big, or you have a resistant dog. How is your handling? Is your foot right up by or on the buckle? Does his collar fit properly, room for three fingers to be slipped under the collar but not more? Is he starting from a "Sit" position? Are you on a slick surface? If the answer is yes to all of these, then you just have to wait him out. Turn on a favorite TV show, set a soda on the counter next to you, put you foot on the lead and wait. You

can give him the occasional stroke, talk to him supportively ("You'll get this, it isn't hard. What a good dog!") and wait.

The normal wait for a resistant dog is one to four minutes. The dogs that resist the most are usually either frightened, dominant or have learned that if they resist you long enough you'll give up. Just stay calm. He is not doing this to annoy you. He does not know what you want yet. Eventually he will comply, and when he does, you will be there to praise and support him. Once you have praised him in the "Down" position, release him with an "OK" and praise some more. It's important that you let him know when the exercise is completed.

Dog resists placement.

If your dog stiffens up or splays out his back legs when you try to ease him over into a "Down," try the food reward method outlined on page 77. After a week of that, go to the enforced down. Severe resistance to this can be a sign of a dog who thinks too highly of himself. Make sure he works for the attention he gets. No more free lunch for him. Taking him down a few notches mentally will improve your chances with "Down."

Dog panics when learning the enforcement down.

This response calls for an immediate halt to the process. Although the method can work well for these dogs, they need specialized handling to succeed. Go back to placement and food methods for three days, then try again. When you do, start with your foot halfway down the lead. Allow the dog to relax with that amount of pressure, then slowly tighten the lead over a five-minute period while praising

A happy Blackie gets his reward. The owner's foot is right up by the clip, and he's praising Blackie in a way the dog obviously enjoys. Blackie is using a buckled-back Woodhouse collar.

him supportively. Shoes with a heel make this slow tightening a simple task. Stroking him occasionally will help to relax him. Your dog is just unsure what is happening and why; once he relaxes, he will respond appropriately.

Dog bites the lead.
Clever dog. Spray the lead with Bitter Apple and then proceed.

Dog lies down when you tell him to sit.
This is a normal stage in teaching "Down." It signals you that it is time to separate the two commands. From now on command the dog to down from the standing position only. If he does not, put your foot on the lead and guide him down. Keep up the praise.

Dog gets up immediately.
Keep your foot on the lead. This will prevent him from being a Jack-in-the-Box and allow him to get some praise in the proper position. Soon he will relax and stay down. When he's relaxed for 15 to 20 seconds, release him with a clear "OK" and praise him some more.

Dog rolls on back.
Not exactly a problem, but it can get messy if your dog does it outside. The way to fix this is to ignore him when he flips on his back: quiet praise when he is upright, silence when he flips over. Also, try using only verbal praise, as bending over is a dominant posture causing a shy dog to belly up immediately.

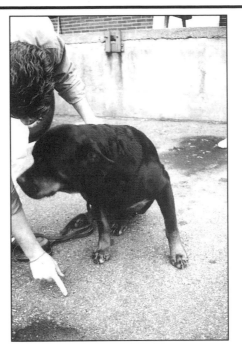

It is easy to get into the habit of pointing to the ground to get your dog to lie down. This limits how you can use the command. I also don't like how close this man's face is to his dog. This dog happens to be sweet, but it's a risky thing to do when working with a dog resisting the "Down."

This Dalmatian is learning the enforced down. He is resisting at the moment. Notice the buckled-back Woodhouse. Never introduce this command on a slip-type collar. I am stroking him gently to relax him. Slowly I'll tighten on the lead, drawing him downward a bit at a time as I do. Don't rush this command. Taking plenty of time the first few "Downs" will save you lots of time down the road.

"Let's Go"

Unlike "Sit" and "Down," which your dog does several times a day on his own, walking on your left side is a strange behavior for a dog. Without training he sees no point to it at all. He thinks "Hey, we're both walking in the same direction. What's my owner's problem?"

People try to teach their dog this command by pulling him back to the correct position every few steps while repeating the command. This makes little sense to the dog. While you're thinking "Boy, do I wish he'd stop dragging me around," your companion at the other end of the leash may be thinking the same thing. In fact, he'll pull even more in an effort to get away from the pressure. He may pull so hard he chokes himself. That's dog logic: something is pulling on me, so I should struggle to free myself.

The way to teach this command is to make the dog understand the importance of following you on a loose lead. One of the keys to success is properly holding the lead. (See pages 84–85 for full instructions.) Always put the thumb of your right hand through the lead, closing your hand around the loop. Now rest your right hand by your belly button, relaxed, and keep it there. The right hand's job is to hold the lead. It rarely does anything else. The left hand will be your active hand. You will use it to correct your dog in a variety of manners. Combining proper leash handling with turns, changes of speed and side steps will teach your dog to pay attention to you. Every time he stops watching you, change direction, give him a quick, horizontal, slightly downward pop on the lead, then

Max is showing how it's done. He is happy and relaxed. Focused on me totally, mouth open and happy, tail wagging. See my right hand resting by my belly button, how loose the lead is, how I am praising him.

praise him. Your attitude is "Gee, that popping thing just happens to dogs who aren't paying attention. I had nothing to do with it. I'm thrilled you decided to watch me." For full instructions about how to give a correction, please turn to page 88.

Your goal is for your dog to walk on your left side, his head even with your left knee, lead loose, happily following your every move.

I'm just holding out the lead like this to show you how loose it is. When you do it, keep that hand by your belly button. My left hand is off the lead, Max is paying close attention.

The lead is still slack. He and I are doing just fine. He's not a "highly trained" dog. We asked his owner to lend him to us because he looks so adorable. I worked with him for a few minutes and this is what I got. It's not magic; it's just the right methods applied in the right way wrapped in lots of praise.

TIP

THE DIFFERENCE BETWEEN "HEEL" AND "LET'S GO"

There is no magic in words. Dogs do not understand language. I personally have trained dogs in Russian, Italian, Hebrew, German, Japanese, Czech, Spanish and English. It doesn't matter what words you say as long as you are clear about exactly what you want. Train him to walk by your side at the command "Car wax" if you like. Know what you expect, transmit it to the dog, and praise him when he is right, and he'll learn.

Personally, I use the command "Let's go" because Barbara Woodhouse did. It is easy to remember, and the two syllables make it simple for beginners to step off on the second syllable. Too often "Heel" is chanted at the dog without any understanding of what it exactly means or how to precisely teach it. I use "Let's go" for controlled, attentive walking so that everyone can start fresh, with no preconceived ideas about how much the dog knows or how to teach it.

Flynn isn't perfect all the time. Here my right hand is over my belly button. My left hand holds the lead close by Flynn. Note all the slack between my left and right hands. You need that slack.

Since he is not paying attention to me, I let go with my left hand. After all, he doesn't *have* to pay attention, does he?

But when he's not paying attention, I'll immediately go to my right in the opposite direction. See my two hands, together, by my belly. I'm on my way. He catches up soon. One reason we don't have a complete series of these pictures is we couldn't get Flynn to look away again after the first two times.

LUNGE WORK

The first task is to educate your dog to keep a sharp eye on you. Beginning dogs are often so enthusiastic about life that you can't take two steps without them being at the end of the lead dragging you all over. If you own such a dog, start with lunge work. Lunge work is the art of surprise. All of a sudden instead of trailing obediently behind him, you become unpredictable. He doesn't have to watch you, but when he doesn't, you're going someplace else.

This is the only "Let's go" technique that requires you to have both hands on the leash most of the time. Hold the loop as usual over your right-hand thumb and form a fist around the rest of the loop. With your left hand, grasp halfway down the lead so that the lead is taut between the dog and your left hand and then slack between your right and left hands. In this position, give a nice clear "Let's go," step off with your left foot, and GO!

Most likely your dog will forge ahead. As the lead tightens, simply release your left hand, quickly put your left hand over your right, holding both to your belly. At the same time, pivot 180 degrees to the right and head in the opposite direction with determination. Do not look back. Physics being what it is, the lead will tighten, correcting your dog. Praise enthusiastically; encourage him to hurry to your side. When he is back in position, return your left hand to the middle of the lead and continue as before. Keep praising: it makes you more interesting to the dog. You will have to do this four or more times before your dog begins to get the message that watching you is important.

RIGHT ABOUT TURN

Once your dog is beginning to pay attention while walking, it is time to get that left hand off the lead. Do this as soon as possible. It will prevent you from getting into the bad habit of holding your dog in place. Remember, a tight lead encourages the dog to pull.

Holding the lead in your right hand only, put the your thumb through the loop and gather up the excess slack. The lead should be hanging down, forming a "U" shape between you and the dog. It should not be so loose that you or your dog could trip over it. With your dog sitting by your left side, with his head even with your knee, command "[Dog's name], let's go," at the same time briskly stepping forward with your left foot.

Praise warmly as he stays by your side. If he begins to pull ahead, pivot 180 degrees to your right and continue. If you feel any tension on the lead, put your left hand on the lead, reach back toward the dog, snap forward and downward, then release. Do not pull or drag on the dog. Continue praising when the dog is back in the proper position.

This is an excellent turn to use when your dog begins to pull ahead, is distracted, or starts to cut in front of you.

As Piper starts to pull ahead, I do a right about turn. My hands are ready to give a correction but he does not need one. He corrects himself and catches up like a good dog.

LEFT ABOUT TURN

The left about turn teaches the dog that you need the space directly in front of his nose and may, at any moment, be using it. This realization convinces him to keep his head close to your left knee, out of your way.

As you are walking along in a "Let's go" with your dog in the proper position or just beginning to think about pulling ahead, put your left hand on the lead, halfway down it. Snap back toward your dog's tail, stepping directly across and in front of him with your left leg. Continue to turn left until you are going in the opposite direction. This is a wonderful way to teach dogs not to forge ahead.

When you make this turn, you may bump into him. Do not avoid doing so. If you stay out of his way, he will never learn to stay out of yours. Walk right in front of him. Keep your feet close to the ground and don't use more force than you need. Praise him well when he gets out of your way. Timing is critical here. If you are correcting too late, be careful not to fall over the dog!

Topaz is in excellent position, but I don't think she's really paying attention. I'm going to prevent a problem by reminding her now to watch me carefully.

With my left hand on the lead, I get ready to snap back and step across in front of her with my left leg.

There I go. Oops, she bumped her nose. No harm done, but she wasn't quite in the right spot.

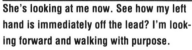

She's looking at me now. See how my left hand is immediately off the lead? I'm looking forward and walking with purpose.

Don't stand there looking at the dog. They won't be able to tell you anything.

And away we go. Topaz is paying close attention to me now.

RIGHT TURN

The 90-degree right turn is a quick way to correct your dog without turning all the way around. I like to combine a quick right turn with a quick left turn to get the dog's attention without having to stop my forward progress.

The 90-degree right turn should be crisp and military. Dogs learn more easily if these turns are square rather than circular. As the dog begins to get distracted, say nothing, simply turn 90 degrees, put your left hand on the lead and give a quick horizontal pop forward and release. Continue in the new direction, praising.

Topaz is just beginning to pull ahead of my left knee. Time to do something!

I decide to turn right 90 degrees. Note my foot coming around. My left hand is going to the lead, getting ready to correct if I need to, but Topaz is noticing, so no correction will probably be necessary.

And away I go. Topaz is a bit behind, but if I correct her she'll back off even more. Instead, I'll praise her and play a bit to get her enthusiasm up.

Scooter is not paying close attention as we approach this left turn.

I cut her off at the pass.

Now her head is up!

LEFT TURN

This 90-degree left turn improves your dog's walking. As with the left about turn, snap back and step across with your left foot, only square the turn and continue on from there. Combinations of left and right 90-degree turns are challenging for the dog, fun for you and educational for both.

As your dog improves, stop correcting. It becomes unnecessary if the dog is in the proper position by your left knee. You do not have to look at your dog to check his position. If your lead is loose, all is well. If it is tight, correct.

Now you can start playing follow the leader with him. Get to an open area and do all kinds of turn combinations. The more interesting it is, the more attentive he will have to be to keep up. Have fun! Move in deliberate, even strides but turn every which way. Have an "Uh-oh, you missed me!" attitude if you have to correct him. The more fun you have, the more attentive he will be.

SIDE STEP

This is an easy, effective correction for sniffing or not paying attention and a terrific choice on a crowded street where you have little room to turn. As you are walking, step sideways with your right foot. Imagine stepping from one side of the railroad tracks to the other. That is the correct movement. Do this if your dog's attention is wandering. It is also excellent for dogs that mouth your feet and jump up when being walked. It is a gliding sideways motion followed by a sideways snap if the dog fails to notice your departure. Praise is heaped on after the correction to reinforce the value of staying near you. "I had nothing to do with it, darling." You tell the dog "It just happens to dogs who don't pay attention to their owners." Smile and continue.

This little American Cocker Spaniel is not paying close attention. It's time to do something!

I sidestep; she doesn't even notice.

She gets a pop for that.

Then lots of praise! Notice that her tail is up—she's having a good time. My left hand is off the lead immediately after the correction.

Here's a quick way to test your dog's attentiveness when you don't have the time or inclination to turn in any way. This is a fun pop quiz for your dog. As you are walking along, switch into low gear, move slowly. Most dogs will miss the transition. Place the correction at the moment he misses the transition and his head pulls past your knee. Once he masters this, then try going faster. Take off at a brisk pace. Once he is enjoying that, shift into normal speed abruptly. It's the dog's responsibility to notice. If he does, praise!

Changes of speed are hard to capture on film. I am going fast with Topaz, and then I go back to normal suddenly. She doesn't miss a stride, paying close attention to my every move. Good dog!

Halt

Teaching your dog to stop and sit quietly on your left-hand side takes some practice and a special technique. Prepare for the halt mentally a few steps before you actually stop. Coming to a halt is a four-step process.

1. Take the lead in your left hand about halfway to the dog.

2. Reach your right hand over and across your body to take the lead from your left hand.

3. With the lead in your right hand, bring it to your right hip as you would for a sit. Allow the lead to slide through your fingers so that it remains taut.

4. Just as you bring the right hand into position, take your final step, planting your right foot and bringing your left foot to meet it. As your left foot swings into place, you command "Sit" and give the hand signal with your left hand. Does it sound like a lot? It is at first.

For his part, the dog should slow as you slow and respond promptly to the "Sit," his head even with your left knee. When he does, praise him lavishly. This is new, and new efforts are always praised warmly even if they are not done perfectly. Chances are you made a few mistakes, too. If he does not sit, it is an easy enough task to reach down with your left hand and place him into position as you would for any other "Sit."

Common mistakes are pulling the lead too tight, which forces the dog to sit crooked; giving the command while walking, which makes it tough to obey and giving the command after completely stopping, which allows the dog time to get distracted. Give the command *just as* the left foot is swinging into position, the leash is brought to your hip, and the hand signal is given.

This technique takes a bit of practice. Work on one part at a time. Try it without the dog. This may feel strange, but if you don't do the movements well, how can you expect your dog to respond well? Practice walking through it first, timing your feet, hand signal and voice. When that is comfortable for you, add in a leash without the dog. Go through the shortening motion solo for a few rounds. When you feel reasonably in control, add the wild card: your dog.

Step 1

Step 2

Step 3

Step 4

Here is a typical situation. This enthusiastic German Short-Haired Pointer will drag you all over the place unless educated not to.

Big or small, if they aren't paying attention, they get a pop. Things to notice in this shot are how the dogs ears are flapping but the dog himself is not moving, and that I am snapping the lead sideways, not upward. This means you small dog people *have* to bend.

Tina says no. Don't stop as I do for this picture. To get her going, I just brought the lead across my legs and kept walking. The minute she started moving with me, I praised, then stopped (a reward in itself) and praised her some more.

SOLVING COMMON "LET'S GO" PROBLEMS

Dog pulls ahead.

Timing is of the essence. You need to place the correction *just as* your dog's nose goes ahead of your knee. If you correct him after this point, it will be hard for your dog to understand the exact position you want him to maintain. Some dogs shoot forward so fast that it is tough to get the proper timing. In that case, say "Let's Go," pivot 180 degrees, then go. Any and all turns are helpful for this type of dog; left about turns are particularly good if you can do them just as the dog is pulling forward. If his shoulder is already even with your left leg, you'll probably trip over him.

Dog lags behind.

Do NOT correct. That will only make him lag more. Dogs lag for a number of reasons. If your leash has a big buckle or an overly long collar, you may be smacking him in the face with the buckle when you walk with him. I'd hang back too. If your corrections are too forceful or frightening, he'll lag. Maybe he can't keep up or he is unsure about what you want. It's also possible he's just being difficult.

First, make sure your collar and lead are the proper size and length so that he is not being hurt. No choke collar should have more than two to three inches extra when you tighten the collar snugly around the mid- point of the neck. If he is frightened, you may need to use a nontightening collar. Some shy dogs get spooked when the slip collar tightens, and overreact. Pretty soon they don't want to walk at all.

If all is well—you know he can keep up, and you're being fair—and he still lags behind, then walk faster. If you slow down as he slows down, he'll only learn that slowing down works well. So speed up. Follow the leader is the game here. Being decisive in your movement is vital! If you don't look like you know where you're going, don't expect the dog to follow. Praise him happily as you speed along. Do not correct.

The best thing to do is bring the lead across your legs and anchor your right hand by your right side, at the outer seam of your pants. Hold it there. As you walk, your leg will pull him up, then release, pull and release in an even rhythm that most dogs respond to well. When he catches up, praise him for 10 to 20 steps, then squat down, praise him more. Tell him what a terrific thing it is he just did. Continue to praise as you start again. He'll soon be trotting at your side.

Dog stops.

You don't. Keep going. Do not turn toward or look at the dog or discuss it with him. Act as if nothing were happening. The moment he starts to walk again, squat down, call him up to you and praise him. Do not, under any circumstances, go to him. That will only reward him for stopping. Most dogs will bounce around behind you for a few steps and then, realizing you're not paying attention, get up and trot along.

If you've been picking them up when they stop, you've got a harder row to hoe. Put a buckle collar on him, then tie the lead to you in the house and have him follow you. There the flooring is gentle on his feet and you won't be going far. He'll figure out it's easier just to come along than to resist.

Dog jumps up.

Sidestep, correct, then keep going. The side step is the single best answer to a dog that jumps while on lead. It gives you a better angle of correction. You may need to do a few before he gets the idea, but he'll get it.

Dog puts foot over lead.

Smart dog. It is another way some dogs have learned to stop their owners. He flings his foot up. You stop and untangle him. He flings his foot up. You stop. . . . get the idea? Guess what I suggest: don't stop. He'll hop along for 15 to 20 feet, then he'll unhook his paw and walk like a real dog. If he doesn't, stop—do not look at or speak to him, no acknowledgment whatsoever—unhook his paw, and keep going. After a few three-legged races he'll decide this isn't working as well as it used to.

Dog cuts in front of owner.

Do lots of left turns and circles before he cuts in front to teach him to stay back. Be sure you walk through him if he is in your way. If you step around him, it won't teach him anything. When he cuts in front next time, put your left hand on the lead, midway down, and snap it out to the left. If he is big or gets all the way across before you get a chance to do this, turn to your right. Turning to the right almost always puts the dog on your left in the proper position.

Dog cuts in back of owner.

Two techniques work well for this habit. The first is an easy one. When he cuts behind you, *keep walking* while you pull your lead to the right (across your body). Keep walking, keep pulling, and it will bring him around to the proper position. Your other option is to reach back with your left hand and correct out and to the left. Keep moving. As with all the other corrections, timing is critical. Try to correct *just as* the dog considers cutting behind. It is much easier to get the dog back into the proper position at that moment than when he is all the way behind you.

Increasing Your Control

Now that your dog understands his basics, you can add "real-life commands" to his vocabulary. These are the words I use to direct a dog's actions away from unwanted behaviors toward good ones. Unless you can do this, you are stuck either reacting after the fact or trying to prevent the bad behavior through restraint. How many of us hold our dog back as a guest enters our home, or grab the lead up short and tight when we pass another dog?

Restraint creates resistance. Your goal is for the dog to control himself around distractions. This goal can only be achieved through careful teaching and practice in controlled situations. Translated, that means don't expect the dog to spit out a chicken bone he found in the park if he won't drop his toy on command in the house. Always establish control in a quiet environment before you expect obedience around distractions.

Winston starts out slow but then . . .

"Out"

Getting dogs to spit things out of their mouths is necessary. Not only do they have a tendency to pick up valuable things like eyeglasses or a shoe from one of the only pair of comfortable dress shoes you own, but they pick up dangerous things like pieces of glass, not to mention the disgusting things like decomposed rodents or used tissues they find in the street—things you don't want to have to touch. Most every dog learns quickly to clench his teeth, lower his head, and resist with every ounce of his being your efforts to pry his mouth open. Luckily, you can teach him to spit anything out of his mouth.

First off, you must give the animal a way to win. Look at this scenario: Your dog has a dead thing in his mouth. He enjoys having a dead thing in his mouth. You see that he has it. You yell and give chase. He runs away. You do this for a while, then you catch him. You are annoyed because you've been running for a bit now and are feeling pretty foolish, angry, frustrated and tired. You pry open his mouth while yelling at him "Drop it." He finally does. You yell at him some more for having picked it up five minutes ago. What does your dog learn?

. . . grabs the bone and pulls it out of my hand. (Not an easy thing to do!) He wants it and hunkers down to try and keep it.

He learns that it is fun to have the dead thing in his mouth and a real drag to let you catch him. Canine moral of the story: run faster next time.

Regardless of how disgusting the thing in his mouth is or how long you have been chasing him or how angry you are that he has done this, you must—I repeat, *must*—praise him when the thing leaves his mouth. Once he has it, it is too late to teach him not to take it. The only thing you can hope for is to teach him to spit it out without any fuss. Stay focused on what you need right that minute, not on what he should have done five minutes ago.

To start teaching him to spit things out, put him on his lead and training collar. Have him sit, and face him. Offer him an object that he enjoys, can't swallow and is large enough for him to have in his mouth while you hold another piece of it. Praise him and allow him to hold it for a few seconds. Hold the lead about two feet from his collar. Leaning slightly toward him, making solid eye contact, calmly tell him "Out." Do NOT try to pull it out of his mouth. That will only make him hold on to it more tightly. Instead, hold on to it and give a quick downward or horizontal pop on the lead. You may have to do this two or three times before

I tell him "out" and give him a correction.

he opens his mouth. Do not pull on him or try to drag him away from it. Use quick, clean downward or horizontal snaps.

Once he has released it, put the object behind your back out of his view and praise him immediately. That was perfect! Make a big to-do over him for spitting it out. Now do it again. Always praise the moment he begins to loosen his grip on the object. Only correct if he does not voluntarily obey.

Soon he will be spitting it out with no fuss whatsoever. Once he is at that level, start offering him different things. Socks, shoes, bagels—anything he covets. Always begin with the things he finds mildly interesting and work up to the things he is wild about. If at any time you feel nervous or he looks like he may be thinking about being aggressive, stop. Get professional guidance before you go further.

Your praise should match the difficulty of the command. If he spits out a tennis ball: "Good dog." If he drops a bone he found in the park, "Good boy! What a fine dog! Amazing!" Don't be stingy. That kind of obedience deserves bonus praise and play. If you don't let him know how pleased you are with his response, he'll be likely to choose the bone next time.

It took a couple of pops before he spit out the bone. I immediately praise him for complying.

Now he won't even taste it. What a good dog!

"Off"

Jumping dogs are almost always our fault. Few of us can say with complete honesty that we NEVER pet our dog when he jumps up. Rewarding him with a pat or a kind word every so often is enough to keep most dogs jumping. The first one you have to control if you are going to teach this command is yourself. You can't pet him for jumping in the morning, then scold him for doing the same thing later in the day. He can't tell the difference between blue suits and blue-jeans.

Everyone in the family should comply, all agreeing never to pet, speak kindly to, throw a toy for or give a treat to a dog that has only two feet on the ground. This includes lap draping, where your pet lays the front of his body across your lap. Any time he has two feet off the ground he should be ignored or corrected. Once everyone agrees to this, training can begin. If you can't come to a unanimous agreement about this, then don't correct the dog for jumping. It isn't fair. If you can't be consistent, don't expect your dog to be.

Start by setting him up. Put the dog on leash and collar at times when you suspect he will jump. Be prepared when family members come home,

when you are romping with him or getting his dinner ready. Teach him that no matter what you do, he has to keep four feet on the ground.

Keep hold of the lead about two feet away from the collar and keep it loose. If it is tight, reach in toward the dog to get some slack. If you try to correct with a tight lead you will only pull the dog. Pulling allows the dog to lean his body weight against the lead, something I am sure you've noticed. Even a small dog seems to weigh a lot when he is pulling on the lead.

As he goes to jump, tell him "Off" in a calm voice. Immediately give a quick sideways and downward snap on the lead. Do not snap backward as this will put pressure on his trachea. A good, quick sideways snap will put him a bit off balance. He'll have to hop off and put his feet back on the ground to recover. The moment those four feet touch the ground, immediately praise warmly but not wildly. If you are too enthusiastic, he will jump back up.

Now you need to tell him what you want him to do. Instruct him to sit, make sure he does, then praise some more. Your dog is self-serving. He is jumping to get attention. When he stops getting attention for jumping, he will stop jumping. It usually takes about three times for the dog to be convinced.

Here we set up the situation so we can correct Jim at exactly the right moment. This was a very difficult series to get because once we did it, the dog wouldn't make the same mistake again.

SOCIAL EMBARRASS-MENT

Social pressure is a factor just about everyplace, but nowhere does it affect a dog owner more than in the city. Train your dog on a city sidewalk, and strangers will glare, stare, mutter or make comments. These same people, not remembering you from weeks before, will tell you how terrific your dog is when he is behaving well.

There are ways to handle this. Praise happily and steadily. People don't mind the occasional fair, unemotional correction if it is surrounded by praise. Force is not the key to correction. A good, clean sideways pop does not move your dog an inch. And lastly, do not pay attention to the strangers. Refuse to make eye contact or acknowledge them in any way and they'll move on. This may seem rude. It is rude. But in a city where thousands of people consider themselves experts in dog behavior, believe me, it is necessary.

What do I do if my dog is not on lead? There are several ways you can handle this. Number one is plan ahead. You know your dog's going to jump at certain times, so don't be surprised. Plan for those occasions and get the lead on him.

If you can't plan ahead, such as when you are coming home from work and he has no lead or training collar on, you can do one of a few things. Use the keys that are in your hand. After you command "Off" calmly, toss the keys down by his back feet. The noise will startle him, and he'll pop off to investigate. (Note: Do not use this method on tiny dogs as the keys could hurt them.) Or you can use a shake can behind your back to reinforce your command. If that does not work, toss it down by his feet—always praising when he gets off and instructing him to sit so he can learn what he is supposed to do.

The easiest correction you can try is just standing there, arms folded, looking at the ceiling, ignoring him completely. In a few seconds he'll stop, cock his head and wonder what's wrong. The moment this happens praise him warmly; do not pet him unless he sits. If he jumps again, ignore him again. This clear contrast allows many dogs to quickly learn what the desired behavior is. Please don't use this if your dog can knock you over. Training is not supposed to be painful for either of you.

If you don't want your dog to jump, don't reward him when he does.

"Leave It"

Distractions are the bane of a dog owner's existence. They make walking your dog a chore, serving a meal a challenge and going to the vet's a nightmare. Suddenly your calm, affectionate pet becomes a straining, leaping beast gasping for air as he drags you toward whatever it is that interests him. Squirrels, other dogs, pieces of paper blowing in the wind, cats, children on bicycles, garbage on the street, birds, rats, and kids playing ball are a few of the things dog owners dread. Shouting "No!" doesn't help. Holding them back only makes them pull harder. The command to teach is "Leave it," meaning "Leave it alone *right now*." Teach this command indoors in a quiet area and then, as his understanding improves, move to more challenging things. Your goal is for him to avert his eyes from what interests him the moment you give him the command.

Put your dog on his leash and training collar. Start with treats. A hard biscuit is good. Break a few into small pieces. Pick up one whole biscuit and a small piece. Grasp the lead about two feet from the collar with one hand. Show the dog the biscuit in the other, tell him "Leave it," and then toss it some distance from you. You need the distance at first so you'll have time to correct him when he leaps for it. As he starts for the treat, give him a quick, sideways snap on the lead. He may take two or three of these before he stops dragging forward. Praise him the MOMENT he stops moving toward the treat. Do not wait silently to see if he's going to try again; assume he won't and praise him to the hilt. Give him the small treat in your hand. Tell him how spectacular that was. Then do it again. Soon he will focus on you when the treat is thrown, looking for his praise and reward. Perfect!!

Continue this training, adding in

First the puppy sniffs the bread. Then I toss it down and tell him "Leave it". A quick correction convinces him he did not really want it in the first place. Then I praise him.

more difficult objects—favorite toys, more tempting foods. Then go to more difficult surroundings—outside, in the park. Always keep the dog on lead during the training process. Praise the dog whenever he obeys.

As soon as your dog responds consistently, then start weaning away the treats in that situation. If you start something new, begin with treats, then cut back. If you praise enthusiastically before, after and while you give the treat, the dog will not mind when you stop using them.

Here is one of my classes practicing "Leave It" on the stairs. Notice the woman on the left. The leash properly over her right thumb. Her left hand poised by the lead, ready to correct if her dog so much as looks at the other dog. She's doing a great job!

Mastering Time and Distance

These next three commands—"Wait," "Down"/"Stay" and "Place"—all involve a time element. Just like the capital letter at the beginning of a sentence and the period at the end tells us we are dealing with one complete thought, the command at the beginning and the "OK" at the end define these commands for the dog. "OK" is the universal release for all commands. "Wait" stops the dog at doorways, corners and getting in or out of the car. It means pause for a second. It does not tell the dog how to wait. The dog can sit, stand, or lie down as is his preference. He can't move forward. "Wait" ends with "OK." "Stay" means "Don't move a muscle until I release you with 'OK.' You must stay in the position I left you in, regardless of what goes on around you." "Place" is a "Go there, lie there, and stay there" command. It is used around the house when you need your dog to be out of the way but not out of the room. If you teach the dog to place on a bed you can travel with, it gives the dog an easy home away from home when you're on the road.

"Wait"

Begin teaching the "Wait" command on lead with his training collar on, inside your home. Walk up to the front door. Put the lead in one hand. With the lead loose command "Wait," then open the door. *Just as* the dog begins to move forward, give a quick sideways snap on the lead. Correct him *just as* he moves toward the door. Do not wait until you are looking at his hind end—at that point it's too late. If that happens, simply bring the dog back inside and try again. Praise the moment he stops trying to get out the door. Then tell him "OK" and go out the door, you first, him politely following.

It is critical that the lead be loose as you open the door. A tight lead will guarantee that he will fight you. There is no shame in having to do this a few times until you get it right. You are both learning many new skills and it is not easy. Be patient with yourself and your dog. Soon you'll both get it!

This dog likes to bolt out doorways. Giving the "Wait" command, I correct him *just as* he starts out the door. He doesn't make that mistake twice.

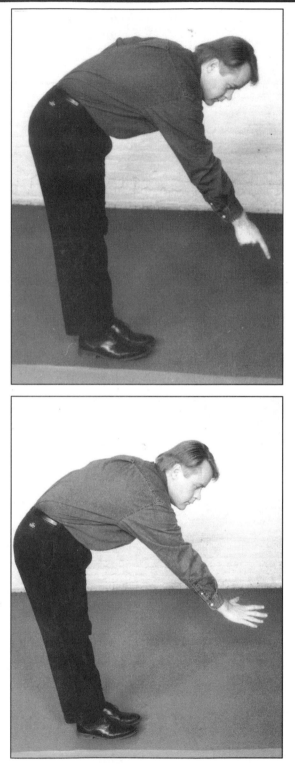

"Down" / "Stay"

"Down"/"Stay" means "Stay right there until I come back and release you. Don't move a muscle." It is a terrific way to get your dog back under control after he has been a jerk. Used daily, it can support your leadership without being confrontational. If your dog ignores you, is aggressive, hyperactive, wild, obnoxious or just generally a handful, work on this command. These dogs need help learning self-control.

When teaching "Down"/"Stay" you are working with three different variables. How long the dog has to stay, how far away you are and how much is going on around the dog—time, distance and distraction—are what you have to overcome before your dog will stay reliably.

The mistake people make is they try to address too many variables at once and in the wrong order. Conquer one at a time in this order: time, first; distraction, second; and lastly distance. The two most common errors are backing out of the room to see if the dog will stay there and standing silently, waiting to see how long he'll stay. You want your dog to be successful at first to build his confidence. If he gets corrected frequently, he'll become nervous. Nervous dogs make more mistakes. Practice for a few seconds at a time at first. Even if it isn't much of a "Stay," that doesn't matter—it is fun, he is successful, and you can praise him. Once he learns the basic concept of stay, you'll be able to increase difficulty quickly.

The "Stay" hand signal has two parts. First, point at your dog and tell him "Down," then open your hand and tell him "Stay." Bend at your waist so the commands are right in front of his face.

Begin teaching this command with your dog on lead on your left-hand side in a "Down." Place him in a relaxed "Down," so that he is over on one hip, not lying sphinxlike. Once he is down and comfortable, step off with your right foot and pivot in front of him. Bend at the waist, point at him, saying "Down," followed by an open hand in his face as you say "Stay." The voice and the hand work in unison.

Now, keeping the palm open toward the dog and still holding the lead, stand upright and step away from the dog at a normal speed. Rushing away will encourage him to follow. If you are slow and tentative, he will pick up your insecurity and become doubtful himself. Be careful to keep the lead loose at all times. Stand quietly while you praise him softly. Use any words you want but do not say his name. He'll want to come to you, which is not what we want right now.

After just a few seconds step back to him, placing your foot down on the lead close to him but not causing any pressure on his collar. Now bend and stroke him calmly. If he gets up prematurely, the foot on the lead will correct him without any fuss. Praise is not his signal to get up, "OK" is. Make him wait for that. Continue to tell him what a fine dog he is. Then clearly tell him "OK" and back away from him. Praise now should be more lively to urge him up and to you.

Do this repeatedly until he understands that he is to wait for you to return and tell him "OK" before he gets up.

Doing lots of close "Stays" in different situations and for different lengths of time builds a strong foundation for the command. Notice how relaxed Walter and Chester are. Chester is advanced enough that he does not need the hand signal to constantly remind him what to do.

Once he understands this basic concept, you can start pushing him to stay for longer and in more difficult situations. Always work on one thing at a time. Lengthen the "Stays" indoors until he can stay for 10 minutes or more without a fuss. Once he has gotten to this point, go back to short stays but add to the equation a rolling ball, a dropped treat or some other temptation. Since you are adding a new feature, you want to shorten the "Stays."

Expect only a 10-second stay around a ball at first. When he stays successfully, end with a happy "OK" and play ball for a minute. When he can do 10 seconds easily, work up to 30. When teaching "Stay," always try to build on success rather than focus on correcting mistakes. If your dog is constantly getting up, he has been pushed too far, too fast. Go back to the start and stay at that level for a week before you attempt to do more. "Stay" is only possible if the dog is

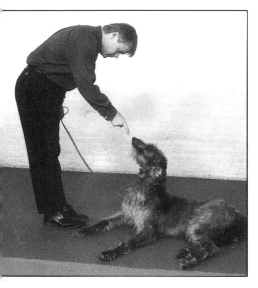

Piper is in a relaxed "Down," lying on one hip. He's likely to stay put in that comfortable position. Always have a lead on your dog when you start a new command.

He looks away for this part of the hand signal. Don't worry about that. It is his responsibility to know what's going on, not yours to try to get his attention.

I've stepped away but am keeping my hand signal up to remind him to stay put.

relaxed and confident. Corrections that raise tension and nervousness are counterproductive to the "Stay." Use the "Stay" frequently—when you're on the phone, watching TV, cooking a meal, doing the laundry. The more you integrate it into your daily routine, the more responsive your dog will be.

When outside, work on short "Stays" until he can control himself around all these new smells, sights and sounds. Once he is relaxed and attentive again, then start demanding longer "Stays." Keep him on lead outside unless you are in a safe area.

The last thing to work on is distance. Again, because you are adding something new into the equation, everything else should be made easy. As you start getting farther away from the dog, work for shorter periods in areas with few distractions. Once the distance is understood by the dog, then expect longer "Stays." When that is under control, then start adding in distractions. Always build slowly, on a foundation of success.

When I return, I praise him while he is lying down . . .

then release him with an "OK" and praise him some more.

It is not uncommon for people to get into correction cycles with their dogs. One trainer I know has sensitive little Shelties, which have a difficult time staying. It was a painful process to watch. The woman tells the dog "Stay" in a threatening tone. The dog tenses up immediately. As she walks away, the dog begins to look around; anxiously it creeps toward the owner. "No!" shouts the trainer, as she strides quickly toward the cowering dog. "No, bad dog," she says as she drags him back to where she left him, corrects him firmly, angrily tells him to stay, and leaves. The dog is beside himself with panic. Upset, he wants to be close to his beloved owner, so he immediately creeps after her. This infuriates the trainer . . . and on they go.

It's a true story. You would think a trainer would know better, but they don't always. She needs to do short "Stays" near her dog, with loads of praise to relax and calm this animal. Anger never helps fear. It only makes it worse. Training is not a confrontational exercise. If you can remember this, you will avoid many training mistakes.

If your dog gets up while in a "Stay," simply walk back to him silently and calmly, reach to the midpoint of the lead, and with quick, sharp snaps lead him back to the spot you left him in, then snap him downward into a "Stay." It is briskness, not force, that works here. This is meant to be annoying, not painful. Then flash the "Stay" hand signal in his face and walk away; say nothing. Quietly start praising him if he holds it.

If your dog repeatedly gets up, do many short "Stays" with plenty of praise for not moving. Return to him frequently to praise him or give a small tidbit. Stepping on the lead as you arrive will prevent him from standing up prematurely. If he gets up silently, step on the lead. Be calm and deliberate. Speed or anger will only create problems such as running away, jumping back or fear. Successful practice is much more important than correcting the mistake. Go back to your basics and make sure he understands the concept of "Stay" before you push him to higher levels.

If your dog still is getting up, then step on the lead. Have him hold the position for a minute or so, while you praise. Then release with "OK" and praise some more. As he relaxes during practice, step back with your other foot to get some distance. Slowly raise your toe off the lead and see if he stays. Then draw your foot back until you are standing a few feet away. If he gets up, guide him back into place with your foot. This will give him the idea without having to fight with him.

Owners who frequently call their dog from a distance out of the "Stay" are training their dogs to get up. Only call the dog from a "Stay" when he is highly successful at staying, and even then only once every 7 to 10 times you have him stay. More than that will create anticipation and mistakes.

I quickly step in and put my foot on the lead to correct Topaz as she considers getting up.

Working around all kinds of distractions is critical to developing a reliable "Stay."

If your dog creeps toward you, do a few more weeks of close "Stays" for long periods. Chances are you moved too quickly to distance work before your dog really understood what you wanted. Be sure to praise warmly and consistently to relax him and build his confidence. Feel free to return to your dog, praise him or give him a small treat, then leave again without releasing him. If he gets up, just guide him back down without comment.

Work up to distance slowly. Don't go from close to the dog to out of the room in two days. Only add a few feet at a time, always returning and praising him frequently. Note the distance at which he has trouble—some dogs can't tolerate the owner being more than 6 feet away, others 10. Whatever it is, practice staying just shy of his trigger point. Do lots of 5-foot stays for the 6-foot worrier.

If he still creeps forward, try running a long lead from the dog, to a table leg or tree behind the dog, then back forward to you. This way, if your dog creeps, you can stop his forward motion by simply tightening on the lead.

Marc gives Ike the "Down" hand signal as he tightens up on the long line. Unable to move forward, Ike lies back down and gets praised.

"Place"

This useful command means "Go to a designated place and stay there until released with an 'OK.'" It's convenient when traveling, around guests, during meals or anytime you need the dog out from underfoot but not necessarily out of the room. I like to use a blanket or towel as the designated area because I travel a great deal and these are easier to pack than beds and baskets.

Begin with the dog on lead. Have a treat in one hand. Command "Place!" and point to the bed. Now walk over to it, encouraging the dog along the way: "What a good dog, that-a-way." When you arrive, guide the dog onto the bed with the treat, then hold the treat down to the floor, which guides the dog into a "Down."

Ruby eagerly heads for the bed on the "Place" command.

I use the food to guide her into the "Down."

Once he's down, give him the treat and praise. Immediately tell him "OK" and praise. Back away and make sure he gets off the bed. He has to learn that "OK" means "All done." Praise him some more. Repeat until the dog walks onto the mat and lies down in a relaxed manner.

Now you begin to teach him that he has to stay put. Again using treats, stand up and step away once the dog is down. Immediately step back, praise and give a small treat. Repeat this process. If the dog gets up at any time, use quick little pops on the lead that make the collar jingle to get him back to place. Use one pop per step. The idea is that the corrections are annoying, not "teaching him who's boss." Force will create resistance. Once he is back to place, give a downward pop for the down. Say nothing, give no treat.

Stepping away, I praise her calmly as she holds the "Stay." She's licking her lips in anticipation.

"Good girl!"

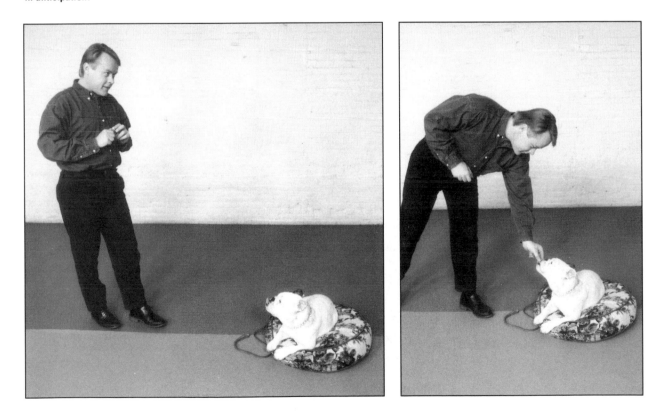

As he catches on to the bargain—"I lie here and you reward me. I move and I get that strange chinking thing on my neck"—he'll be staying there like a champ. Over time, reward less frequently. When he can stay in place for 15 to 20 minutes, then start moving farther away. As you begin this new phase, be sure to shorten the length of time. Anytime you add in a new variable, always make everything else easier. Once he can handle you walking farther away, then add in time again. Soon the dog will be staying for long periods with no food rewards at all. Make it fun for your dog. Say "Place" and run back to the spot. Use the command from different directions and distances. No matter what level of training you're at, keep up the warm praise throughout. One client forgot her dog was in place and went to the movies. Going above and beyond, the dog was there when she returned! Now *that's* a good dog.

"OK" releases her so we can do it again.

"Come"

I've saved "Come" for last because it is a difficult command to teach a dog. It almost inevitably involves asking the dog to leave something it enjoys and come do something it likes less. From your dog's perspective this does not make it a fun command. Your job is to make it as enjoyable as possible so your dog is willing to do it. "Come" is also the command people seem to get the most creative with. Go to any park and you'll hear all the renditions. There's the Bribery Recall: "Cookie, girl, cookie. Come to Mommy, sweetie. Do you want a cookie?" Next is the Multiple Call Recall: "Daisy, come. Come, Daisy, come here, girl, come. Come. Come!" The dog eventually wanders over. The Or Else Recall is a common one: "Come here right now!" must be bellowed in a threatening tone for the dog to respond. My favorite is the No Call Recall, which involves chanting the dog's name without ever telling it what you want it to do. "Deacon, Deacon, Deacon . . . " The funny thing is that all these dogs could come immediately, on the first call, if the owners understood a few basic principles. The most important thing to remember is that the dogs learn to respond at the point where you make them respond. If you call him 10 times, then go get him, he'll respond on the 10th command or stand there waiting for you to come to him. If you call him repeatedly, get annoyed, and then go get him, he'll learn to respond when you sound annoyed. If you only get enthusiastic when you have a cookie in your hand, then your dog will learn to come only to a cookie. It is up to you.

As with all training, start in a situ-

ation where you have physical control or can teach easily, then progress to more freedom. So many people call complaining that their dog will not come to them outside, and when questioned they admit that the dog won't come inside either. If you don't have a strong first step, then don't move on to the second.

The first step is done on lead either inside or outside. While walking the dog, walk backward and call the dog. As the dog turns to follow you, continue to walk backward while you praise her every step toward you. After she has walked 10 feet or so toward you while you retreat happily, stop, continue to praise. As she approaches, slide your hand down the lead so that when she arrives you have her on short lead, making it easy to control her and to prevent her from running past, which I call Coming and Going. It is a typical happy dog thing to do. You call them, they bolt to you; your heart soars, then plummets as they bolt right on past, running huge circles as you call them over and over. Prevent this game from even beginning by keeping control of the dog throughout the training process. Doing this 5 to 10 times a day will soon have your dog turning and coming to you happily on the first command.

Meanwhile, you and your assistant can begin recall games in the house. The most fun and effective is the Run Away game. Have your assistant hold the dog silently. You play with the dog, get him real worked up, then run out of the room. As you disappear, call happily "Dog, come!" and praise him to the heavens. The assistant releases your dog, who 9 times out of

As we are walking along, I back away, calling Lady to me.

I back away, praising her. Lady was found on the street at age eight. She is a bit nervous with me, so I am making myself as small as possible to appear less frightening. You don't have to bend over this much.

GOOD OWNERS, GREAT DOGS

10 stampedes to find you. When he arrives, command "Sit," praise him merrily, and repeat. Only do this 2 or 3 times a session, as you want to keep him interested. If he seems to be slowing down, quit while you're ahead. Also, try ignoring him for an hour before playing this game. That usually gets their attention.

An occasional surprise, a toy, or a treat given unexpectedly every seventh or eighth time he arrives will pique his interest. As he learns to enjoy this game, hide. Make it increasingly difficult for him to find you. This added challenge builds some dogs into a recall frenzy.

"Good girl!" I scratch her chest to encourage her to sit up. She looks happy, doesn't she?

Since she is shy, I am using my hand to support her head as she sits. Otherwise she would lie down.

I stop and am shortening on the lead.

Next you move outside with the long line. A long line is any 20- to 30-foot lead that can hold your dog at a full run. The goal of this training tool is surprise. Put it on at the same time you take off his 4-foot lead. Keep it loose as he begins to sniff around and play. Do not allow it to tighten until you give a well-timed correction. When he is distracted, call him with a clear "Dog, come." If he comes, praise him happily. If he pays no attention, give a quick, sharp snap on the long line. Be sure to make the snap horizontal to the ground. Then follow immediately by praise to draw him to you. Always be sure that the lead is not wrapped around a leg before you snap. After that first correction, put him back on his 4-foot lead and take him home. Once he knows he's on a line, no further training can be done that session. Always quit after that first, initial surprise correction.

This dog just stands there looking at me when I say "Come." That won't do. I'm stepping forward and putting my left hand on the lead in preparation for giving a correction.

Here's the correction.

That did the trick. I'm praising her as she comes to me.

As she approaches, I'm shortening on the lead.
That worked well.

Dog runs off. First of all, do *NOT* chase her. She'll figure you are coming along with her and run farther ahead. If she is still close or looping around you with glee, tell her "Down" in your most serious, intense voice. Use your biggest hand signal and step toward her. If she pauses for a moment or glances your way, command again. This is one of the few times that you can repeat the command and sound as serious and threatening as possible. You are trying to switch her into a submissive frame of mind. When she downs, praise her calmly as you approach. If you sound angry, she may run away from you. If she starts to get up, down her again. When you reach her, take her collar calmly, stroke her calmly, and snap on the lead calmly. Why stroke her? You do want to be able to catch her, don't you?

Your other chance is to run *away* from her. Clap your hands, laugh, call her, sound like you're having a terrific time. Few dogs can resist chasing after a happy owner. Once you have her back, praise her as always. Now, give yourself a sound scolding. What is an untrained dog doing off lead anyway? It's the number-one way to be the proud owner of a dead pet.

Dog won't allow you to put the lead back on. This habit comes from being grabbed and leashed immedi-ately. When your dog comes to you, squat down, reach underneath his neck, and grasp the collar. Praise him, stroke him, make a fuss for at least 10 seconds before you clip on the lead. That way he'll link coming to you with praise, not being caught. If he still is being difficult, use a food reward. Hold it in your fingers so he has to lick at it to get any. Keep your hand close to your body making him come all the way to you to get it. Use your free hand to scratch his chest, then casually grasp his collar. After you have hold of him, give him the treat. Praise as always.

Dog comes halfway and then stops. Here is a dog who has learned to distrust you. All it takes is one angry greeting, and your dog may decide to check your mood before he comes any closer. Since stopping annoys most people, he gets yelled at for stopping. That convinces him that it was a smart thing to stop. If your dog stops, try walking backward, bending over, clapping your hands and praising him. Try squatting down. Most dogs have not been corrected by a squatting person and find the position unthreatening. Use food reward when he arrives, holding it in your fingers and allowing him to lick at it as you stroke him. Then put the lead on and practice. Play recall games in the house. Make it fun. He'll soon barrel up to you, not wanting to miss the good time.

Telling Tales

When Mrs. F. asked if it was okay that she only played with her dog four to five hours a day, I knew the dog was getting more attention than it needed. When I entered the home and saw wicker baskets full of toys, all for this tiny little spitfire of a dog, I knew I had some serious work to do, but not with the dog.

As I entered the apartment, Tidbit spun in circles barking. Mrs. F. laughed and picked her up. "Bitty excited to meet the trainer?" she asked the dog, stroking her affectionately as the five-pound bundle of Maltese energy squirmed and barked in an effort to say hello. Mrs. F. was in her fifties, graceful, gracious and charming. She had no children. We all sat down on the couch. When Mrs. F. put her down, Tidbit immediately climbed to the back of the couch and ran to me, leaping and jumping at my head. "Is this normal?" I asked. "She loves people," Mrs. F. said by way of explanation.

Tidbit wasn't papertrained, she barked too much and had nipped Mrs. F. several times. "I'm so hurt," said Mrs. F., referring to her emotional state. "I love her so much but she bites me. Doesn't she love me?"

"This has nothing to do with love," I explained. "She's a dog. She sees things like a dog. What she sees is that you wait on her hand and foot. If there's reincarnation, Mrs. F., I want to book my next life as a dog in your house." Mrs. F. laughed.

Mrs. F.'s concern for the dog's emotional state made setting up a training schedule an ordeal. To the idea of confinement to help with the housebreaking, she countered with "But she'll be so unhappy." She'll be more unhappy, I told Mrs. F., if she can't travel with you, go to stores or visit friends because she isn't paper-trained. If you don't train her you are limiting the life she can lead with you. If you love her, train her so she can come with you.

The instruction to train the dog to sit, down, leave it and come was met with an "I don't need her to do those things. I just want her to stop biting me." Training is not a matter of I'll take one of these and two of those. One behavior can affect all the others. Mrs. F. had to change almost everything she did with her dog if she hoped to change the dog's behavior. She did it. It was hard for her, but she did it.

◆

Buster was a mess. His coat was matted all over, he was filthy, and it smelled to me like he had an ear infection. This big, happy Poodle/Newfoundland cross was not a stray. He was not abused. He was owned by lovely people who had more household help than most of us have family. The home was palatial, elegant and pristine.

Part of the problem was that the people were novices. Part of the problem was they had a high-maintenance dog that required daily grooming (or a close shave) to stay neat and clean. And the rest of the problem was that the family was not used to having to do this kind of work because they hired help to do that and the help didn't want to care for this mammoth dog. Consequently everyone looked the other way and nobody took responsibility.

Between phone calls, Mr. and Mrs. T. outlined what they wanted. "He chewed the couch in the den," Mrs. T. started. "And *when he's outside, he refuses to come back in." I nodded. "He doesn't bark at the door," Mr. T. added. "He's not much of a watchdog. One of the reasons we got him was for some kind of protection. We love him, but I think he's a stupid dog."*

The story was predictable for this kind of well-intentioned situation. Nobody walked him, someone let him out when he stood at the door. He slept alone in the kitchen (too dirty to come upstairs, which was beautifully done in white carpet). No one taught him anything. He just hung around the house. The most attention he got all day was from delivery people who played with him briefly when they dropped off the dry cleaning or flowers or groceries or what have you. He didn't bark at the door, he wagged his tail. I told the T.'s that they were fortunate they had such a nice dog and to have lost only one couch. Buster was bored, lonely, uncomfortable and underexercised. They were shocked to hear that initially, then shocked again when they understood what had been happening. Like most people, they loved their animal, just misunderstood what he needed and wanted. We got him groomed, trained and organized. Now he sleeps on a dog bed in their bedroom, lies at place on a mat in Mr. T.'s study and is a fully integrated part of their life. He barks at the door now that it is *his* house, filled with *his* people.

◆

Agatha was a full body wagger, bending her body into a "U" with every wag. An adorable, black-and-white American Cocker Spaniel, she peed the minute I squatted down to say hello. "Agatha," Mr. G. moaned. "She does this all the time," he complained as he got the paper towels. "She's ruining the floors." It was true. The

finish was coming off the wood in spots. This wetting is a common problem with cockers. It can be resolved, but it is only made worse by complaining, correction or anger.

I asked Mr. G., to show me what he and Agatha could do. He started with "Sit." "Aggy, sit?" he asked sweetly. Agatha bent herself into a pretzel wagging but made no move to obey. "Aggy, no. Sit." Agatha froze in place, lowered her head, and waited. "Sit!" he repeated, shoving her bottom to the floor. Agatha rolled over on her back. "No," he said, using the collar to lift her back into position. When he released, she rolled back over, peeing a bit. "I've been working on this for months," he complained. "She just is so difficult." He went to pull her back into a "Sit." "Stop," I said. "I get the picture."

The thing to realize, I told him, was that you both want to get it right. She's not trying to be difficult and neither are you. Once you both understand each other, you two will be great together. I went on to explain that the rolling over was submissive. She was trying to tell him that she understood he was annoyed. She was apologizing and asking him to stop being aggressive toward her. When he lifted her back into the "Sit," she figured he was correcting her, so she apologized more, rolling over and peeing this time. This frustrated Mr. G., who felt the dog was being knowingly difficult. So he got angry. The more angry he got, the more she apologized, and around we go. . . .

It doesn't matter how long you work with a dog if you're working incorrectly. It can be years. The dog's failure to progress is 99 times out of 100 due to human, not canine, error. Reevaluate your techniques. Try to figure out how the dog is reading your messages. Problems that have taken weeks or months to develop are not going to disappear in a few days. Changing behavior takes time, patience and the right methods.

By toning down his voice, placing her instead of correcting her, using some food reward to get her mind off her worries, and upping the praise considerably, Mr. G. got himself and Agatha on the road to becoming a happy team in no time.

◆

Nevel looks like a mad scientist, hair sticking out in all directions. One ear stands up, the other does not. With his bright eyes and nice canine grin, I like him on sight. The presenting problem is barking.

Nevel barks in the car. Not an occasional woof but nonstop, top-of-the-lungs, barking. The owners, who have a country home 2½ hours from the city, make the drive weekly. Nevel barks the whole time.

When Mr. and Mrs. S. come to me, they have already been to two trainers and a behaviorist. They've tried air horns, squirt bottles filled with lemon juice, yelling, crating the dog in the car. The last trainer advised stopping the car, pulling the dog out by the scruff of his neck, shaking him and yelling. Now Nevel is aggressive to anyone who reaches for him in the car, a sensible canine response to what he viewed as random human attacks.

Nevel's owners kept trying until they found something that worked. Persistence is a key to all training. Locating the right trainer for you and your dog can require as much patience and persistence as training the dog itself. Notice how the methods used on Nevel focused on punishing him for barking. No one bothered to try to teach the dog what was wanted or reward the dog for the good behavior. By the time the owners found me,

Nevel was eight years old and had been barking like this for years. I resolved the problem, but it took a few months and a variety of methods to do so.

How do you find a qualified trainer? Trainers are not licensed. Anyone can hang out a shingle and call himself a trainer. When you are looking for a professional, ask for recommendations both from clients and from other dog-related professionals. Veterinarians and humane societies are the best resources for names. Anyone can come up with clients who are happy. Be wary of trainers who use a membership in an organization as proof of their expertise. Some of these groups have high standards. Some don't.

Once you locate someone, talk to him or her. Does he guarantee? Beware of that. That's similar to doctors guaranteeing you will get well before they see you. It can't be done. Training is a combination of you, your dog and the trainer. A trainer can and should promise he'll do his best but beyond that no one without a crystal ball can see.

Find out what methods he uses. He should have a wide variety of techniques to choose from, depending on you and your dog. A trainer who uses one method exclusively tends to blame the dog if that method is not effective on that dog. Every animal is different. A good trainer has a range of equipment, methods and ideas for any problem.

Remember, you are hiring this person. Feel free to stop the session at any point to ask questions. Explanations should make sense, and your dog should be responding. Praise should be given out three to four times more often than correction. Hitting, yelling, shaking, throwing, hanging by the collar, tying up and harsh corrections are not needed. Corrections are a part of training, not its focus. They should be fair, quick, wrapped in praise and effective.

If you feel comfortable with the trainer and the method and are seeing the results you want, then that trainer is right for you. If you don't, find someone else.

Dog training is not an adversarial activity. Good training results in the dog liking the trainer.

Frequently Asked Questions

My dog is five years old. Is it too late to train her?

Not at all. Dogs are social animals, accepting of changes in leadership at any age. It may take her a bit longer than a pup to understand—you're working against five years of guessing. Once she comprehends you're trying to teach her something, she'll learn whatever you teach her quickly.

My dog bumps into me all the time. He's even knocked me over a few times outside. Why does he do this?

There are two types of dogs that do this. The first is the touch-insensitive dog. Classically a sporting breed, bred to run through briars and swim in cold water to retrieve game, they just aren't aware that they have knocked into you. If they are aware of it, they mean it in only the nicest possible way. The other type knows full well he is making contact. He's doing it to make a point. Subordinates do not bump leader dogs often and never without repercussions. He is telling you that it is your responsibility to get out of his way. He needs an attitude adjustment. Use your "Off," "Sit," "Wait" and "Down" commands to gain the right of way.

Is allowing my dog to sleep on the bed bad?

If your dog is otherwise well behaved, it is not a bad thing to let him sleep on the bed. Tri is always on our bed. Caras comes up when invited. Piper prefers his dog bed. If you are single and hope not to be one day, don't let the dog sleep up there all the time. Insist that he wait until he is invited. Have him sit, then say "OK, up" and pat the bed. If he jumps up on his own, put him off and make him wait. Otherwise, the next time you have a friend sleep over, you may find that three is a crowd.

A friend tells me I should roll my dog over and pin him when he is bad. What do you think?

I think it's unnecessary and know it is dangerous. One 12-year-old boy heard about it, used it on his dog, and got a bite on the face for his trouble. I don't like methods that involve confrontation. If the dog chooses to accept them, they work fine. But what if the dog takes offense. What do you do then? And where does it leave you emotionally? You've pinned your dog and he snaps at you—what do you do then? How do you get both of you out of this situation without being hurt either emotionally or physically? All in all, the physical methods requiring brute force and aggression are not necessary or safe.

This is embarrassing, but my dog mounts me when I train him. Can I stop this?

First of all, don't be embarrassed. He is not making a pass at you. He is trying to keep his position as the leader of the group. When you train, you are taking the leadership role. If he thinks he's the leader, he will consider you rude and uppity to be commanding him. He's telling you that when he mounts. There are three things you should immediately do if your dog starts this behavior. First, do the side step as instructed on page 143 and keep going. The side step gives you enough room to give a good correction. Do not turn toward him and try to push him off. That will only make him fight you. Secondly, no more free attention or praise. He works for everything or gets nothing. He needs an attitude adjustment. Thirdly, neuter him. This bold, pushy behavior is a prelude to more serious aggression. He obviously is not making good use of his hormones and doesn't need them.

Whenever I walk him, my dog holds the lead in his mouth. If I try to get it from him, he thinks it's a game. Help!

Chances are someone used the lead to play tug-of-war with your dog when he was a pup. When they're young, it's pretty cute when they grab the lead; as an adult it is obnoxious. Never train your puppy to do something you do not want him to do as an adult. Stop all tug-of-war. Spray the lead with Bitter Apple right before the walk. If he grabs it, do several "Downs" in a row. That often takes a dog's mind off of being playful. If that does not work, take the lead on either side of the mouth and, using your wrist, snap it down and out in a "J" motion. Remember to praise your dog the moment he releases the lead. Also, shortening up on the lead so it does not dangle in front of his face will help him to resist the temptation.

I've heard of group classes, private training and sending your dog away to be trained. What kind of training is best?

Group classes are for an owner who has the time to train and for the dog who has no real problems other than he is out of control. Pick a class that is limited to 10 or fewer and that uses methods that make sense to you. Both the dogs and the people should be having fun and having some success.

Private training is for people who don't have the time to go to class every week and for dogs who have specific home-related problems such as housebreaking, chewing, barking or aggression. It is individualized to suit your needs. Choose a trainer who has professional references from such sources as veterinarians or humane societies. You should like them and see that their methods are effective with your dog. The trainer's job is NOT to train the dog but to teach you how to train the dog. After all, you'll be the one working with the dog most of the time.

People who have no time to train or who have dogs that have advanced problems may find that sending the dog away for a few weeks is the answer. It is an excellent way to get things started, but you will still have to earn your dog's respect when he returns. The trainer will teach the commands and teach the dog to respect and respond to him or her. That respect can only be transferred to you through hard work and consistency on your part. Sending the dog away is a shortcut, but it is not a miracle. If you do not work with your dog, he will not listen.

What do you think of attack training?

I don't like it. Bringing out the aggression in an animal is not a game. Once your dog learns the joy of biting—and most do enjoy it—he will not be a pet anymore. Just like when you load an antique gun and display it on a table, it is not just a piece of art anymore.

To own such an animal, you have to have absolute control over it—

meaning, if your dog is chasing a squirrel and you say "Come," he stops in his tracks and responds immediately without hesitation or question. It may sound impossible, but it's not—it's necessary. A dog in the full swing of aggression is more focused and excited than when he is squirrel chasing. If you can't control him then, you have no business considering attack work.

A well-trained dog is the best security. Kesl is protection trained, but Sarah has never used it, although she lived in a rough part of town for a while. Just seeing a huge Bouvier walking at heel, on a loose lead, obeying every command immediately, made people wonder what else he might know. If you want a good defense, train your dog well. It's the best deterrent there is, and the safest.

PART 4

Under-
standing
and
Solving
Canine
Problems

Basic Retraining

Most dog owners encounter a canine problem at one time or another. Dogs are not wind-up toys. Some are easy to live with, creating few problems; some are not. They have their own distinct personalities and quirks. Labeling certain behaviors as "bad" is a subjective judgment on our part. A dog that barks nonstop when left alone in the country is not a problem. A dog that does so in the city means an eviction notice. A dog that growls at strangers in a tough part of town may be highly valued, whereas if the dog lives in a family of five kids, with their friends coming and going, that behavior is a dangerous, unwanted trait.

"Bad" behavior is not bad from the dog's perspective. It's normal dog behavior that we humans cannot tolerate. Don't assume your terrier feels remiss about digging up your flower bed. He does not. He had a glorious time doing so and would do so again given half a chance. That's an important realization. Behavior can only be changed within the normal limits of your dog's temperament and breed.

Your guard breed may never be wildly friendly to strangers. Your retriever may always pick up every stick he sees outside. Even Lassie wasn't Lassie, but several dogs trained to do specific tasks.

I use Lassie as an example because it is easy to compare your current dog to the image of a past, problem-free, perfect pet. After 10 or so years with an animal, it is easy to forget problems there were in the beginning. Each dog has his own strengths and weaknesses. With the proper direction, most dogs can become wonderful additions to your family.

Problem correction is more advanced than straight obedience work. To correct problems effectively, you must develop an understanding of how a dog thinks so you can anticipate what he is about to do, understand why he is about to do it, and redirect him to a more appropriate behavior.

The first step to developing that kind of understanding is taking a good, solid obedience course and listening closely to your instructor. He

This ten-year-old Afghan is lure coursing. This is a sport where dogs earn ribbons and awards for chasing after a rag being dragged at high speed around a course.

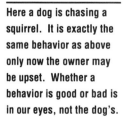

Here a dog is chasing a squirrel. It is exactly the same behavior as above only now the owner may be upset. Whether a behavior is good or bad is in our eyes, not the dog's.

or she will undoubtedly be able to give you insights into what type of personality you are dealing with and what the most effective methods will be for your dog.

There are certain tools that you'll use to correct any problem behavior. The first tool is obedience work. Obedience work does so many good things that I will not be able to cover all the benefits here. Command training asserts your authority in a nonconfrontational way. It builds communication between you and your dog, making it easier for both of you to understand each other. Trust is created through positive obedience work, and attachment is deepened. Developing a common language, which is what this work does, allows you to tell your dog exactly what you want him to do, instead of yelling at him to stop doing the unwanted behavior. It calms nervous dogs, relaxes tense dogs, tempers aggressive dogs, and gives confidence to frightened dogs. Every dog and owner can benefit from learning and practicing obedience work.

The other important tool is you. TEAMwork (discussed in detail on pages 34–39) is the foundation of good dog management of any kind. Knowing how to use your voice so it makes sense to your dog, using words in a way the dog can understand, correcting him without creating fear, praising him properly, and doing it all at the proper time are critical skills to develop if your dog is to be able to learn from you.

The last tools that are important before you can start retraining your dog are the physical training tools you'll need. Crates are a key to almost all problem correction. Their selection and use are discussed on pages 42–43. Some people have an immediate dislike of the idea. Unfortunately, its use is dictated more by the dog than by you. One of my clients never liked the idea and refused to do it. She took great care to puppy-proof her home, but the pup still got hold of an extension cord. She came home to a mess. The pup miraculously survived, but she had defecated all over the house in a panic and the electricity had burned a quarter-inch gash in her mouth.

We do not live in a dog-safe world. I could fill this book with stories of dogs who jumped out of windows, ate razor blades, swallowed string, and died. I do not mean to be morbid. It's just that if you love your dog, do what is right for him and keep him safe.

Training collars have to be fitted and used properly to be effective. There is a right way and a wrong way to put on a training collar. They can only work from *one* side of the dog. Please look at pages 78–79. Take care to learn how to put a training collar on properly. Collars have to fit to work. All too often I see training collars that are overly long. Not only does this make the correction ineffectual, but it can allow the snap to hit the dog in the face when walking or being corrected. Use a lead with a small or medium-size clip. The big, heavy clips can whack the dog on the chin and tend to weigh down the collar, keeping it tight all the time. Use the proper equipment, fitted properly. Take your dog to the pet store if you need to; don't try to guess what will fit.

Problem correction is gratifying work. Once you learn the basics—understanding your dog; teaching him to respond to direction; using your voice, body language and the correct timing to communicate effectively; and educating yourself about the proper use of training equipment—you can start changing your dog's behavior.

This is not always a do-it-yourself job. Finding a good trainer or behaviorist who will answer your questions, give you clear and sensible direction and help you interpret what is going on can make problem correction simpler, quicker and more enjoyable for all concerned.

If your dog does not respond to a command, make him! Commands are never optional, especially for a problem dog.

How Well Trained Are You?

Before you blame your dog for his behavior, take a close look at your own. What he learns is up to you. How he behaves is up to you. If you want him to change his behavior, the chances are excellent that you will have to change yours first. Over the years, I have noticed a few common mistakes people make with their dogs—mistakes that often lead to problem behavior. Let's look at some of these before we start trying to work with the dog.

ARE YOU OVEREMOTIONAL?

I remind clients all the time to relax. Housebreaking mistakes or jumping up may be annoying but they aren't felonies. Take a breath. To teach, you need to be calm, relaxed, enthused and clear; if you are not, don't expect the dog to respond the way you want. Yelling, screaming and hitting are not helpful. They invariably make matters worse, adding new problems to the list you already have. Dogs may respond temporarily out of surprise, intimidation or fear, but they have not been taught exactly what you want so they will make the mistake again.

ARE YOU INCONSISTENT?

How can you expect consistency from your dog if you can't get it from yourself? Are you consistent about your word usage, or are you a bit casual, maybe giving the command "Sit" one time and "Sit down" the next? How about your expectations? You say "Sit" and he lies down, but you let it slide? How about your praise? When he grabs his leash and tugs on Saturday morning, you laugh, but when he does it on Monday morning, you get annoyed? Do you praise your dog when he does listen? Your dog will never know more about what you want than you do. Decide what behaviors you want and don't want and then stick to that decision. If you do your part, he'll do his.

ARE YOU EXERCISING HIM ENOUGH?

If your dog is behaving poorly, up his exercise. This is especially true for sporting, terrier and Nordic breeds and mixes. (Nordic includes the sled dogs: Huskies, Malamutes, Samoyeds.) Many dogs need an hour or more of hard running a day to behave like civilized pets.

ARE YOU COMPLAINING MORE THAN PRACTICING?

It's easy to complain about your dog. It is much harder to take action. Training is not magic. It takes work. Dog training is wonderful. Work effectively with the dog and he'll improve. If you're working frequently but not seeing the desired results, question your methods, not your dog's abilities.

ARE YOU MISINTERPRETING HIS ACTIONS?

Be absolutely sure you understand *why* he is doing something before you try to change his behavior. Once I walked into a home, and the unneutered male Yorkie immediately clamped on to my leg, humping madly. The owner cooed, "Oh, isn't that sweet? He's hugging you." This is *not* an affectionate gesture. It is an extremely assertive act, especially to a stranger, and points to serious aggression, present or brewing.

Here are some behaviors that are commonly misinterpreted:

If you cuddle with your dog on the couch, don't be upset when he sleeps there when you're gone. You can't have it both ways.

Submissive Wetting. Dog means: "So sorry." Owner thinks: "Spiteful!"

Growling. Dog means: "Back off." Owner thinks: "He's talking" or "He doesn't really mean it."

Pulling on Lead. Dog means: "Let me get away from this choking feeling."

Owner thinks: "He must be stupid if he's choking himself like that."

Chewing Your Favorite Pair of Shoes. Dog means: "I'm frightened. This smells good, like my owner." Owner thinks: "He's getting me back for leaving him alone."

ARE YOU REPEATING YOURSELF?
If you repeat commands, you are begging to be ignored. Obedience on the first command is not optional. It may save his life, and it will certainly simplify yours. Give the command once. Enforce it immediately. Praise him right away.

ARE YOU BORING?
If you are bored, surely your dog will be. You set the tone for your dog. Having fun is not just a nice idea, it's necessary. Praise him, surprise him, enjoy yourself! Both dogs and people learn quickly when the teaching is fun!

With dogs you'll get back what you put in. These two work hard and the results are impressive! This dog was not easy to train but the owner persevered and the dog learned. Bravo!

Common Keys to Problem Correction

Changing your dog's behavior is up to you. Aggression, barking, digging, fear—most things dogs do that we don't like—are normal canine behaviors. It is our lifestyle that makes them unacceptable to us.

Behaviors are changed by first stopping or preventing the unwanted behavior, then teaching the dog the desired activity. This teaching is best accomplished through practice, praise and persistence. Most all behaviors can be influenced if you use these three principles.

Dog training is a skill. As with any skill, practice is necessary to become good at it. Without practice your dog cannot possibly learn. Practice does not simply mean obedience work. It also means setting up the problem situations and consistently teaching him what you want and don't want. Whether it be jumping up, barking, aggression or digging, all dogs need to be taught how to do the right thing. Be sure to build a *strong foundation* of basic obedience before you try to apply the commands in more distracting circumstances.

Praise is vital and something many of us stop doing when we have a dog that is a problem. Clients tell me that they feel like the dog's name is "No!" Emphasizing the positive is mentally important to both you and your pet. Every dog does a few things correctly. Heartfelt praise, used consistently, brings the fun back into dog ownership.

Persistence is the last ingredient for success. You have to be more persistent than the dog. Some of you own dogs that have learned to wear you down. Somewhere in the past you tried to wait them out and failed. A typical scenario is this: You sit down to dinner. The dog comes over and stares at you. You ignore him. He woofs quietly, you ignore him. He begins to bark more loudly. You decide that you are not going to give in to him anymore. He barks—and barks—and barks. Somewhere into dessert you've had it. You can't take this noise anymore. You toss him a leftover roll to shut him up. That works. You've just trained your dog to bark throughout a complete meal because maybe, just maybe, you'll give in. You have to outlast your dog.

This dog has occasionally been fed from the table. She now anticipates it, waiting patiently and drooling, hoping for another morsel. If you don't want a dog who begs then don't feed the dog from the table. Your dog will only be as consistent as you are.

No petting for dogs that are pushy. Once she obeys me and sits, I'll give her the attention she wants.

Praise can never be over-emphasized. The more fun you both have the more effective the training will be. Remember: focus on the positive.

TIME TO HEAL

Problems usually take weeks, months and even years to come into full bloom. Changing these behaviors takes time too. Sometimes a great deal of time. Impatience is a sure way to slow the learning process. Learning takes as long as it takes. Proper methods, practice and setting up the situation can all help the process along, but whether it takes a week, a month or six months to learn not to urinate in your dining room is up to the dog. As a teacher, you must adapt your methods and schedule to your student. Try not to be disappointed if his schedule is radically different from yours.

You're Grounded!

Is your dog being rude, unresponsive, distracted, out of control? Does he consistently break house rules? Then ground him! Grounding is a simple process that calms, sweetens and refocuses your dog in just a few days. Here's what you do. Your dog must

1. Say "Please." Dogs say "Please" by obeying commands. Before you give him anything he enjoys—petting, praise, food, play or privileges like getting up on the furniture or sitting on your lap—a command should be given and obeyed *first*. Are you getting him a treat? He should sit. Are you doing him a favor, like getting a toy or letting him outside? He should say "Please." Are you responding to a request for a pat or a drink of water? That's definitely a place for "Please."

You do a lot for this animal. We should all live the life our pets do. No bills to pay, free room and board, free health care, loads of love and attention, daily play time—life for your dog is pretty good. Dogs maintain rank through day-to-day interaction, so having your dog obey you frequently throughout your day keeps him from getting any ideas of competing with you. Besides, a little "please and thank you" never hurt anyone.

2. Be Pleasant. When you're grounded, part of the deal is being on your best behavior. Certainly you should not shove your little brother into the wall as you walk out the door, tackle your father when he comes home, or expect the whole family to politely step around you if you block the door. Same rules for your dog. If he's in

your way you tell him to move and make him do so. If he resists, leave the lead on and guide him out of the way. If you're walking out the door, don't allow him to shove you aside so he can go first. Put him on lead, teach him "Wait," and make him do so. Jumping up on you without permission is absolutely out. Nudging you with his head or paws to solicit attention is over with. No more leaping onto your bed or lap without permission. Make him sit or down before you allow him up. Then praise him and reward him by inviting him up.

3. Do Chores. Doing chores is a time-honored parental mechanism for attitude adjustment. It works just as well for dog owners. "Chores" for your dog are obedience routines. Three short five-minute sessions a day will go a long way to bringing your dog's attitude around. Praise him plenty, but make him work. Obedience work calms the nervous dog, gives confidence to the shy dog, softens the tough dog and relaxes the aggressive dog. It's the closest thing to a cure-all there is in the world of canine problem correction.

4. Organize His Free Time. His free time should be limited. Keep him on lead near to you most of the time. Give him a toy or two to play with, but hold on to the lead. When you move, he moves. The more he follows you, the more he will see you as his leader. Use commands often and indiscriminately, always insisting he follow through. Why? Because you say so, that's why.

5. Go to His Room. Most "problem" dogs benefit from a crating schedule. Even if you are home all the time, crate him for at least three hours in the morning and three hours in the afternoon. This helps to establish good behavior, stop destructive cycles and teach him to sleep when you're out or busy. Make it a routine. Do a short obedience session when he comes out of the crate. This will calm him and teach him to listen when he is excited.

6. Get Less Attention. Many problem dogs get way too much attention. If you're averaging more than 10 minutes of attention per hour when you are home, then you need to cut back. Attention means talking to or petting. Lying at your feet, doing obedience and taking a walk do not count. What I'm talking about are the 10-minute petting sessions on the couch as you watch the news, the unconscious stroking as you read a book, or the nonstop conversation when you get home. Going over to your dog and petting him is particularly detrimental. Dogs cannot help but interpret this as submissive behavior on your part. Stop all of that. If you want him to be enthused about being praised, make him work for it. If it is a little more rare, it will be a little more dear. The more direction you give him, the more attention he'll get!

7. Do 50 Downs a Day. The military loves push-ups. Why? Are they fiends about nice pectoral development? I doubt it. Push-ups are terrific attitude adjusters. There is nothing like being flat out on the floor taking orders to make you feel compliant. It's the same with the dog. Dogs that down willingly without a second thought are rarely problems. Dogs that resist the command often are. Fifty "Downs" a day for a few weeks will make obedience

second nature for your dog, mentally making him more accepting and responsive. Don't do them all in a row. Throw them at your dog when he least expects it. If you have him down every time you interact with the dog, you'd be surprised how close to 50 you come.

This much change can be stressful to your dog. Plenty of exercise is required to help him through the first few weeks of this new program. If done properly, your dog will be getting lots of attention, just in a more productive way.

If your dog wants something, make him work for it. First Caras sits . . .

. . . then he gets his toy! He thinks sitting is great!

Housebreaking Problems

Housebreaking problems can have many causes. Sometimes the dog was never completely housebroken in the first place. Sometimes a change in schedule or family situation sets off a bout of mistakes. Occasionally a medical reason can be the starting point. If your previously housebroken pet is now peeing or defecating in the house, the first thing to do is call your vet. At other times there is no discernible reason why it begins. Whatever the reason is, confinement, diet, schedule, structure, praise and proper cleaning are the answers.

If you have a dog with a housebreaking problem you have already gotten loads of advice from friendly, well intentioned "experts." This advice usually causes more problems than it cures. Let's go through some standard suggestions:

"Rub his nose in it."

Not only is this disgusting, but it makes no sense to the dog. What it does teach the dog is that you are not to be trusted. This break of trust will hurt your recalls and obedience and create anxiety for the dog. That extra dose of anxiety can create *more* housebreaking problems, not less. It can also start a dog chewing, barking or becoming aggressive.

"Clean it with vinegar and then put vinegar on his nose."

This is another must miss. Incomprehensible to the dog, it creates fear of you (and possibly of salads).

"Yell at him when you catch him."

This creates a lot of fear of you. Volume does not teach the dog what he is supposed to be doing. What he learns is that you don't like it when you *see* him urinate. He then starts hiding when he pees inside and refusing to pee in front of you outside. Both behaviors make training that much more difficult.

"Spank him with a rolled-up newspaper."

This and other violent "methods" are the major cause of anxiety, submissive urination and aggression problems. Hitting won't help. He may cower when you come home, but wouldn't you? That doesn't mean he understands that he should have held it until you returned. Dogs do not enjoy being beaten. He is not being spiteful—he does not understand. You may think he does. You may think he should. But he doesn't. Assume he knows nothing and start from the beginning.

"Tie him near it and leave him there for a while."

If you teach the dog anything by this strange procedure, you will teach him that being near his mess is OK. Achieving a clean house requires that your dog *want* to stay away from his mess, a desire most dogs are born with. Tying a dog near his mess erodes this necessary instinct upon which all housebreaking is built.

Successful housebreaking is about education not correction. Where a dog goes to the bathroom is largely a routine. By setting up a regular feeding, watering, crating and walking schedule, you create a routine for the dog. While he is in training, he will not be unsupervised in the house. Keep him on lead near you. If a dog makes a mistake during training, chances are it is *your* fault, not his. The good news is that the vast majority of dogs get housebroken, one way or another. We are just teaching you the quickest and best way.

To those of you who do not have housebreaking problems with your pet, this picture may seem a bit crass. But for those of you who have struggled with this particular behavior, a dog doing his business outside is a thing of beauty and a joy forever.

Diet and Feeding Schedule

What you feed your dog can have a big impact on his housebreaking. Until dogs are fully housebroken—(and there is no halfway; half-housebroken is like being partially pregnant)—he should be fed two meals a day of regular food, in regular amounts, at regular times. Free feeding is not a good idea until after the training process is completed.

All those little extras your dog loves and you love to give him have to stop, at least for a while. Extras can throw off his drinking habits and his bowels. You don't want any changes in those for a while. "Less active" or diet foods are extremely high in fiber. If you have to feed them, be aware that your dog will be defecating more often and more copiously.

Feeding him at radically different times will not help matters. Half an hour one way or another won't matter, but if you vary by hours in either direction, you're asking for trouble. If you're regular about his feeding times, he'll be regular in his bathroom habits.

If your dog urinates small amounts frequently, consult your vet. Urinary tract infections can cause this. If your dog urinates large amounts

Any change in diet can cause housebreaking problems. Don't allow your dog to eat things off the street.

frequently, he is drinking large amounts. Dogs cannot generate urine out of thin air. It can't come out if it didn't go in. I like to offer my dogs water before they go back into their crates. Giving water before the walk or right when you come in from one can lead to problems. Most dogs need to urinate 20 to 30 minutes after they drink, although individual dogs vary. So if you give your dog water, and then take him for a walk for 10 minutes and come home, you may have a mistake 20 minutes later.

Your dog needs about one cup of water for every eight pounds of body weight daily. A 48-pound dog should be offered six cups of water a day. I'd offer it three times a day, two cups at a time. They don't have to drink it, but they can if they want to. Some dogs are real waterholics. They'll drink til their belly is distended. Check with your vet if your dog does this. There are some dogs who just like to drink a lot, but this could be a sign of a medical problem.

If your dog seems terribly thirsty, try giving him an ice cube or two. That will quench his thirst without overburdening his bladder. If it is hot out, you will need to offer him water freely and walk him more. If you have any questions about these instructions, check with your vet before starting.

The crate is a problem dog owner's best friend. Use it while your dog is in training. It will speed up the training tenfold.

Special Housebreaking Problems

Leg lifting is normal dog behavior. Lifting in your house, however, is a statement. This can be a difficult problem to solve once it gets started, so don't delay.

LEG LIFTING

Indoor leg lifting has little to do with housebreaking and a lot to do with a bad attitude. Dogs who lift in your home are marking *their* territory with *their* urine, telling you in no uncertain terms that this is their house. Resolving this problem takes time, persistence and supervision. First of all, neuter your dog. This lessens his desire to rule the world and makes him more accepting of your leadership. Neutering may not thrill you, but how does living with a decade of urine on your furniture strike you? Neutering is not a cure-all nor is it a frontal lobotomy, but it does influence your dog's behavior in a positive way. It should radically lessen his desire to mark and make him more accepting of training.

Secondly, ground him good and proper. (See pages 190–91.) These dogs need an attitude adjustment immediately. Keep him on lead to prevent marking, work him a lot, treat him as you would any family member who urinated against your couch.

Thirdly, clean all areas properly with an odor neutralizer. Then make sure he spends time there. Feed him in his favorite leg-lifting areas. Dogs don't like to pee where they eat. And lastly, if you catch him in the act, use guilt, not volume, to convey your disapproval: "What is this? This is disgusting. I am very disappointed in you." This has the right tone: calm, deep, serious, authoritative.

DIRTY DOGS

Housebreaking is based on the premise that the dog naturally does not want to go to the bathroom where he eats and sleeps. This innate desire to be clean is the foundation of housebreaking.

Some puppies lose, or never had, this desire. They walk through, sleep in and play on their own feces. Pet-store pups or ones from dirty kennels who have been forced to live in their own filth, pups crated too early and too long who were forced to dirty themselves, and some pups who just don't care can have this problem. The third category is rare. The first two categories are correctable, if you use the proper scheduling and technique.

Number one is stop all crating today! Put him in an area set up with papers in back, open crate in front (see page 46). A narrow hall or bathroom is ideal, so there is less of a chance of him making a mistake. Given an opportunity to be clean, most dogs get back in the habit. After two weeks of this, start to put him in the crate for brief periods, no more than two hours, when you are home and can watch him. No bedding of any kind in with this individual! After two weeks crate for no more than four hours at a time. If the mistakes start happening again, go back to the papers. Some dogs never learn to hold it properly, and keeping papers down for them will be a necessity. This is rare, one dog out of a thousand, so don't worry about it. The majority of pups and dogs, dirty or not, eventually get housebroken.

Unable to Make It through the Night

Some dogs have a real problem holding it overnight. If you feed them at 6:00 P.M., they need to defecate at 3:00 or 4:00 A.M. Ugh. If you continually wake up to a dirty house or crate, try this. Feed him dinner at 10:00 P.M., right before his last walk. The eating will stimulate him to move his bowels. We've found this a simple and effective solution for many dogs who come to us with chronic night-soiling difficulties. Often, after two to three months on this program, they can be switched to a more normal mealtime with no further complications.

Submissive Wetting

Dogs that urinate when you greet them, go to pick them up or scold them are *not* making a housebreaking error. This is called submissive urination and is a fairly common behavior problem in dogs. *If you scold him for it, you'll make it worse.* Submissive urination can be an inherited trait (some lines of American Cocker Spaniels are notorious for it). It can also be the

result of overcorrection. By being too loud, angry or harsh, *you cause* him to submissively urinate.

Solutions are straightforward. Ignore the dog for the first 10 minutes you are home. Do not look at or say anything to him. Do not bend over or reach for the dog. Allow the dog to approach you, while you are squatting and turned away from the dog. Scratch his chest; do *not* reach over his head. Stop all yelling at or hitting the dog. Build his confidence through fun, upbeat obedience, emphasizing praise. Be patient. Tossing a treat to him when you walk in can replace his nervousness with eager anticipation and stop the wetting.

Spot Wetting

Some dogs develop a favorite spot to urinate indoors. Normally this an out-of-the-way area like the formal dining or living room, under the piano, in a guest room or possibly the room of the lowest-ranked member of the family—an infant or young child. Regardless of where it is, it is a problem.

First, what's his walking schedule? Every dog needs at least three walks a day, ideally four. If he is getting less than that, you are leaving him no other option.

Next, talk to your vet. Make sure this is not a urinary tract problem before your start trying to stop this behavior. Females coming in or out of heat often develop spot-wetting problems. When mistakes are made, clean up with an odor neutralizer. Nothing else effectively removes the scent.

Once that is done, bring that area into the mainstream. After it's been cleaned, feed him there, make him do "Down"/"Stays" there; teach him that this is a part of the house he'll be using frequently in the future.

Frightened dogs such as this one are often submissive wetters. Build her confidence and she'll get better. Correct her and she'll get worse.

Using obedience establishes your leadership and encourages him to respect your home. Keep him on lead near you to prevent mistakes. Monitoring his water can also help. If he's drinking a great deal, then you'll have to walk him more or limit his intake.

If you catch him in the act, use guilt to shame him: "What is this? Shame on you." Then forget about it and clean up. You *must* catch him in the act; two minutes later is too late. He shouldn't have been out of sight anyway.

URINATING ON EVERYTHING OUTSIDE

As much as your male dog wants to stop and urinate on everything, he does not have to. If you allow this, he'll make you stop at every object, making a trip around the block a 40-minute excursion. Take him out, and walk him back and forth in front of your home. Tell him what you want by saying "Hurry up." Allow him to urinate three times, then go for your walk. Tell him "Let's go" and go! If he tries to sniff, give a "Leave it" and correct him if he fails to respond. Walk at a brisk pace. He'll soon learn to empty himself quickly and to keep up with you the rest of the time.

One advantage to this, besides actually being able to get somewhere, is that your dog may be less aggressive toward other dogs on the block. When he lifts his leg on objects, he is marking them as his. When he lifts on a series of objects, he is marking that whole area as his. When an area is "his," he can—even has to—challenge other males in the area. No marking, means no claiming means less aggression. It's not a magic solution, but it will help dog fighters become more manageable. Also, neuter him, please.

URINATING WHEN ASLEEP

This is not a housebreaking problem. Some dogs leak urine. This is not common and usually correctable. If you find a puddle under your dog when she wakes up, don't scold her; take her to the vet.

OLD AGE PROBLEMS

One sweet couple called me in because their beloved old dog was going to the bathroom all over the house. I told them the truth. She was old, she was having a hard time controlling herself, she was getting forgetful. It happens. If your older pet begins to make mistakes, put down papers, confine her to a small room, and walk her more frequently. Don't correct her. If she could help it, she would. Call your vet. A diet change may be in order.

Paper-Training Problems

DOG MISSES PAPER—BY A LITTLE

Urine sometimes runs off the paper and onto the floor, leaving a scent mark for the dog. He sniffs the spot and squats, his bottom six inches or more from the paper. Make sure you are cleaning *under* the papers daily with an odor neutralizer. Also, slip a sheet that has been urinated on under the clean ones toward the middle of the area. That will draw the dog fully onto the papers before going.

MALE DOG LIFTS LEG AND HITS WALL NEAR PAPER

Neutering may make him lift less. Try taping a piece of plastic to the wall and run it in under the papers. Then

IT'S FOR YOU

When Ms. L. got on the phone, Miranda, her three-year-old Shih Tzu, defecated in the living room. Sometime during the call, Miranda would peek around the door and stare at Ms. L. Ms. L. would put down the phone, go into the living room, see the dirty deed, scold Miranda, scoop her up, put her on the papers and praise her for being in the correct area. She hoped this would convince the dog to go on the papers. It didn't.

What Miranda did learn was how to call her owner. Instead of saying "Come," she defecated, but the owner response was the same. The owner came when Miranda "called" her. Miranda got praise and attention after she called. Miranda learned how to control the show.

The problem was resolved when the owner stopped responding. She kept her near her on lead, especially when she was on the phone, to prevent the problem. She put the dog on a crating schedule and taught her to run back to the papers when she needed to go. She grounded her, too. Being as bright a dog as she was, Miranda understood what was wanted.

take two sheets of newspaper and wad them into a ball. Put that in the center of the papers. This will give him something to lift on. Praise him when he does so, and in a few days he's likely to forget about using the wall.

DOG MISSES PAPERS BY A LONG SHOT

Many paper-trained dogs are terrific when they are in "their" rooms but won't run back to the papers from elsewhere in the house. This common problem is usually due to nobody teaching them that they are supposed to run back to their papers when they need to go. Crating is the easiest way to teach them how to do this. Here is a sample schedule for a dog six months old or older:

Crate Overnight. Walk him to papers first thing in the A.M. (no later than 7:30 A.M.); tell him "Hurry up"; praise and give a treat when he does go. Once he has done both, allow him one hour of free time, then feed and water him in his crate. Keep him crated until next walk to papers.

12:00 P.M. Walk him to papers; tell him "Hurry up"; praise him when he does. Once he does both, allow him one hour free time, then water him in his crate. Keep him crated until next walk.

5:00 P.M. Walk him to papers; tell him "Hurry up"; praise him and give him a treat when he does. Once he does both, allow him one hour free time, then feed and water him in his crate. Keep him crated til next walk.

10:00 P.M. Walk him to papers; tell him "Hurry up"; praise him when he does. Once he does both, allow him free time until bed. Crate overnight.

Teaching the dog the "Hurry up" command makes the training easier for both you and your dog. See page 54 for full instructions. Walks outside for exercise can be done at any time. If you want more time with your dog, keep her on lead near you before you crate her. Always take the dog to papers whenever you take her out of crate. And trust your judgment. Many owners "know" when the dog needs to go, but don't always act on that hunch. If you think she has to go, take her to the papers and tell her "Hurry up!"

Crating forces the dog to hold it so she needs to go when she comes out of the crate. One of the difficulties with paper training is the dog never has to learn how to hold it. You never are quite sure when she needs to go, so it is difficult to instruct her properly. By directing her to the papers, you are teaching her to run to the papers when she has the urge to go. If you have a large home, you may need to put down two or three sets of papers in convenient spots.

When you let her out of the crate, walk to the papers with her, telling her "Go do hurry ups." If your dog is likely to head off to parts unknown, walk her to the papers on lead. Once there, encourage her to go, telling her "Hurry up." If she goes, celebrate: "What a fine dog!" Praise her and give her a treat. If she does not, either confine her to the area or keep her on your lap or crate for half an hour and try again.

As your dog gets the hang of this, start having her run back from different areas of the house. Use enthusiasm and praise; soon she'll be bolting back to those papers when she has the urge to go.

Dog Walks Off of the Papers Midway Through

One of the most frustrating problems a paper-trained dog can have is when he starts pooping on the paper but walks as he is going, so that he ends up off the paper. You can't correct the dog; after all, he started in the correct place. You can try putting the papers in a tray and encouraging the dog to use the back edge of the paper. Using a low-lipped tray works well for some dogs. Others won't hop in at all. Put a few sheets of paper under the tray to keep it from slipping or rattling against the floor. Encourage him to defecate to the rear of the papers by slipping a sheet of paper that is damp with urine under the clean paper in the desired area.

The scent will stimulate him to go there.

Dog Tears Up Papers

This is great fun for most dogs, a real mess for you. Use newspaper, since ripping up wee-wee pads seems irresistible to some dogs. Tape the newspaper down at the corners. Or spray the edges with an antichew product and allow it to dry. This will taste bad but not smell bad to the dog. Or put a shake can up on a shelf, windowsill or counter above untaped papers. Tape thread to the can and run the thread along the wall to the papers. Tape it to a back edge of the paper so the dog will be unlikely to knock into it by mistake. Then, if she pulls the papers, the can will fall. Dogs don't like surprises.

If you have a paper-training problem with your dog, stay with him when he's on the papers, try to "catch him in the act" and praise him. If you don't let him know what you want, how is he going to get trained?

Separation Anxiety

Separation anxiety can come in many forms. When left alone, a dog with separation anxiety may bark, chew, salivate, urinate, defecate, dig or become overly active. Although we will deal with each of these problems individually, they are actually symptomatic of a larger problem, fear of being left alone. This can be a chronic problem, or it can be activated by a move, shift in schedule, marriage, divorce or other lifestyle changes.

Being social creatures, dogs are often upset by our comings and goings. They have no idea where we went or when we'll be back. All they know is one moment their group is here, the next it is gone. The dog is left alone without a clue of what will happen next.

Some dogs take this in stride, curl up and go to sleep. Others become anxious. Dogs that have been abandoned before or caught in correction cycles with their owners—many adopted dogs, for example—may become very anxious. They have every reason to be. There are things you can do to

Few dogs like being left alone, but most learn to accept it. If yours doesn't, don't leave him loose. Dogs can destroy an astounding amount if they have the desire and the opportunity. If you know you have a problem, don't set yourself and your dog up, confine him!

help your pet calm himself, and those things are what we cover in this section.

Treat your comings and goings as if they are an everyday occurrence (which they are). If you behave with your dog as you would behave with a roommate, then you can't be too far off. Can you imagine a roommate bouncing in the door after a day at the job, jumping up and down, hugging you, saying "Have you missed me? Were you good?" You'd think they were nuts! You'd be right. *Ignore the dog for 10 minutes before you leave or after you arrive home.*

Establish and maintain your leadership position. Grounding your dog has a calming effect on your dog. When he trusts that you are the lead-er, he'll relax about what you are up to. If he is the leader, then he is obligated to attempt to control what's going on. When he can't, he'll get tense.

Babying him is the worst thing you can do. You will make him feel *more* insecure, not less. Imagine you are lost in the woods. Two people come down the path. One says, "This is the way back to town. Follow me," and the other says, "You poor thing, isn't this awful. What do you feel like doing?" Who would you latch on to? Well, if your dog has separation anxiety, he is "lost in the woods." Give him someone to follow.

Exercise him. If he is tired, he will be less likely to cause problems. Morn-

Dogs with separation anxiety need to do a lot of mental work. Karen makes Maake wait at every curb until Karen says, "OK." A good habit as well as good training.

A tired dog is a good dog.

ing exercise before a long a day alone is mandatory. Get up earlier if necessary, but he has to run hard for at least 20 minutes before you leave. An upbeat, happy obedience session will tire your dog mentally, reassure him of your leadership and start the day off right. Be sure to have fun, using lots of praise to motivate your dog.

Prevent problems. Crating is often the right tool for the training process. Until he can control himself, you must assist him. This includes crating when you are out or anytime you cannot watch him. Many anxious dogs actually enjoy being in a smaller, limited area, just like a little child might prefer to stay in his own room rather than wander around an empty mansion. Some dogs build themselves up into a state of near hysteria, pacing back and forth in front of the door; crating limits this movement and so derails the hysterics. Once he relaxes, you can give him more freedom again, but until then, crate him.

Practice coming and going for short periods of time. Most damage happens right after you leave, which is why whether you are gone 20 minutes or 5 hours the house looks the same when you return. By practicing this part, you will teach him how to accept your departure, going a long way toward eliminating the problem. Leave the dog out of the crate. Put on your coat, step out the door, step *right back in,* calmly praise the dog. Calmly tell him "Down," calmly give him a tidbit, calmly leave, calmly come right back in, calmly tell him "Down," calmly leave. Do this until the dog seems relaxed, even eager for you to depart, and downs himself when you come back in. Leave a lead on him for this training if he is hard to down. **Always** remove it if he is going to be unsupervised. As he improves, leave for longer periods—30 seconds, a minute—always returning calmly, always downing him, always praising him.

Now, you will have to do your whole leaving routine, getting on your coat, locking the doors, ringing for the elevator or getting in the car. It will help to calm him if you leave a piece of worn clothing in with him, an old sweatshirt for example, and the radio on. Do this for at least one week before going to the next level. Some of you may have to do this for a month or more.

Once he is calm about all this, take off the lead and step out for 3 to 5 minutes. One or two of these a day is good. When this presents no problem, go for 10 minutes.

Now you are ready for the big time. Before you take a short trip—

say, to do some shopping—exercise him, do some training, ignore him for 10 minutes, then leave. Pick up a paper, get a cup of coffee. Cross your fingers and return. No matter what you find, do the same routine. If there is a problem, go back to shorter time periods for a while. If not, don't get excited. Stay calm, progress slowly. Don't rush things. Stay with half-hour periods for a while, then go to an hour. Progress slowly. If you press this and he gets nervous, you will be back at the start before you know it. **Whenever you have to leave your dog for real, crate him until the training period is over.**

Regardless of what he has done when you return, you **do not** punish him. Dogs can become the focus of a bad day; don't let that happen. He is anxious. Punishing him will make him more anxious. He will become worse. You will punish more and—You're in a correction cycle. Stop!

A client recently came to me with a 3 1/2-year-old Shar Pei. This dog was destroying his doors, scratching, chewing, salivating, basically losing his mind when left alone. He had been told to come in, yell at the dog and beat him with a rolled-up newspaper. Guess what? The dog got worse! The poor thing was then pronounced "untrainable." It took a few weeks, but this "untrainable" dog is coming along just fine.

If you take a trip away, board him. Do not leave a dog with separation anxiety at home when you go away, even if a friend or housesitter will be there. Doing so can escalate the problems you are having. From your dog's perspective it is his worst nightmare: you leave and you don't come home! He'll be anxious for months after that!

Chewing

Chewing is natural for dogs. Problem chewers do so because it is fun, because they are bored, improperly trained, anxious or have too much energy. Fun is a main reason that dogs choose to chew. When they unstuff a pillow, shred a pile of newspaper or peel your wallpaper, they are having a grand time. All that scolding you did when your dog was a pup simply got translated into "Don't let Mom catch me chewing." So they don't touch a thing when they are in view; but take a shower or go to the store, and you can find a minor disaster.

Solving this is threefold: prevention, direction and correction. Prevent the problem by crating the dog. Direction means teach him to chew dog toys. Try a rope toy or a sterilized bone stuffed with cheese. Rawhides and cow hooves are other canine favorites. Encourage him to select those objects. Play with them: rub your hands over the toy, then give it to him. Teach him the toy's name by saying it, then walking to the toy with the dog. Divide his toy collection into three parts and rotate the toys daily. This way he'll have something "new" every day to play with. Correction involves having the objects he chews correct him. Using shake-can booby traps or Bitter Apple, you can make what used to be fun to chew an unpleasant experience. A shake-can booby trap is made by putting three cans on a table. Tape a piece of thread to the cans, then tie the thread to an object your dog likes to chew. Put that object within easy grasp. When he takes it to chew on, the cans tumble down. Surprise!

A chewer needs an appropriate outlet. Rawhides are cheap compared to new shoes or a couch. Don't skimp on dog toys.

As with all problems, up his exercise and ground him. Stress release and strong leadership improves most dogs almost immediately. Diet can be a factor as well. Be sure to feed a quality, brand-name food.

Boredom is often the underlying cause of chewing. If you have a bright dog who basically lies around all day doing not much, this could be a key to his chewing problem. Do all of the above but pay close attention to exercising him both mentally and physically. Using commands frequently, especially when unexpected, challenges your dog, establishing a needed attitude of respect. Obedience work gives him the attention he craves in a constructive way.

If your dog is the anxious type, constantly nudging you for attention, spinning in circles when you come home and wanting attention for hours, look at the section on separation anxiety for guidelines.

Improper training is the cause of many destructive chewing problems in adult dogs. If you gave him a shoe to play with when he was a pup or played tug-of-war with a sock, do not be surprised that he is chewing your belongings today. You taught him to. Keep your things put away, don't use them for toys, and booby-trap a few items with shake cans to break this cycle.

Use a crate to prevent chewing, calm the dog and begin solving the problem.

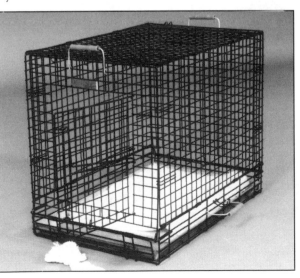

Excessive Barking

Dogs bark for a variety of reasons: they hear a noise; they're lonely; they want your attention; they're having fun; they're frightened; or their toy has rolled under the couch. It's their way of letting us know they need or want something. It also can be a warning that something is not right or that someone is near the house. Some breeds just enjoy barking, doing it recreationally to pass the time. Barking, however, can be obnoxious. Dogs who bark all day can cause trouble with the neighbors. Dogs that bark at you are nerve grinding. Barking, however, can be dealt with.

Excessive barking can't be eliminated by yelling. When you give a good yell, the dog just figures you're joining in. If the dog's barking is due to fear, he is likely to apply your upset to the situation, not his behavior. For example, the dog is barking at a stranger. You get tense. "No, be quiet, no!" you yell. The dog will come to your defense, blaming your upset on this new person in the house, not on his behavior, and bark with new enthusiasm.

If your dog starts to bark at something or someone, give the down command and make him do it. Assuming a submissive posture on your command will quiet many dogs immediately.

Barking for Attention

Your dog looks at you and barks. He barks at you to throw the toy, get off the phone, fix him dinner or simply to give him attention. The best way to solve this problem is to take the bull by the horns. He wants your attention so much? He can have it! Leave the leash on him. When he starts this routine, calmly pick up the leash and drill him on his obedience. "Sit, down, sit, down, come, sit, down, come, wait, OK, down, stay, OK, come. . . ." Do a demanding, no-nonsense drill for two minutes. Do many "Downs," as dogs have a harder time both mentally and physically barking in the "Down" position. Don't give him much praise. At the end just drop the lead and walk away. Most dogs, stunned, mind their own business for a while. Do this every time he starts up. You can also tell him "Quiet" and give a quick leash correction. See page 81 on how to give a correction. That works for some dogs. Be sure to praise him when he quiets down.

Barking When Left Alone

This is common, especially after vacations when the dog gets used to having someone around full-time or after moving when everything is new. To find out when and how long he is barking, leave a tape recorder on. I had one client who discovered that the neighbors scratched at the door during the day, causing the dog to bark. Then they complained about it! We found out by the taping.

Once you know exactly what is going on, your first task is to get your dog used to being alone. A crate is an invaluable tool, allowing you to practice with the dog when you are at home. See pages 42–43 for complete instruction. Crate him in 20- to 30-minute increments at first. Put a piece of clothing you have worn in with him; your smell will comfort him.

Work up to longer periods. Make your comings and goings calm. Revving him up emotionally is doing neither one of you any good. Increase his exercise. A tired dog is more likely to be a quiet dog. Ground him, because grounding helps every dog. Practice leaving and coming back in, starting with short periods away. Praise him calmly but warmly whenever you return to quiet. At first, stay away 5 minutes, then 10, then 15, etc.

Leaving a radio on can help to block out noises and is company for the dog. Keep him away from bark-producing windows, like the one that overlooks a sidewalk, and leave him good toys to play with, like a sterilized bone stuffed with cheese. Exercised, structured, confined and entertained, the vast majority of dogs stop their nuisance barking quickly.

Barking at Sounds

Leave the lead on in the house. When he starts barking, first praise him for doing his job, then tell him "Stop it," call him to you, and down him at your feet. Praise him when he's there. Giving him something else to do is critical to success with this command. If he does not respond to your commands, then pick up the lead and correct him for not complying. See page 81 on how to give a correction.

The woman at the coffee shop wanted to know what she could do to stop her dog from barking.

"When does he bark?" I asked.

"All the time," she replied. "It's in the backyard."

"You can't stop it," I told her, "unless you bring the dog in."

"Can't do that," she said." It's wild in the house."

I sighed. Such a waste. The dog separated and lonely, the owner unable or unmotivated to teach him how to behave.

No dog should be kept tied outside for long periods. It's no place for a social animal like a dog. Bored and lonely dogs bark, dig, whine, pace and become aggressive when tied because they are miserable and have nothing better to do. They are also at the mercy of other dogs, children or adults. Bring the dog into your home, train him and make him a family member or give him to someone who will. Animals are not like toys to be picked up and put down at will. They are living breathing beings who need your constant interaction to be happy, healthy and sane.

Enforce your instructions, then praise him at your feet.

Shaking a shake can behind your back or tossing one down by his feet can reinforce your command to stop it. Praise immediately if he stops.

Barking at the Doorbell

Dogs quickly learn to link the ringing of the doorbell or buzzer with the arrival of guests. Once they put this together, some will bark nonstop from the first ring to the guest entering the house, working themselves into a frenzy doing it. Have the dog on lead. Set up the situation. Praise him for alerting you, then take control by commanding "Stop it." When he does, praise him. If he doesn't, give him a horizontal pop on the lead. The moment he stops, praise him warmly. Tell him what you want by commanding "Down" and then praise some more. Practice this. Have someone ring the bell or buzzer repeatedly over a 10-minute time period. Soon your dog will know to be quiet when you say "Stop it" and "Down." Giving him a food reward when he is quiet will help to link silence with pleasure.

Don't do this.

Whining

Few things in life are as grating as a whining dog. Stress and anxiety cause a lot of whining. Whining can also be a sign of frustration: being caught between what he has to do and what he wants to do, he whines. That's why a dog may whine when learning "Down"/"Stay." He wants to get up, he has to lie there; he is torn, he whines. I take that as a good sign. It means the dog knows what he has to do but is complaining. With more practice the whining will naturally stop.

The one thing you never want to do is reward whining. "Oh, my poor baby, what's wrong?" is rewarding. Stroking the dog nervously as he whines is definitely rewarding him. Ignore whining. Give him other things to think about by practicing commands. Act as if he was behaving perfectly normally. He'll forget his worries soon enough and quiet down.

What does not work is to correct the dog. Correction can raise the dog's anxiety level, leading to an increase, not a decrease, in whining. Instead, work him, ground him, and pay no attention. As the dog gains in confidence, he will lessen his noise.

Certain situations will start many dogs whining. A car ride, a visit to the vet, another dog, all can cause a whining spree. Command "Stop it" and praise if he does. Using obedience commands in quick succession works well to assert your authority, calm him and give him something else to think about.

Whining dogs need to think about something other than their worries. I use puppy push-ups. Sit, down, sit, down, sit, down . . . a few minutes of this and most dogs just want to be left alone.

Hates to Be Handled

Some dogs hate to be brushed, held or touched in certain areas of their bodies. Many dogs dislike having their feet handled; a good number don't like their rears touched. The younger the dog is when you start handling training, the quicker he will learn. Dogs of any age can be taught to accept handling if it is made pleasurable.

First, put the dog on lead. As always, if you do not have verbal control, you must have physical control. Begin by doing something the dog enjoys, like scratching him behind the ear. Speak to him warmly. Then, continuing to chat cheerfully, run your hand to the area he does not like touched; casually brush over it. Do not miss a beat in your praise. Be confident and casual. If you hesitate, you relay your concern to the dog, cuing him to tense up. Go back to scratching his ear or massaging his shoulders. Do this over and over. As he gets relaxed, pause over the trouble area. Give him a treat, gently tickle that area, then go back to scratching his ear. Do this for a few days. Soon he will be quite relaxed about being touched.

If he fusses, tell him "Stop it" in a no-nonsense way and give a quick lead correction if necessary. Then go right back to praising him and practicing. This is not a confrontation or a negotiation. Deal with the resistance decisively but do not dwell on it.

Dogs that are fussy about being groomed can be retrained in a similar way. Start at a point he feels comfortable with; this may be you stroking him. As he is lying there, happy and relaxed, pick up the brush and gently brush over him once. Then pet him some more. Make this casual. Repeat this until he pays no attention to the brush.

Now, with lead and collar on, start to brush him. Be careful to be gentle. One big reason some dogs come to resent grooming is that it hurts. If he is matted, get him professionally groomed. If the dog is sensitive, use a soft brush or be careful to brush the hair, not rake it over the skin. Brush a small section at a time,

Handle your dog's ears, feet and tail when you praise him and soon he'll think that it's good fun.

then take a break; praise him, give a treat, play a bit, then do a bit more. It is not important that you groom the whole dog right now. Your goal is for him to learn to enjoy brushing. Once that is accomplished, doing complete groomings will be a breeze.

If at any time he attempts to mouth you, tell him "No bite" and give him a quick pop on the lead *just as* his mouth opens. Develop an "I'll have none of this" attitude. Tone is critical. "No bite" should be confidently matter-of-fact, not loud or frantic. Then go right back to brushing. Start with the praise the moment he removes his mouth.

Struggling dogs can be difficult to handle. This usually develops from the misguided habit of releasing a dog when he struggles. You think: "Poor thing, he wants to get up." Your dog learns struggling earns him freedom. Dogs that struggle should get a lead correction and be told "Stop it." When he has lain quietly for a few seconds, release him with an "OK." Do not try to groom the whole dog at once. It is good enough

that he learns that calm behavior gets him a quick release. Then go back and do a bit more later. Working on lots of "Stays" with this type of dog will help as well.

Most dogs who have trouble sitting still or who have certain body parts they don't like touched benefit from gentle massage.

Long-haired dogs in particular need to accept all kinds of handling calmly.

Car Travel and Its Problems

There's nothing like a carsick dog to take the fun out of a family outing. Most pups grow out of carsickness, but the ones who don't need special handling. First, do everyone a favor and don't feed the dog for four or more hours before you leave. If he skips a meal, that's OK. Once in the car, don't try to soothe the dog, stroking him nervously, trying to make him feel better. You won't.

If you have a choice, don't introduce your dog to car travel in a standard shift car or in heavy traffic. All the shifting and stop-and-go can make any pup woozy.

Take short trips to fun places. Go to friends, return a video, or drop off dry cleaning—take the dog in. The more fun he has, the more relaxed he will be. Eager anticipation and fear are not compatible. If every time he gets in the car, he ends up at the vet, he'll soon dislike riding in one.

Some dogs never vomit but do salivate profusely. Take towels along and let the dog be. With experience, he'll relax. Keeping the dog down in

With the leash running from the dog, between the seat cushions and to me, I can control the dog without much effort or distraction.

the footwell of the car helps as well. He'll feel better if he can't see out the windows.

Crating the dog when you travel is the answer for many dogs. They feel more secure and relaxed in their haven. Buying a grid to fit in the bottom of the crate will allow any fluids the dog does produce to pass through, keeping him neat and dry.

Dogs that are hyperactive or chronic barkers in the car are best put in the backseat on a lead. Run the lead through the crack between the front seat's back and seat or, if you have bucket seats, under the front seat. With the lead attached to your dog's collar in the backseat and you holding the lead that runs through or under the front seat, it is simple to control your dog. If he begins to bark,

pace or try to jump into the front, command "Down" and pull up on the lead. This familiar downward pressure on the back of his neck, cues him to lie down. If he resists, steady pressure will eventually get him down. Always praise and release the pressure the moment he complies. By telling the dog "Down" every time he gets overly active or starts to bark, you are teaching him what you want him to do. It is not uncommon for dogs to start downing themselves after a few weeks of consistent practice.

Do not allow your dog to stick his head out the window. Not only can he damage his eyes this way, but what if he jumps? I've seen dogs that have leaped from cars going 35 miles an hour. The dogs lived but only after painful, and costly, surgery.

Don't do this either.

Hyperactivity

When you restrain him, he gets more frenzied. When you yell at him, he gets more wild. When you correct him hard, he gets worse. You have a reactive dog. The good news is that he is 100% trainable. Reactive dogs have a hard time calming themselves down. They tend to take every emotion you send their way and magnify it. You are upset, they get more upset. With these animals it is mandatory that you be calm, dead calm. If you are calm, they become calm. There are no tricks, no shortcuts. Commands are neutral; correction unemotional, direct and over with. Concentrate on timing and structure rather than force. If you try force, they will get anxious and active. Praise is warm, kind and not too excited.

My personal experience is that the reactive dog is mentally sensitive, eager to please and intelligent. When approached as stupid, stubborn, difficult or untrainable, he becomes those things. With your proper handling and patience, he will a become responsive pet.

If your dog can't sit still, has been described by those who love him as "wild," and generally has the energy of 10, then you probably have a hyperactive dog. The most effective approach is to exhaust him mentally and physically, not to fight with him trying to force him into behaving.

What people see as hyperactivity may be normal for a dog of his age and breed. A young Weimaraner may be endless motion, but I'd be worried if he wasn't! If your dog is easier to live with on the weekends and during vacations when he gets more time outside, then exercise may well be key.

Mental exercise is of equal, if not greater, import. Giving him structure and directing his behavior creates parameters for him that he may not be able to create for himself. Obedience work helps to calm and focus such dogs and is a part of your daily life with these animals, not a special occurrence. "Down"/"Stays" are vital in teaching overly active dogs self- control. Ground him, not as a temporary measure but as an ongoing management plan. Truly hyperactive dogs will need structure their whole lives.

Overcorrection and lack of proper teaching can cause hyperactivity. Unnecessarily rough or loud handling can raise a dog's anxiety level, causing him to become hyperactive. A lack of leadership upsets every dog, making some overly active. We've all seen toddlers who were out of control because the parents simply refused to set any boundaries for them. Dogs react the same way to a lack of structure.

Diet can influence hyperactivity. If your animal is young and overactive, he may need to come off puppy food at seven or eight months of age. Read labels. Foods that are high in protein or fat may just be more than your dog needs. Don't be conned into believing that more is necessarily better when it comes to nutrition. A moderate food is best. I often suggest a diet change for overly active or sensitive dogs with positive results. Although it's rare, I have seen cases where the dog improved 75% in the first week after changing to a milder or different type of food. Also, talk to your vet. There are some medical conditions that can cause hyperactivity.

Digging

Dogs dig. They dig because they are bored. They dig because they enjoy it or to make a cool spot to lie in. Fixing it is not easy. Here are some digging corrections that sometimes work.

Put his feces in the bottom of the hole before you refill it. Most dogs are repelled by that. Once he digs into it, he'll usually avoid it in the future.

Booby-trap him from the house. Try lobbing a shake can or two in his direction when he starts to dig. This is most effective if he does not see or hear you do this. Shake cans falling from the sky are an excellent deterrent.

Some dogs are genetically driven to dig—terriers and Nordic breeds, for example. Try focusing them on an engaging game; a Boomer Ball sometimes works well. These hard, plastic balls last forever, and once the dog learns how to push them with his nose, he may entertain himself for hours. Only use this toy in a fenced-in yard.

Prevention is the best cure. If your dog is outside, supervise him. If you can't supervise him, don't leave him out. That's the best, guaranteed solution to a digging problem.

Tri certainly is having a fine time digging out this hole.

Fear Reactions

Fear is one of the hardest problems to solve. It can also be tough to diagnose. Many dogs are aggressive due to fear, and the aggression will not be resolved until the fear is addressed. To work with canine fear successfully you need to remember two things. First, fear takes as long as it takes to go away. That means, drop all your expectations about what your dog "should" know or how far along he "should" be. He'll get over it on his terms not yours. If you push him in any way, you will go back to the beginning or worse!

Secondly, you cannot solve this problem by empathizing with him. He is already frightened; he does not need you convincing him he is right to feel this way by becoming upset along with him. If the plane is having engine trouble, do you feel better if the pilot sits with you, saying "What's the matter? Don't be scared"? You need the pilot up there flying the plane, saying "Everything is under control. We'll be landing safely in five minutes." To your dog, you're the pilot and he needs you flying the plane.

To solve fear problems you have to show your dog what the normal reaction should be. If you want the dog to be happy, you be happy. If you want him confident, you be confident. He will take the lead from you, so don't let him down. Ignore whatever he is doing and act as if all is well.

Do *not* try to force the issue. If he is scared of skateboards, people in hats or the trash can on the sidewalk, do not drag him up to it. This will make him resist. Do not allow people to approach him; that will only spook him and force a retreat. Fearful animals are more comfortable approaching at their own speed. If he is hesitant, stand near the object or person yourself and speak in a relaxed, happy tone. If he comes up, don't make a big deal out of it, just praise him warmly as he moves toward it. If he chooses to withdraw, that's fine too. Just stop praising him.

Give him attention for courage and ignore fear. It is easy to give him

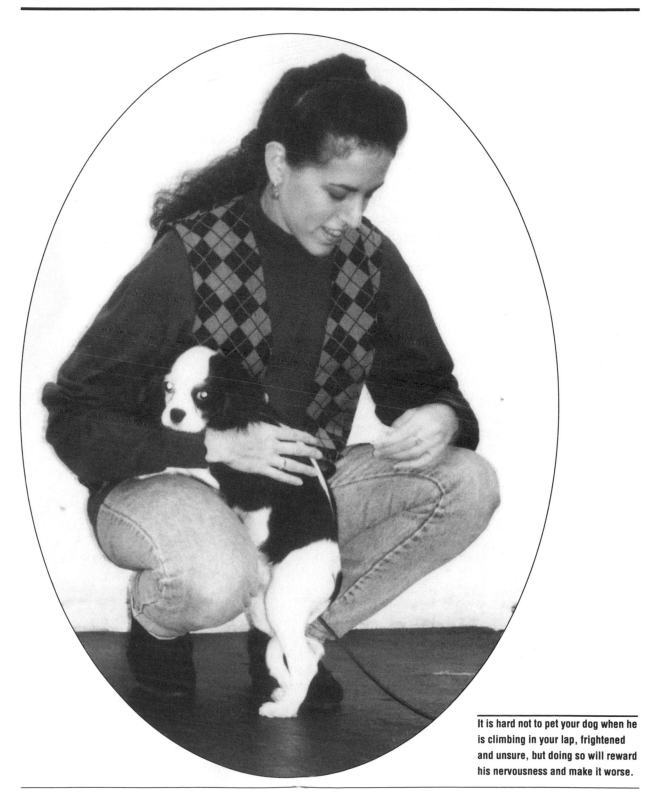

It is hard not to pet your dog when he is climbing in your lap, frightened and unsure, but doing so will reward his nervousness and make it worse.

lots of attention when he is frightened, but he will misinterpret that as praising him for the fear. This is not good. Ignore a frightened dog, focus on his courage, and soon he'll be making efforts to conquer his nerves.

Practice your obedience. Work especially hard on your "Down"/"Stay." This will help develop his self-control. The more positive structure he gets, the calmer and more confident he will be. Fearful dogs need to think about other things; listening and obeying you will help take his mind off his worries.

Setting up a self-rewarding system can help your pet conquer his fear. Many dogs are frightened of vacuum cleaners. I just leave one sitting out with treats placed all over it. It may take a few hours, but he'll start trying to get those treats. I'll squat by the vacuum and hold out a treat to encourage him. If he takes it, great! Next, I hold it out again, only I don't quite extend my arm. As he comes toward it, praise! Soon he'll be coming right up to the dreaded vacuum.

Now that he's approaching the vacuum with ease, let's turn it on. Most dogs will jump back when you do that. Make it a game! Turn on the vacuum, praise enthusiastically and give a treat. Turn it off, silence. Having fun is contagious.

If strangers are the fear, have them sit down and ignore the dog. Lay a trail of treats from the dog to the stranger. Use more and better treats the closer you get to the person. Then give your volunteer a few of the best treats to hold. If the dog ventures forward, do *not* look at the dog or say his name. Focusing on him can spook him. As he comes closer, warmly praise him. If he makes it to the stranger, great! Have the guest toss a treat in his direction. If the dog accepts the treat, have the guest hold one out to him, still not looking at him in any way. If he takes it, wonderful! You're on your way.

Do this several more times before you have your guest softly speak to the dog as he takes the treat. If he accepts that, have the guest look in the dog's direction. Do not rush this. It may take 1 or 20 visits to reach this point. Allow your dog to set his own pace. Link his forward movement with the words "Say hello." This will give him a verbal cue, helping him to relax and gain confidence. Take whatever time he needs. Rush him and you'll undo all your good work.

If your dog is hesitant, you can speed up the process by fasting the dog before the guest arrives. Skipping a meal will not harm your dog but will make him more eager for the treats. Also, find a treat he really likes. One frightened Rottweiler would only work for meatballs. Messy, but effective. Cheese, boiled chicken, biscuits or freeze-dried liver treats are more the norm. Have no pride in this area; do what is necessary.

If your dog is afraid of certain noises, try to get a recording of them. Music stores often carry sound tapes of thunderstorms rolling in. If your dog hates street noise, rent a video with some wild chase scenes in them, full of squealing tires and screeching brakes. Play these when your dog eats. Start them at very low volume. Over the next few weeks, raise the volume bit by bit, until he can tolerate loud noise without concern.

If sudden noise is his problem, make a game out of it. When he is a good distance away from you, bang two pots together, gently. Laugh, toss him a treat, run around. If he comes toward you, praise him and put the pots away. If he is too scared, you have done too much too soon. Make less noise next time. If you genuinely have fun doing this, your dog will soon come to view it as a bizarre but enjoyable game.

Feeding him in metal bowls and mixing his food with a metal spoon can help associate the sounds of metal on metal with pleasure. Sound sensitivities can almost always be made better if you progress slowly and let your dog be your guide.

Marc Street demonstrates the right way to greet a fearful dog. He is squatting low and reaching under her chin so as not to frighten her. Notice how the dog is looking at the owner for guidance. Her owner is praising enthusiastically for being such a brave dog!

TiP

MAKING MATTERS WORSE

Two parents in the playground are watching their children play. Suddenly both children take a tumble. One parent walks over. "Boom, boom. Oh, well," she says, setting the child back on her feet and brushing her off. "You look fine, go play." The parent smiles, unconcerned. The child hesitates, looks up at her mother, and goes off.

The other parent rushes over. "Are you OK? What a terrible fall! You poor thing!" he gushes, hugging his child close to him. The child looks up at him, sees his concern, and bursts into tears.

Fear is one of the hardest problems to work with because people naturally want to fix it. They try to make the dog feel better by reassuring him. You can't make fear go away. All you can do—and a hard job it is too—is set a fine example for your pet. The more of a leader you are, the more he will trust your perspective. Use obedience; make him work for his praise. Set a happy enthusiastic tone, and your dog will adopt it. **Act as you want your dog to act.**

The Role of Exercise

Stress affects dogs just as it can people. Think how stressed you would be if your family came and went as they pleased, never telling you where they were going, when they would return or what they were up to. A dog, being naturally social, is particularly stressed by the hours of isolation mandatory in today's world. Situations that create stress for you—a new job with different hours, a new child or problems in your relationship—can all add up to increased stress for your dog.

Like humans, dogs need to release stress. Medita-tion and biofeedback are not possible, so exercise and play become the main avenues of release for your dog. The more stress he is under, the more exercise he needs. Playing with other dogs is one of the best and easiest ways to exercise your pet. If you know that schedule is going to be hectic or your new boyfriend is coming over, make time for extra doses of training, running and playing beforehand.

If you have a problem dog, the importance of exercise increases. Having some fun during play can be a good way—and sometimes the only way—to relax with your dog. A good game of fetch, watching him play or working on obedience as a team can remind you of how much you love this animal.

Matisse enjoys a good workout and is a calmer, easier-to-manage dog after she has had one.

Stealing Food or Objects

Many owners have lost some or all of a meal to a quick and silent dog. Virtually every dog owner has seen their pet walk by with something of value in his mouth. Scolding after you catch him does teach him something: not to get caught. That is how sneaky dogs are created. Owners train pets to be sneaks by using the wrong type of correction at the wrong time. The best thing to do is to have the object he tries to steal correct him.

Booby-trapping is the answer for many dogs. Put three shake cans on the table. Tape thread to the cans, then tie the thread to a bagel. A bagel is ideal because it is easy to tie thread to, hard enough that it won't fall apart when the dog pulls it, and mediocre enough that the taste will not be more appealing than the cans are scary. Place the bagel near the edge of the table and wait for nature to take its course. You'll hear the tumble of cans and smile knowingly to yourself.

Do not use booby traps when you are not home. First, a mischievous dog should be tucked safely away in his crate, not loose in your home, and secondly, if he eats the bagel, the booby trap will be useless in the future.

You can booby-trap everything from socks to the pile of newspapers your dog loves to shred. If your dog is a trash can picker, put ground black pepper thickly over the top of the trash. When he goes to take a sniff, he'll get a nose full. Purchasing a can with a tightly fitting cover is another solution.

For dogs who are shake can–wary, drape a paper towel over the cans so

Attaching a shake can booby trap (1–3 cans with thread taped to them and then the thread is tied to the object he likes to steal) makes a nice surprise the next time your dog tries to take it.

they are out of sight. Alternatively, you can watch him closely, and when he walks out of the room, follow quietly. If you can catch him in the act, lob a shake can down by his feet, then get out of sight. Say nothing. It is critical that the can correct him, not you.

If your dog is a closet raider, try resting two cans on the top of the slightly opened door, leaning against the wall. This way, if a curious canine nose nudges the door open, the cans will fall. Dogs do not like surprises.

Leaving a lead on him when you are home makes him easier to catch if he does get something. If you catch him with your best shoes in his mouth, command "Out" and enforce it with a leash correction. If he shows any interest in your tables or countertops, use the "Leave it" command. Regardless of what you do, praise him well when he leaves it alone, drops the object or allows you to take the object from him. Once it's in his mouth, it's too late to correct him for taking it. At that point your only hope is to teach him to willingly drop it.

Caught red-handed! This pug raided the kitchen trash to claim her prize. Booby-trapping the garbage with ground black pepper or shake cans could stop her thieving ways.

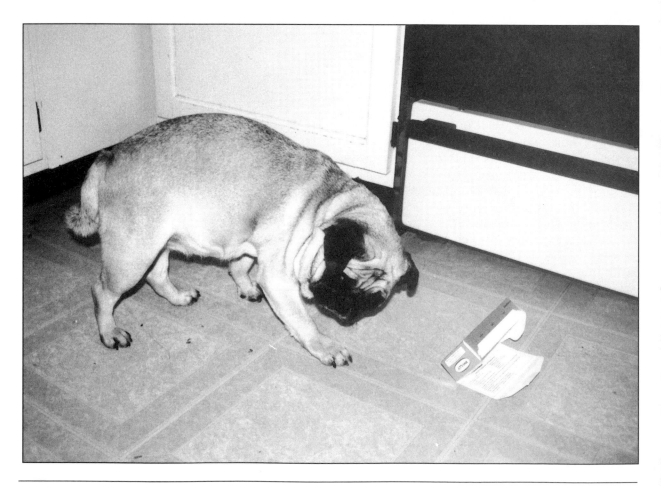

Jumping Up

Jumping is possibly the most common problem dog owners have with their pets. And most of us richly deserve it. When the small puppy arrives in our home, we pet and play with him as he leaps eagerly against our legs. Then when the same animal, now 65 pounds, leaps up, we say "Down," when what we mean is "Off," and scold him. It's amazing dogs don't give up trying to understand us.

If you want to stop the jumping, you must be consistent and stop yourself from petting him when he does. If you pet him for leaping on Saturdays when you are in your work clothes, he will jump the rest of the week regardless of what you're wearing. Dogs have an extremely limited fashion sense.

Jumping is a compliment. He loves you and wants to say hello face to face. If the dog is mounting or mouthing you when he jumps, it is less complimentary and more a statement of dominance. In either case, jumping can knock people down, ruin your clothing, spill your coffee and generally annoy you. So now that you've started it, how do you stop it?

Once you've made the decision that you really don't want this behavior—ever, and it is not a sometimes kind of thing—you can get started. Before you can expect the dog to control himself, you have to teach him what you want. Put him on lead and teach him "Off" as on page 152–54. Once he has the idea—and it will take him a while to believe you since you've been inconsistent with this in the past—you can start expecting him to respond off lead.

Setting up the situation so you

Small dogs are hard to resist but if you pet him expect him to jump all over your guests.

can focus on training the dog, not greeting your guest, is a must. If you don't practice and achieve success in a controlled situation, don't expect control with a stranger at the door. Get a volunteer to ring the doorbell and enter the house on your cue. Have a lead on your dog and command "Off," then "Sit." If he tries to jump, command "Off" and give a quick snap of the lead to one side. Once his paws touch the floor, praise him and command "Sit." Praise him as he sits; you can even have your guest give him a treat while he sits there. Then do it again. You'd be surprised how quickly a dog can learn to control himself when you focus all your attention on teaching him to.

To control this habit, you will have to control all the people who encourage your dog to jump. "I don't mind," they say with a smile. Of course not, they don't have scratches on their legs from an early morning leap or rips in their favorite sweater. Tell kind souls in a friendly but firm way that you were not asking for their opinion on the matter. Regardless of what they say, correct the dog when it jumps. They may not like that, but they don't live with the problem.

If your dog is the savvy type that figures out immediately to mind his manners when on lead but is a jumping fool off lead, try the techniques outlined on page 83.

One of the keys to stopping unwanted behavior is realizing that to remove one behavior you must

If I open the door now, I'll be rewarding his jumping.

replace it with another. If you want him to stop jumping, then give him an alternative. In this case, "Sit" is what you want. As he approaches you, tell him "Sit" before he reaches you. When he obeys, scratch him and praise. If he jumps, tell him "Off" and then "Sit" again. You have to train him how to greet you. This will take a few weeks, but it is well worth the years of jump-free living you and your dog have in front of you.

All Jim wants is a little attention, but he's not going to get it for jumping up!

After he sits, he gets the attention he wants. He even gives me a little lick on the face.

Doorway Etiquette

Here is a trouble spot in most dog-owning households, the area where dogs push, pull, scratch, shove and jump to get in or out. To get some order, put your little whirlwind on lead.

Rushing out the door is countered by teaching "Wait" (page 159) and insisting on compliance. Practice going in and out several times a day. As soon as he realizes that self-control, rather than brute strength, will get him out the door quickest, he'll sit all a-quiver, waiting for your "OK."

Pushing you aside as he bolts out the door is disrespectful and rude. Work on the "Wait" command, then make sure he does. If he tries to shove you

This kind of behavior is obnoxious and potentially dangerous. It is also all too common.

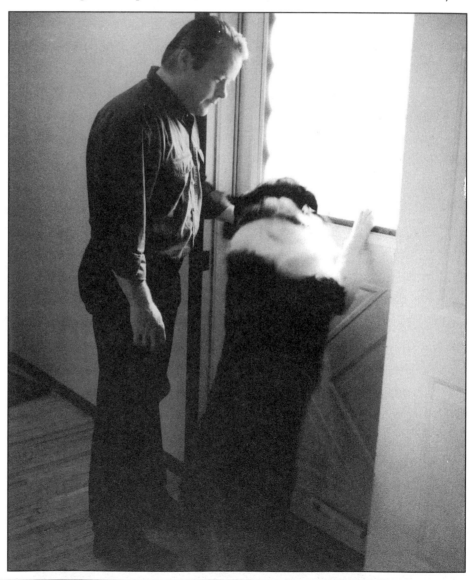

aside, give him a leash correction. He richly deserves one. Praise him enthusiastically when he gets the message.

Jumping is covered in the previous section as well as on pages 84–85 and pages 154–56. Jumping and other greeting misbehavior are effectively countered with obedience commands. "Down"/"Stays" are great. Practice them at the door regularly until he is a pro. Then make it a challenge, ring the doorbell, jump in and out of the house, throw toys around—make it a game! By the time guests arrive, they'll be a nonevent.

To stop jumping specifically, set up the situation. Volunteers in casual, easy-to-clean clothes are needed. Bribe friends to assist you by promising them dinner if they help you out. As difficult as it is to believe that your dog can control himself in this situation, he can. Go back to the basics: praise, practice and persistence.

This is better. With a little practice, your dog can do this too.

Eating and Rolling in Disgusting Things

"There's no accounting for taste."

As I was working on this book one day, I noticed a smell—a revolting smell. I checked the bottom of my shoes. Nothing. I got up to see if anyone else smelled it. There was no smell in the kitchen until Caras walked in. I lifted his chin; his brilliant white rough was caked with something beyond description. Whatever it was, or had been, it now stuck with amazing powers of adherence to my dog's coat. I headed him straight for the tub.

Dogs roll in things we make circles around to avoid. Some say dogs roll in things because, in the wild, doing so covers their scent so their prey will not know the dogs are nearby. All I know is that some dogs love to indulge in canine cologne. You have a chance of stopping your dog if you can get a strong "Leave it" or "Come" in right before they begin. Once started, good luck. Their eyes glaze over with ecstasy. Inevitably, they run to you with pride afterward, dancing happily around you as you gag.

As for eating things, most dogs will eat other species' feces if given an opportunity. Putting him on lead and using your "Leave it" command if he shows the slightest interest is the best and surest way to avoid poop breath. Developing a good response to "Leave it" will save you, some of the time. Prevention is the best program.

The majority of dogs scorn canine leavings, although not all. Many clients remember to tell me this as the dog is licking my face. "Oh, yeah," they add, "he eats his own poop." Timing is everything.

Eating his own feces is a disgusting habit and often is difficult to stop. There are numerous theories about why dogs do this: a nutritional need, a genetic trait, a learned behavior. Whatever its causes, dogs who like it really like it. There is a product called Forbid that has been known to be an effective deterrent. Ask your veterinarian about it. When this is put on the dog food, it apparently makes the poop taste bad. If you see no improvement in three days, stop. It works immediately or not at all. (Adolph's Meat Tenderizer or Accent works on some dogs.)

I've had some success calling the dog to me right after he defecates, putting him in the house, spraying the poop with Bitter Apple then letting him back at it.

The other option is to lie in wait and lob a shake can at him as he goes to nibble some. Don't say anything. If he links the correction with you, that will only inhibit him in your presence. That's not much help.

A few clients have had success with a diet change. A few very rich foods seem to lead to more of this type of problem than others.

One of these methods may help you, but many cases are tough to stop. If nothing else works, prevention through supervision and picking up after the dog may be the best answer possible.

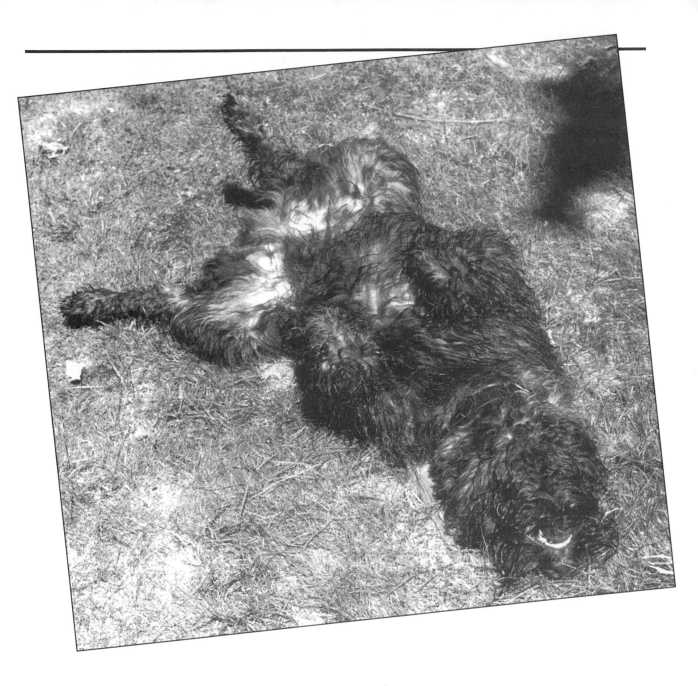

Kesl loves to roll in anything. Here he is taking advantage of a dead mouse, if my memory serves me. Dogs will be dogs.

BARKLEY: The Finicky Eater

My favorite finicky dog story is Barkley, the Scottish Terrier who would only eat if his owners went into the hallway outside of their apartment and rang the doorbell. I still don't know quite how that developed, but I think it's a pretty complex trick for a dog to teach two human beings. This dog arrived at Family Dog, our training facility, with precise feeding instructions: Barkley is to receive 15 pieces of dry dog food, half a jar of chicken baby food and a quarter of a cup of cottage cheese. Anything else, I was assured, he would not eat. I asked the owners if this was how they wanted it. They said, "No, but he starves otherwise." (Fat chance—this dog is serious about his food. He has them preparing special meals and standing in the hall. He'll never starve himself.) I assured them that in the 20 years I had been doing this work, no dog had ever starved himself.

First we put Barkley on a regular feeding schedule of regular dog food. We used the dry dog food he was used to and mixed it with its canned companion product. We gave him two meals a day, each left down for half an hour and then removed. No snacks, no apologies. He nibbled at this but, after two days, was not eating as well as I wanted or he needed to. So we went to plan B.

Plan B is the crazy dog-owner syndrome. First, I made the dog food, mixing it slowly, making "yummy, yummy" sounds as I did. The whole thing was a production. Barkley was not interested. As I bent down to give it to him, I put it right under his nose, then took it away and threw it out. Barkley looked surprised.

At dinner I went through the same the preparation. This time Barkley was considerably more interested. But just at that last moment, as I put it right under his nose, I decided not to and I threw it away.

By the third meal, he was jumping up and down. I went to put it down, pulled it away, looked at him for a minute and put it down. He ate with gusto. He now eats anything you put down for him without question. His owners were thrilled. Barkley's one-day fast did him no physical harm and a lot of mental good.

Dogs who get people food quickly lose interest in dog food.

Inappropriate Sniffing

Dogs greet each other by sniffing each other, often in private areas. They extend this behavior to us, at times with disarming vigor. One of our celebrity clients owned a hard-core crotch sniffer. This dog has enthusiastically bumped and snuffled some of the most famous crotches in the country. This was a problem made worse by the fact that this dog was an enthusiast of his sport, often ramming into this most private of areas at full speed. He actually knocked one of our employees right off his feet. The poor man was not able to stand for quite a few minutes. Crotch sniffing is not always a laughing matter.

Dogs that stick their noses up skirts or into crotches must unlearn this persistent but natural canine behavior. Working with the dog on lead, just as he goes to take a sniff, tell him "Leave it" and give a sideways pop on the lead. Then redirect him with a "Sit" and praise him.

It is natural for people to hop up or out of the way when a dog does this, but he will interpret that as submissive behavior. If your dog sniffs you, step forward, into him, and make

This normal canine-to-canine greeting is highly unacceptable canine to human.

GOOD SCENTS

Your dog's sense of smell is unimaginably better than yours. I am quite sure dogs think of us as nasally retarded. Lucky for us, dogs are willing share their talents. Here's just a few things that dog's can do with their nose:

• Find drowning victims. Search-and-rescue dogs are rowed out onto lakes in boats. They bark when the boat is over the victim.

• Find human bones. Search dogs have located bones several years old when out searching crime areas.

• Locate termites. Dogs, often beagles, are trained to check for termites in your home.

• Locate gas leaks. Dogs can find minute leaks from natural gas lines 20 feet or more below ground. Leaks so small that our most sensitive equipment cannot detect them.

him back away from you. Use your best, no-nonsense tone, the same one you'd use if anyone else did such a thing. "Are you *nuts*? Stop that!" Be serious, not emotional.

Dogs can also be taught not to sniff endlessly when out for a walk. If he attempts to stop to "read the doggy newspaper," tell him "Leave it" and keep moving. If you stop when he stops, then he's trained you to stop. If you don't mind him taking a sniff now and then, allow him to when *you* want him to, not when he's in the mood. Walk right up to the lamppost, fire hydrant or garbage bag, tell him "OK" and let him sniff. After a few seconds, tell him "Leave it," then "Let's go." If you do not let him know clearly when he can or cannot sniff, he'll keep trying thoughout his entire walk.

Here I am practicing "leave it" with Topaz. For dogs that are devoted garbage hounds, practicing this command in all different areas with all sorts of temptations is necessary.

Running Off

Dogs, unneutered males in particular, like to roam. Bored dogs—dogs kept in the backyard or left alone too much, who get little training and less fun—roam because they aren't attached or happy at home. If you want your dog to attach to you, spend time working, training and playing with him.

Some dogs roam because they get rewarded for doing so. If your dog is a trash picker or compost raider, he will be strongly motivated to take off for a quick snack. Even a trained dog can get interested in a smell and take a stroll if left outside unsupervised. The best protection is a fence, dog run or a walk on the lead. Allowing dogs to run free causes dog bites, car accidents, maimed or killed livestock and wildlife and adds greatly to the pet overpopulation problem. Please do what is best for your dog. Be responsible.

Licking

This is a sweet gesture from a friendly dog, but it can become an unwanted annoyance if you don't want dog saliva on you or if your dog is one of those "won't take no for an answer" types. For a few pushy dogs, it becomes a "friendly" kind of dominance. What starts out as affection ends up as assertion. If someone you like kisses you, that can be nice. But if they kiss you over and over, more than you want, and you back away and protest but they continue to kiss you, you would not call that nice. Do not misread your dog's intentions either.

Pulling our hands away, verbally protesting, backing up and attempting to avoid the licks without putting on the lead and telling him to stop will be interpreted as submissive behavior. Some dogs then lick as a way of soliciting this submissive from you.

Put the lead right on him and tell him "No lick" if he starts. If he stops, verbally praise him—but no petting. If he keeps at it, pop the lead and then praise him if he withdraws. One lovely woman owned a dog that urinated on her pillow—while she slept on it! We worked and worked to resolve this problem. The obedience was strong, the dog was responsive, but the urination problem continued.

Finally, one day I was sitting on the couch, reviewing everything we had been working on, when he walked up and started licking me. Long, intense licks. "Yuck," I said "Does he do this to you?"

"All the time," she said. "Why?"

"Here's the problem!" I said. "This is disgusting and he is being way too pushy about it."

That was the missing clue. The urination stopped when she corrected his incessant licking.

Licking is normally a gesture of affection, as shown here. But when taken too far, it should be stopped.

Aggression

Aggression is the most powerful and effective survival tool a dog has, and they use it on some level throughout their lives. It is a normal canine behavior used to establish and maintain a dog's place in the group, procure or defend his food, protect himself, his territory or his group, earn a mate or react to a real or perceived threat.

Overt aggression is frightening. After 20 years of working with dogs, a deep chest or belly growl still makes my hair stand on end. Aggression comes in two basic forms, genetic and developed.

Puppies six months or younger who are seriously growling, snapping or biting usually have a genetic problem or have been badly abused. Aggression seen before six months of age usually means the aggression came in the pup. In some animals, there may not be much you can do; these pups rarely make safe, dependable pets. A young pup with a serious aggression problem cannot be given away and almost always has to be euthanized.

Puppies like this are the exception, not the rule. I say this to maybe two owners a year out of the hundreds that I see. This type of temperament is one of the major reasons it is helpful to see one or, preferably, both of your pup's parents before selecting him. If that is not possible, temperament testing is a good guide.

Breed can influence aggression. In some breeds, it is normal for pups to be aggressive at an early age. A dominant, assertive pup grows up to be a dominant, assertive adult unless you intervene. Such pups belong in only the most experienced hands, but if you own one and are determined to keep it, hire a professional trainer as soon as possible. Two months old is *not* too young to begin obedience work in a fun, light-hearted way. As soon as the pup is fully inoculated, enroll him in a puppy kindergarten

class. It is never too early to start molding your assertive pup into the safe, manageable dog that you want.

Behavioral aggression usually takes six months to a year to develop. You can see it as early as six months, but it is most common after nine months of age. Its onset coincides with sexual maturity in most cases. This is the "he never did that before" kind of aggression. Aggression builds from the first ignored command to the growl that escalates to a bite. The path between the two is predictable and well worn. My job is to tell you the landmarks to look for so you can avoid this most dangerous and distressing of canine problems.

Aggression comes in many forms and is used for many purposes. Here Rose and Julia are playing. This is a perfectly acceptable use of lower level aggression.

From a Dark Look to a Bite: The Progression of Aggression

Overconfidence is at the root of much canine aggression. Aggression rarely develops overnight. Normally and naturally submissive, a dog has to work up to aggression. He'll begin by ignoring commands. You tell him "Sit." He looks at you and walks away. If you let that disobedience slide, you're on your way to trouble. From ignoring your directions, he will probably move to a subtle threat. You tell him to get off the couch; he ignores it and freezes slightly as you go to move him off. Dogs can certainly give dirty looks and you'll probably get one then. A direct stare is a threat signal. Next, he freezes more noticeably and gives you a hard stare as you approach. He'll then progress to a throat growl both in protest and in threat.

Growls come in three distinct types, the throat growl, the chest growl and the belly growl. The throat growl is level one. It is used by young or inexperienced dogs for their first experimental threat or bluff. It would translate into something like "Hey! Don't do that! . . . Please?" You'll hear this growl during play battles as well. The chest growl is a more mature and serious growl. He is a dog that is willing to put his money where his mouth is, so to speak. If you push him, he'll probably back up the threat with a full set of teeth. The belly growl is, thankfully, rare. When you hear it, the dog is telling you that he *will* stop you if you continue whatever it is you are doing. If you hear it, that deep rumble that sounds like a train coming toward you, stop! You are in danger. One simple rule to live by: if your dog is growling, you've got trouble.

Not all dogs growl before a bite; so don't count on it to warn you. Be aware of the other signals of serious aggression: the hard look, the direct eye contact, the stiffening of the body, the stiff-legged walk, the snarling or freezing in place.

From a throat growl comes a snarl or a fast turning of the head. This is a big step for most dogs. It will take him a while to get up enough courage to try anything more than that. But if he is left unchecked, a half-snap is next, where he bites the air close to you. He

This dog is telling the cat to stay away from his dinner. He uses direct eye contact and a hard stare to get his point across. The cat respected these signals and retreated.

didn't miss. If he had wanted to bite you, he would have. In fact, that's his next move. Normally, but not always, the first bite is inhibited, leaving red marks or bruises on your skin. The dog is now rapidly learning his power.

From the bite that leaves bruises, it normally takes a few more months to get enough confidence for a hard bite that punctures skin and draws blood. A chest growl may accompany this.

Serious biters, the belly growlers, attack, ripping the flesh. They are no longer trying to back you off, they are trying to hurt you. I rarely see this type of dog, as most people take action long before this point.

Your dog may show all these signs or just a few; regardless, they all should be taken seriously. *A growl is a warning. Dismissing, overreacting to or rationalizing this warning will escalate aggression.* The first time—the very first time—you are frightened of your dog, get professional advice. Don't waste precious time hoping it will magically go away. It won't. It will happen again. It will be worse the next time.

The fear biter develops differently. He bites in a moment of panic in an effort to get you to stop whatever you are doing. If a dog is terrified, move with caution! Do not try to make him do something he does not want to do. If a dog is cowering in the corner, trying to run away or under

Eclair is snarling at the camera. What you can't see is that she is nursing puppies in this shot and does not like the stranger and the stranger's camera near her new babies. This type of aggression is common in females with pups and should be respected.

the bed, he is telling you as clearly as he can that he is frightened. If you are fool enough to reach under that bed or into that corner, then you have left him with no other option—he must bite. And he will, sometimes a quick inhibited bite, sometimes a harder puncture bite. Either way, you deserved it.

A dog that is frightened and not on lead should be left alone while you call a professional. Do not punish a fear biter for biting. Any yelling or hitting will only create more fear, increasing, not decreasing, your problem.

Common Mistakes Owners of Aggressive Dogs Make

Owners of aggressive dogs can make mistakes that make matters worse. You must intervene with effective, humane methods as soon as you think your dog is considering aggression. If you're not sure, ask a professional trainer or behaviorist to evaluate your dog.

The first and most common error people make is not teaching or using their obedience work. People save commands for special occasions for some reason instead of integrating it into their daily life. Dominance is psychological, not physical. If you tell him to down and he lies down, you have dominated the dog. Using commands to direct the dog is more effective than reacting to the growling. Remember, the growling is the symptom. Lack of direction, fear or confusion are the real causes of aggression. Obedience is the best, least-confrontational way that there is to assert your leadership, gain control of your animal and keep tabs on his mental state. It's easy and it's fun. There is no excuse for not using it. If your dog is growling, get working!

It is easy to dismiss aggression.

I am demonstrating what **not** to do. If this was a real situation, my tightening on the lead, getting tense and holding my breath would all be danger signals for this dog.

After all, it happens so rarely. Most of the time your beloved pet is an angel, or at least close to one. "He's so good with the family." "He doesn't bite, he just nips a little." "Surely that snap was a mistake." Wrong. A dog that growls is not "just talking." He is not allowed to snap because he was "on his chair" or "had his bone." Those things are yours, not his. You're letting him use them. Keep that in mind.

There are many reasons for aggression but few excuses. *If your dog growls, snarls or snaps at anyone, it is serious. If he puts his teeth on a human being, he is **extremely** serious.* Aggression never gets better on its own, it only gets worse.

It is easy, when the dog starts to growl or snap, to focus on that as the problem. It rarely is. It is the symptom of a larger miscommunication. I was speaking today to friends whose dog is becoming a dog fighter and unreliable around people. This dog had been growling for many months, but they had refused to do anything about it, not wanting to believe that their beloved pet could be aggressive. By dismissing the signs, they allowed an easily cured problem to bloom into a difficult mess. See it early, deal with it early.

Soothing the aggressive dog is another unproductive activity. "It's OK, Barney, it's just the mailman," said with a concerned voice while stroking the dog, is supposed to calm him, but instead it *rewards* him. He mistakes your kind words and gentle touch for praise and increases his aggression.

Once the dog has shown aggression, the "uh-oh" response develops. This is the natural tendency of people to dread dealing with an aggressive incident. When they see a potential one about to develop they tighten the lead, stiffen their body, take a deep breath and say "uh-oh." These things cue the dog that something dangerous is happening.

Overreaction creates more problems for both the dog and the owner. Yelling, screaming, hitting and harsh corrections actually increase the problem. What was a minor attempt to test his boundaries has now been made into a federal case.

What won't go away is your dog's breed. Working and guard breeds have been selected for centuries for their ability to protect their owner, their owner's property and themselves. I have had several incidences of such animals "turning" on their owners, and in *every* case, the owners turned on the dog first. If you attack a dog that was bred to defend itself, what do you think it will do? You purchased him, at least in part, for his ability to defend himself, and he will, against you if you force him. Owning a large working breed entails a high level of responsibility. If you don't socialize and train the dog properly, expect problems.

The most common mistake that develops aggression is lack of proper socialization. Sometimes people don't realize it's important, sometimes life just gets busy, and sometimes people think that by isolating their pet they will create a wonderful watchdog. Not true. A good watch dog knows the difference between friend and foe and he learns to recognize that difference through socialization. Take your pup with you whenever you can. If you have an adult dog, take him to group classes. The more exposure to the world he gets the calmer and more stable he will be.

All dogs need love, but I would never hug this particular dog if he wasn't muzzled. He bites people who pet him. I am doing this intentionally to get him used to human handling. Hugging and kissing the back of the neck is a dominant gesture on my part, one he might interpret as a challenge. If your dog is aggressive, do not do this with your dog.

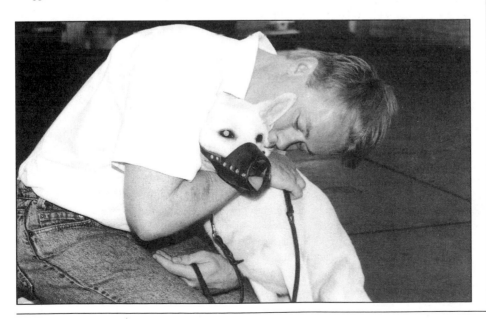

JOHN DEERE: One Dangerous Dog

The three boys met me at the front door. They were all excited that the trainer had arrived. Both parents were home, so we all sat down at the kitchen table to discuss the problem. J.D., short for John Deere, they explained, was beginning to bark a bit at children through the fence. They did not think this was a real problem but were uncomfortable with his behavior. They said he really was a sweet dog, just a bit overprotective of the yard. This was early in my career, before I learned the art of thorough questioning, an art John Deere taught me to cultivate. I said I'd be happy to take a look.

As we stepped out onto the brick patio, one of the largest St. Bernards I have ever seen came running across the yard at me. All 210 pounds of him slid to a halt, hesitated a half-second, and mounted me. Putting a massive front paw on each shoulder, he almost forced me to the ground. I staggered under the weight. His basketball-sized head was next to mine; his low threatening growling filled my ears. I was in real trouble here. "Call your dog," I said through clenched teeth, as I hopped across the patio, propelled sideways with every thrust. It was all I could do to keep my balance under the onslaught. When I spoke, the growl deepened, until it sounded like it came from the center of the earth. If you move, the growl assured me, you will be hurt.

The father had obviously never seen anything quite like this. He stood slack-jawed and immobile on the patio. The wife, equally as mesmerized, had her hand over her mouth in surprise. The three boys, watching from the kitchen window, were howling with laughter.

"Call your dog," I said sweetly as I could under the circumstance. Any strong use of voice would have caused an attack. "Call him, now!" Finally the man snapped out of his daze and called the dog off. J.D. left reluctantly. I leaned against the house for a moment, shaking, adrenaline pumping through my system. As we went inside, J.D. stood at the door, growling.

The parents shook their heads. "What's the problem with these dogs?" they asked me. "This is our third one, they've all been like this." Coincidence? Not at all. They were unknowing experts on how to raise an aggressive dog.

It turns out J.D. had been raised in the backyard, purchased "for the boys." The parents did little but give him food and water. The boys played boy games with the dog—lots of tug-of-war, wrestling and teasing. They and their friends played poke-the-dog-through-the-fence games and laughed when he growled or grabbed the stick. He had never left the backyard. He had never met anyone but immediate family. Now two years old and unneutered, he was king of all he surveyed. J.D. was a disaster wanting to happen.

I told them the truth: "You have no choices. Either you return the dog to the breeder, if she'll take him, or you euthanize the dog." They returned him to the breeder, who herself euthanized the dog six months later. A terrible waste and not the dog's fault.

The Overprotective Dog: The Triumph of Midnight

Mr. M. met me at the door. He was well over six feet and built like a weight lifter. When he shook my hand, I could feel his strength. Midnight met me at the door as well. He yapped as I entered. Running back and forth, trying to drive me out with every step I took in. I directed Mr. M. to put the dog on lead. Mrs. M. complied. When I asked what the problem was, they led me into the bedroom and explained their plight.

Mrs. M. always went to bed earlier than Mr. M., as he worked nights. Midnight slept on the bed next to her. When Mr. M. came home, Midnight would not allow him into bed. Mr. M. had been sleeping on the couch for a month now. The last straw was when he tried to pick up the dog and put him on the floor one night. Midnight latched on to his finger and would not let go. Mr. M. shook his hand but the dog held on.

Hearing this story, I laughed. This man was easily 250 pounds. Midnight was twelve pounds. "Who else could keep you out of your own bed for a month?" I said.

He cracked a smile too. "He scares me," he explained.

"I can understand that." I sympathized. I've been on the end of the lead opposite a lot of aggressive dogs, and big or small, they can frighten anyone.

The problem started with Mrs. M., who was sometimes frightened when home alone at night. She liked it when Midnight started showing signs of protecting her; it made her feel safer. When the dog started growling at her husband, Mrs. M. tried to calm him. "It's only Daddy," she said soothingly, stroking the dog. What the poodle understood was his owner was praising him for growling. If you own a dog that growls at other family members or guests in your home, follow these steps:

• Start working on that obedience right away. It is critical that he take your direction instantaneously and without question. Aggressive dogs have to obey immediately, and that only comes with lots of practice.

• Teach the dog to "say hello." This is done with the dog on lead. Have someone the dog knows and loves walk into the house. Tell the dog "Say hello" as you walk up to the "guest." (This can be a family member at first. As long as the dog loves the person, use anyone you want.) Have the guest stand still turned sideways to the dog, avoid eye contact and hold out a treat as the dog approaches. You walk right up to the person and stand next to them, *laugh* and chat in a *relaxed*, happy way. Be sure to use extra good treats here. Fast the dog for a meal if necessary. Once the dog learns this routine, you can use someone the dog knows a bit less but who is still not a stranger. Repeat until the dog eagerly approaches the person on the command "Say hello." If you find the dog is tense, work outside of your home. Once off their territory, most dogs relax considerably.

You're on your way! Move to more unfamiliar people. The "Say hello" command will not ruin him as a watchdog, so don't worry about that.

CAUTION!

The steps I outline here are general guidelines. If you own an aggressive animal, you should seek professional assistance immediately. Never do anything with or to your dog if you are unsure or concerned about your dog's reaction. Respect your gut reactions; you may not know exactly why you're frightened, but there is probably a good reason. Do **not** proceed. Call a reputable trainer or behaviorist. Aggression is dangerous; never dismiss or underestimate it, or believe it will go away on its own.

Some facts I have witnessed over the years:

• Serious aggression most often develops between the ages of one and three.

• Serious biters are most often intact male dogs.

• Children get bitten most frequently.

• If a child is bitten, it is usually on the face or hands.

• Aggressive dogs come in all breeds, shapes and sizes.

• Once a breed becomes popular, aggression problems are never far behind.

• Most owners knew there was a problem and ignored it, allowing a bite to occur.

• People sue over dog bites these days.

• In cases concerning biting dogs, the dogs always lose, regardless of fences, warnings or innocence. It does not matter.

If someone comes to the door that you don't know, don't tell your dog to say hello.

• He's grounded! He works for everything. No one even acknowledges his existence until he has responded to a command in some way. Second-guessing you—sitting before being told to, say—does not count.

• Get him off your lap, couch, bed or chairs. Being on the same level makes some dogs think they are your equal. Being on the furniture also allows the dog to look you eye to eye as your equal. Bad behavior means he loses all privileges.

• Keep him on lead. You need that control.

• If he is aggressive toward one person in the house, like Midnight is to Mr. M., then all care, attention, feeding and play becomes Mr. M.'s job. Mrs. M. should ignore the dog. Do this for a minimum of two weeks, and Midnight will stop viewing Mr. M. as the villain.

The overprotective dog is no asset. Half the time, people with dogs like this have to lock them in the back room when guests come over. How much protection can a dog be locked away? The best protection in the world is a devoted, well-trained dog. When strangers see a dog perform obedience instantly, they figure that this is something they do not want to deal with. They can't tell just how much training your dog has had.

The Territorial Dog: The Mailman's Nightmare

Most dogs are protective of their territory. Mirko took it to a high degree indeed. When I was called in on this case, Mirko, the intact male German Shepherd owned by the Consulate General of the West German Embassy, had already treed numerous visitors and several gardeners on car roofs and eaten his way through a garage door during a dinner party.

This couple leads a busy life. Between meetings and social obligations, they were seldom home. People came in and out of the house constantly. With no one to guide him, Mirko did what all dogs do when left to their own devices: he reverted to his heritage. A bored Golden Retriever will retrieve balls all day, urging, with wagging tail and eager bark, anyone to throw them. A Irish Terrier will probably dig if unsupervised. Mirko, being who and what he was, decided that his job was to attack whoever came to his home. And he took this job seriously.

Mirko had been worked with, unsuccessfully, by three other trainers before me. They all had concentrated on correcting him, no one bothered

A good fence keeps your dog from wandering but it can also make him confident and bold about protecting "his" territory. Don't leave a dog in a yard unsupervised.

WHY DOGS LOVE TO HATE MAILMEN

Every day your mailman comes up your walk. Every day your dog barks at him. Every day your mailman leaves, going on to your neighbors. And every day your dog thinks that he drove this intruder away with his barking. Doing this daily raises your dog's self-confidence level, leading him to believe he can drive any threat from the door.

Over time, your dog can develop a real drive to get that person who comes up the walk at the same time every day. He'll wait by the window as the time nears. This challenge from an "intruder" and successfully forcing his retreat become the main event in his day.

Poor mailman. All they are doing is delivering the mail. They are not trying to be come the main object of hatred in your dog's life.

to teach him; to take direction or make friends.

I solved this problem using the following tools:

• Obedience must become second nature to these dogs. Do your basics, then work on distractions. The more you can get him distracted and then command him in training sessions, the more immediate his response will be in a real situation.

• Ground him! These dogs need direction and self-control, grounding is the quickest, easiest and most effective way to achieve that control.

• Do not allow him to be harassed. A great many dogs get teased through fences. If you can't supervise the dog, do not put him outside.

• Neuter him.

• Socialize him. Take him every place you can. Enroll in a local obedience class.

• Set up the situation. Have him on lead during all training. *Praise him when he alerts;* after all, you like it that he tells you someone's at the door, right? You just want him to stop after that. After you thank him for a job well done, then command him to down. Correct him if he continues to bark. Praise the moment he stops. If he is calm, teach him to say hello by having guests give him food rewards when you walk him up to them. Be happy. Laughter is incompatible with fear and aggression; use it to set the proper tone.

• Keep him on lead when you have a guest. Not only will these dogs become aggressive when people enter your home, but some will take a nip as the person leaves. Prepare for this by putting him in a "Down"/"Stay" when your guests exit. Praise him warmly for holding the position. If he does not hold it, correct him firmly back into place. This is not optional. He must take his direction from you, not decide on his own what is appropriate for this situation. Obedience must override his desire to attack.

The Fearful Dog

Scotch, a butterscotch-colored mix of Golden Retriever and something, was deathly afraid of the vet. He began to tremble the moment he realized he was nearing the vet's office. His nervousness built in the waiting room. Increasingly tense, he began growling when he heard anyone walking down the hall toward the waiting room. Doing a basic exam on Scotch was a trauma for everyone. He tried to bite the vet and scramble off the table. It took three assistants and a muzzle to make it through a simple exam.

Successfully handling situations like this requires a combination of setting a positive, happy tone and applying appropriate, decisive correction. Be no-nonsense, but do not escalate. You must remain calm if you want the dog to. He's expecting disaster at any moment; anger or upset will support his worst fears, making matters worse.

• Do not soothe, reassure or coddle a fearful dog. You can't make this better for him by becoming submissive and forfeiting your leadership, which is exactly what your dog will think you have done.

• Act as you want the dog to act. This is critical for the fear biter. Laugh, be happy! Few dogs have been hurt when their owner is happy, so the mood relaxes them. Scotch relaxed so much he fell asleep on the vet's table!

• Socialize this type of dog. Enroll in obedience classes, take him over to friends' houses, do errands with him. The more he sees, the less he'll fear.

• Use treats, play or anything the dog enjoys to help change his feelings of dread into eager anticipation and fun! Have your vet be the bearer of treats.

• Handle him frequently at home in ways that vets or groomers have to. This way, when he is at those places, he will be used to what is done.

• Do obedience work. Not only will this build his confidence and calm him, but it will reinforce his image of you as the trusted leader, capable of handling anything that comes your way. With that belief, he will look to you for direction instead of worrying.

• Do not rush the training process. Fear can take a long time to conquer successfully. Gradually introduce the people or situations your dog fears, noting when your dog gets tense. Work slowly, concentrating on setting a relaxed, positive tone. Your dog can sense your moods exactly, so if you're not comfortable, he won't be either. Please see pages 64–65 for more instruction on handling the fearful dog.

If a dog shows fear, respect that. Don't chase after him or you may force him to defend itself.

The Possessive Dog

Ginger, a buff male American Cocker Spaniel, stood over the rawhide. Head low, eyes glaring up at me, body tense, he had taken his stand and dared me to come in after him. I declined his offer. "Ginger, come," I said cheerfully, giving the lead a quick pop. As he came toward me, I praised heartily. "What a good dog!" I said sincerely, smiling.

Just because a dog wants to have an argument doesn't mean you have to do so. By having him obey a command, I taught him an alternative

I just told Caras "Down." For an aggressive dog, I recommend 100 or more downs a day.

behavior and asserted my leadership, without confrontation. Many dogs become aggressive because certain situations almost always lead to a confrontation. The minute the dog is in the situation, he begins to get tense. The vast majority of animals are only too happy to avoid a fight if they are shown a sensible alternative.

After we got past that tense moment, I took out some treats and taught "Leave it" and "Out." These are required learning for the possessive dog. Here are some other ways of interacting with this type of animal:

• Ground him. This is old news, but grounding is always necessary and it *always* works if you really do it, cutting no corners. Daily and integrated obedience asserts your leadership many times a day, preventing him from slowly building to challenge your authority. It also allows you to keep close tabs on his mental outlook. Resistance to known commands is a sure sign of a bad attitude. Even though these are serious sessions, keep them light. All dogs need praise, love and encouragement; you're just giving those things in a structured and positive way. Ninety percent of the time it is the behavior, not the dog, that is "bad."

• Keep him on lead. This type of dog may be ready for trouble the moment you come toward him. Using a lead allows you to prevent aggression by having control without reaching at the dog.

• Stay happy. Few dogs have had

major battles when they are being praised. It will defuse much of their tension.

• Do **not** fight with the dog. When he is over something, growling, this is not the time to train him. Just work through the situation either by ignoring him, calling him or giving him an alternative command. Once past the crisis, kick yourself. The dog is not supposed to get into these situations during training unless you set it up and have complete control.

• If your dog is aggressive around bones, rawhides or some other toy, throw them out. Who needs this in their life? A normally peaceful dog can become aggressive over a real butcher bone, so I don't recommend them.

• Practice giving him the articles and then taking them away. Stay relaxed. Use praise freely. Read your dog! If he looks tense, or you feel frightened, don't try to take it. If that happens, or anytime your dog takes something which you can't get away from him, pick up the lead and work on your commands. Ignore the item in his mouth. The obedience work will assert your leadership without confrontation. A dog will usually drop the item on his own after a minute or two of command work.

• Booby-trap the items he likes to be possessive of with a few shake cans. That will teach him not to take them and run!

Aggression with Children

A parent's nightmare, a dog owner's dread—few things are as upsetting as your dog being aggressive toward or biting a child. The good news is that, considering the number of children and dogs in this country, it doesn't happen very much. The bad news is thousands of children a day get treated by a doctor or hospital for dog bites. That's thousands too many.

The number one cause of bites between dogs and children is lack of parental supervision. Leaving a dog alone with a child is like leaving two toddlers in the same room, one with a pair of scissors. Even the best dog in the world can bite if he is surprised or hurt. Sarah got a call from an upset father whose Doberman bitch had just bitten his toddler in the face. He was frantic.

"What happened?" Sarah inquired.

"I saw the whole thing out the window," he explained. "My boy ran up to the dog and bit her on the ear. She spun around and bit him."

"Where exactly was he bitten," Sarah inquired further.

"He has two red marks at his hair line on his forehead and more under his chin."

This dog had the child's whole face in her mouth and yet did nothing but frighten the boy. She had the opportunity and the reason to do seri-ous damage, yet she chose not to. Now *that's* a good dog!

"Do I have to kill her?" he asked anxiously.

"No! She behaved quite well considering," Sarah said. "Control that boy of yours. The dog sounds fine."

More questioning revealed that the child chased the dog around with a Wiffle Ball bat and liked to stick things in her ears. Here was one patient dog and one foolish parent.

The basic rule to live by with children and dogs is "Do not allow your child to do to the dog what you would not allow done to a younger sibling." This rule covers chasing around the house, harassing, teasing, pinching, kicking, screaming in ears, jumping on top of or otherwise hurting the dog. Breaches of this rule should be handled speedily and with seriousness. After all, even if your dog is saintly enough to tolerate this abuse, someone else's dog won't be. Your child's safety is in the balance.

Some dogs plain don't like kids. If your dog seems to have a real aversion, respect this and keep the two apart. Some dogs have never been exposed to kids. If they reach adulthood without ever meeting children, they may genuinely not know what children are—never mind who they are. Have him meet some quiet, well-mannered children first. Allow the dog to come up and sniff them at his own speed. Stand near the children and chat with them; this will help relax the dog. If he seems tense, tell the children to ignore him. Have them toss treats toward him without speaking or looking at him. Children often stare, a behavior most dogs interpret as rude and some as a threat.

Children being children can

annoy dogs. Screaming, moving rapidly, jumping up and down or running at the dog can frighten some animals, particularly those who have been hit or beaten. These dogs associate yelling, running at them, and fast movements with being attacked. Kids can frighten these dogs, making them defensive.

Because children are young, dogs can perceive them as competitors for rank in the group. Dogs might freely challenge them, though they might not dare to challenge an adult. If your dog is competitive with your child, help the kid out. You hold the lead while the child gives the commands. If the dog does not respond, you enforce the command, but do not look at or acknowledge the dog when you do so. The child praises the dog. This will help to establish your child's leadership without putting him or her in the position of competing with the dog. Once the dog is responding freely to the child's commands, then the child can hold the lead. Use a food reward if your dog doesn't get too wild. Have the child tell the dog "Sit," "Come" and especially "Down."

Children copy your behavior. If you are yelling at or hitting the dog, the child will, too. Not good. Set an example of sensitivity, respect and kindness toward the dog, and your child will follow your lead.

Children need to be taught not to bother a dog when he's eating, chewing or sleeping. But when the children are away or asleep, you should be teaching your dog to accept this type of surprise. Walk up to him while he is chewing a toy, take it away, give him a treat, then give it back. Walk up to him when he is eating, toss in an extra-good yummy, then walk away. Wake him gently from a nap, give him a treat, then leave him be. Do this regularly, but not frequently, throughout the week. If you do it too much, your dog may come to resent the interruptions. The idea is to condition him to wag his tail when a human approaches. With supervision, training and common sense, most dogs can learn to enjoy the company of well-behaved and supervised children.

This dog is obviously relaxed with this little girl. Exposing her belly like that is a trusting and submissive gesture which should be encouraged by the parents and the child.

Dog Fighters

When dogs greet each other, dominance and submission are established within minutes. The dominant dog holds himself erect, moves slowly, or he may playfully put his paws on the other's back. The submissive dog may put his head down, ears back, run off playfully, inviting a chase, and will accept the other's paws on his back. The problem comes when neither dog submits. When they both stand erect, move slowly or try to put their paws on each other's backs, watch out!

Chronic dog fighters are dogs that are dominant, afraid or have been attacked in the past. When they greet a dog, they are tense. Either they attempt to establish their dominance immediately, or they are highly sensitized to any dominant gesture or threat from the other dog.

Dogs can also develop hatred for an individual or breed. Often this is caused by an attack by a particular dog or similar dogs earlier in the animal's life.

This problem can be dealt with in

part, but do not expect that you'll ever be able to let your dog play with other dogs. A fighter may learn some self-control and tolerance, but if a young whippersnapper bumps him or some brash dog tries to mount him, he is unlikely to be tolerant, even with training. Start getting control of this problem with the following techniques:

• Neuter your male dog. Not only will this lessen his aggression level, but other dogs will not be as competitive with him since he will no longer smell like a threat.

• Keep your lead loose. Your corrections will be more effective. If you shorten the lead and hold your breath, as many people do when another dog approaches their fighter, you signal him to become protective. It is similar to you walking down the street with a friend. She gasps suddenly and grabs your arm hard. You're going to go on alert. Something is wrong; you'll check all around to locate and identify the threat. That's exactly what happens with your dog when you tighten on the lead. Be prepared, ready to correct if necessary, but don't telegraph your apprehension to the dog.

• Work on your obedience, particularly "Leave it" and "Let's go." When he spots another dog, take the attitude of "Fine, you can pay attention to him if you want, but I'm going to become very demanding." Rapid-fire turns, speed changes, and command series force the dog to choose between paying attention to the dog and paying attention to you. Be demanding. Eye contact is critical to the buildup of aggression. Use "Leave it" to insist that he break eye contact with the approaching dog. If he has to watch you, he can't challenge the other dog. No eye contact, no challenge, no fight.

• Don't panic. Many of my clients stop dead in their tracks when they spot another dog coming. They wrap the lead around their hands, hold the dog tight to them, hold their breath and generally signal the dog in every way that there's trouble. Keep moving. Sound relaxed, even if you aren't. Start with your turns and commands. Give him something else to think about.

• Ground him! If he sees you as the leader, he will be more responsive to you in this distracting situation.

DISPLACE-MENT BITING

Displacement biting is a dangerous problem. This is when a dog is in an aggressive frenzy but cannot reach his object of aggression, so he turns his aggression on the closest thing to him. I've seen dogs like this, one a top show dog, attack other innocent animals and people when in this state. Such an animal is unstable and extremely dangerous. Do not attempt to correct this type of dog when he is in an aggressive state. Movement around him at those moments will simply focus him on you. When dogs like this are highly excited, they are not in their right minds. They will not "see" you as the person they love. He will not know what he is doing or has done. Immediately seek the advice of a qualified professional trainer or behaviorist. This is not a problem you should attempt to handle by yourself.

Good Dogs, Foolish Choices

The butler opened the door with the hand that wasn't bandaged. I heard a big dog barking somewhere in the house. The family met me in the library: the father, an intellectual businessman; his cherubic daughter, a sweet, polite and beautiful girl of six; and his teenage son, tall and thin like his father. The father explained that he had purchased this 18-month-old intact male Rottweiler with impeccable bloodlines, the best money could buy, when he was in Germany. The dog had been raised in the breeder's backyard. They had owned the dog for two weeks and it had already bitten four people.

The dog was a solid, gorgeous Rottweiler, an easy 135 pounds. He trotted into the room, off lead, circled the table, then sat in front of me attempting to make direct eye contact. When I put on the lead, he attacked me. He continued to attempt to do me serious bodily harm for five minutes (an extremely long five minutes) during which time he showed a high level of intelligence and problem-solving ability. He did what I had never, in my 20 years of doing this, seen a dog do. He put his two front paws over the lead, pressed down hard, grabbed a section of lead in his mouth, put his paws above on the lead, pressed down hard, and grabbed higher up. It took all my skill and experience to avoid being mauled by this dog. To make a long story short, I recommended placing this dog with a professional breeder. They did.

Not all mismatches are so obvious. A dominant dog can be tough on an owner that wants to be able to cuddle the dog nonstop. A fearful dog can be miserable in an active, loud family. A normal, healthy terrier may lose patience with the physical maulings of a toddler. These are not bad dogs, they are just the wrong dogs for their situations. Some popular breeds are not good choices for the novice owner. Research before you buy. This is 10 years, or more, of emotional, time and financial commitment, not something to be done impulsively.

Sometimes you can work a bad selection out, sometimes it is kinder and easier for everyone to place the animal in an more appropriate home. If it is a pure breed, contact the rescue group for that club, if there is one. If your dog is aggressive, you have few options. A shelter usually cannot adopt out such a dog. If you don't tell the new owner about the problem and a bite occurs and they find out that you knew the dog was aggressive, you could be in legal trouble. So if you suspect that you and your dog are mismatched, get some training, get the word out, and often you can place the animal in a loving home if you are willing to take some time doing so.

Not every breed is for everyone. The larger, assertive breeds demand a high level of expertise to own and train successfully. Learn about your breed before investing emotions and finances in one that may not work out for you.

The Predatory Dog

Dogs love to chase balls, sticks, cats, squirrels, bicycles, kids on skateboards—just about anything that moves. The predatory dog chases with aggression thrown in. His ancestors had to kill for survival, and those instincts are alive and well in the predatory dog.

Almost any dog can become dangerously aggressive when he is chasing an animal, runner or bicycle. If two dogs are chasing the animal, the danger to the chased increases dramatically. Once dogs form a pack, all their primal buttons are pushed.

If your dog is a predator, take the following steps:

• Work on your obedience until "Leave it," "Let's go" and "Come" are well instilled. If you can't get an excellent response to these words under normal circumstances, forget stopping him midchase. Make him choose between watching you and watching what he likes to chase. Use 90-degree right turns and right about turns to get his attention. Correct him if he misses your turn. Praise him well if he follows you.

• Do not encourage him to chase. Often a puppy or dog is egged on by someone saying "Go get 'em, boy." Don't add fuel to the fire.

• Set him up on a long line. Let him think he is off lead, then point him at an animal or thing he loves to chase. When he takes off after it, wait until the long line is just about taut and say "Come" in a calm voice. When he hits the end of the line, laugh and praise him back to you. Tell him to sit and go home for the day. Do it again tomorrow. If he is a big dog, you may have to let him start his chase and then run in the opposite direction to get up enough velocity to make an impact on his focused brain. A pair of gloves makes this easier on your hands. Your goal is to teach him that you have the power to reach him at a distance and that "Come" means right now!

• Set up the situation if he is a car chaser. Have an assistant throw water balloons or three shake cans loosely tethered together at him from a moving car. Never leave a car chaser off lead and unsupervised.

Sarah took this picture in Turkey from a boat. There was nothing she could do to prevent it or stop it. The cat ran off, apparently unhurt.

More about Aggression

THE ABUSED DOG

These poor dogs have been beaten in a previous home. Now, in certain situations, they get ready for battle. You'll see them tense up, freeze in position. Do not fight with them. Do not yell at them. Such treatment will only reinforce their fears. Laugh, praise them, call them to you. By behaving as if nothing is wrong, you are teaching them nothing is wrong.

Use obedience training to build you dog's confidence in himself and his trust in you. A hesitant dog will benefit from food reward. It lets him know that you are "good news." Don't make excuses for a dog's behavior because he was abused; that does not help the dog. He needs to feel like part of a team, and obedience work is the best way to establish that.

THE FERAL DOG

Feral means wild. Dogs become wild not just from running loose; if they are left in a backyard to raise themselves, they can be just as wild as a raccoon. If a dog spends his puppyhood in the wild, he will never make a reliable pet.

It may break your heart, but it is rare that such a dog can adjust to home life.

PACK BEHAVIOR

Six otherwise well-behaved dogs that had been let out of their kennel by the 10-year-old left in charge got hold of a toddler when the parents were not around. The 10-year-old tried to stop the attack with no success. The toddler was horribly mauled when the police rescued him.

Chances are, the dogs did not start out aggressive. Maybe one grabbed the baby's hand because there was a cookie in it, or pulled at the diaper because it smelled interesting. When the child began to flail his arms, other dogs became curious. Was this a game? Maybe one bounced at the child, or the child got frightened and began to scream. Once that started, the dogs would have become highly agitated.

Do not allow your dog to run loose. No matter how wonderful, how trained, how socialized your dog is, he is still and will always be a dog. Children and dogs should always have adult supervision. Always. Do not forget that.

THE ORPHANED DOG

Orphaned pups, even those raised with care, can have real and irreparable problems. Pups learn from each other, and from Mom, about how to inhibit aggression. Without that early experience, inhibition never properly develops. These normally sweet animals can become dangerous in a matter of moments. If you have an orphaned pup, put him with older, well-socialized dogs as soon as possible. A dog that will be tolerant but will pin the pup when he needs it is worth his weight in dog biscuits. Early training is a must!

A puppy play group, such as this one at Sarah's and my business The Family Dog, will alert you to any serious problems early. Serious problems are uncommon; mostly, it's just lots of fun.

TYSON: The Dangerous Dog

I first met Tyson in a puppy play group we used to run at our training facility on the West Side of Manhattan. Sarah called me in to take a look. When I entered the room, Tyson, a handsome five-month-old Dalmatian, was hiding in the corner. Whenever another pup came by, he cowered into his hiding spot more. When no other dog was bothering him, he entertained himself by digging at the shadow on the floor. I knew we had trouble.

As he matured, he became increasingly odd and aggressive. Finally, one day when we were boarding him, he snapped at the veterinarian, Dr. Freedman, who had squatted down to say hello. Tyson wagged his tail, came on over, and then, as he got petted, spun suddenly and snapped at the veterinarian's face. When I saw friendliness turn to aggression in an instant with no warning or reason, I called the owner and said that the dog should be destroyed. She became angry, not wanting to believe her beloved pet was dangerous. She picked him up and we did not hear from her until she called six months later. She had just euthanized him. She had tried other trainers and gotten a full medical workup, but after Tyson savaged her twice while she was stroking him, she knew she had no other choice. (On a happy note, we found her another dog, a delightfully odd-looking Deerhound mix. They are happily devoted to each other.)

Some dogs are crazy. And when they are, there is little you can do. The common type of insanity is Tyson's, a link between pleasure and aggression, that makes them unpredictable and dangerous. His owner had no other choice. She tried every avenue, gave it her best shot. Sometimes, euthanasia is the kindest and only option.

MEDICAL SOLUTIONS

Neutering: I recommend that all dogs that are not stable in temperament and of champion quality be neutered. All dogs with aggression problems should be altered no matter how beautiful they are. Neutering is not a miracle cure, but it does do two things for dogs with these problems. One, it makes them more accepting of your leadership, and two, it will lessen other dogs' aggression toward your dog. Both sexes are considerably stabilized by the operation. And for all you men out there that can't separate your feelings for your own body from your feelings about your dog, get over it. Just because you are able to control the dog, that doesn't mean your wife or children can. They are surely more important than your dog's testicles.

Drugs: Although I do not recommend them often, there are drugs available that can help to relax your aggressive dog, making retraining more simple and effective. Some relaxants are also disinhibitors, meaning if your dog gets aggressive, he will bite harder and faster. Be sure to discuss with your vet all the possible impacts on your dog before you start him on any drug. Any drug therapy must be done under veterinary supervision. NO EXCEPTIONS.

When No Solution Works: Euthanizing the Aggressive Dog

Choosing to take the life of an animal you care about is a miserable choice. When there are medical reasons, it is a hard choice. When there are behavioral reasons, it is even harder. It is tough not to say to yourself "Maybe if I tried one more thing, read one more book, did something differently, this would stop."

Trust that if you are considering this option, you have tried everything you can think of, have sought the proper advice from more than one source, and no improvement has been seen. The heartbreaking thing about aggression is that a dog with this problem is fine 90% of the time: friendly, loving, playful, sweet as long as things are going his way. The question is, when things aren't going his way, that other 10% of the time, what does he do?

If your dog has bitten repeatedly and seriously, if your dog's aggression is unpredictable, if it seems to be getting worse despite what you are doing, if you have discussed the problem with a trainer or behaviorist and a vet and they agree, then you have to consider this option.

There are dogs out there that will never be pets. Dogs that, through an accident of genetics, trauma or training, are too aggressive or unpredictable to be safe. Frequency does not necessarily define the problem. Your dog may only bite occasionally, but if it is serious, you've got a real problem.

If you can't keep the dog, you can't give him away either. Skipping over the legal implications, you're probably the best home possible for this animal—definitely, if you're concerned enough to be reading this book. If you love him, don't let him be bounced from home to home, probably to be treated with less love and understanding than he is getting with you, only to end up confused, bewildered and alone, in a cage, to meet his death among strangers.

If you love your dog, end his life with as much love and caring as you had him live it.

Living with the Older Dog

There is gray around his muzzle. He is slow in getting up in the morning, taking a few stiff steps before he loosens up. He doesn't respond to his name as readily as he used to and sleeps a great deal of the time. He's getting old.

Dogs age at different rates. The average 50-pound dog usually lives a 10- to 12-year life. In general, the smaller the dog is, the longer he lives. A Yorkshire Terrier or Chihuahua can easily live til 15 or older. The reverse is also true, the bigger they are the younger they die. An Irish Wolfhound or Great Dane is gray at seven and frequently dies well before 10.

Regardless of the breed, prepare for some new needs and special problems that come with age.

BEDDING
Even if your dog has never used a bed before, choosing instead to lie on the cool tile or by the door, he will want one as he ages. The beanbag beds work well as do the ones made for older dogs. Avoid beds that require a lot of climbing into and out of. That can get difficult as he ages.

INCONTINENCE
Dogs can lose bladder control as they age. If you begin to find puddles around the house, you can either walk him more often or confine him to the kitchen or bathroom, with his bed and papers. Do not punish him for these mistakes; if he could help them, he would. *Take him to the vet when this starts;* a diet change or medication may help.

BLINDNESS
If your dog starts losing his vision, see the section following this one on training the special dog.

DEAFNESS
See the next section for instructions on working with a deaf dog. Even if you have always walked your dog off lead (something I never encourage), put him on lead now. He can wander off at this age and not hear your calls. Don't take that chance.

This lovely old face belongs to Brandy. Muzzle graying, eyes clouding, Brandy is a beloved member of the household, as the bandana attests.

Diet

Many dogs reach this advanced stage in life fat. Even if they are not heavy yet, it may be time for a senior diet. These diets, especially formulated for the older dog, put less strain on his kidneys, are lower in fat and easier to digest. Speak to your veterinarian if you have any questions.

See Your Vet

From here on in, see your vet twice a year or as often as he recommends. Health problems caught early are easier to deal with than those left to develop into problems. He will probably need teeth cleaning on a fairly regular basis as he ages.

Protect Him

Active children, noisy crowds, loud parties which he used to love may now confuse or annoy him. Watch for his reaction. If he wants to be left alone, make sure he is.

Boarding

As he matures, try to locate a friend or professional service that will take care of the dog in your or their home.

Brandy enjoys her bed, using it to take naps and just to rest. Older dogs should have a comfortable spot in every room you all spend time in. It doesn't have to be fancy, an old folded blanket is fine.

Even the best boarding kennel in the world can be stressful on an older dog. Keeping him in a home environment can make your being away easier on him. When you do travel, call your vet and make arrangements in case your dog needs care in your absence. Tell this to whoever is caring for the dog and leave the telephone number and detailed directions to the veterinary hospital. Regardless of the care given, some older dogs will get sick when you're away. It is easy to blame the kennel or housesitter, but it probably was not their fault. Change of any kind can be stressful on the older dog.

GROOMING

Dogs that actively wore down their nails as younger animals may need regular pedicures as they slow down a bit. Overly long nails can be painful for the dog and make it difficult for him to get good footing. Regular brushing and weekly health checks will keep you aware of lumps, warts and skin changes as they develop.

Older pets often crave your attention and affection. Go on and give it to them, they deserve it. Frequent handling ensures that you will notice any lumps or physical changes as they develop.

Saying Good-bye to Your Old Friend: Euthanizing the Older Dog

A dog can easily be one of the longest and most steady relationships we have in this day and age. They see us through marriage and divorce, hiring and firing, childbirth and the death of loved ones, without ever wavering in their devotion.

Losing such a friend is devastating. The fact that he is an animal and not a person does not, as some mistakenly believe, make the loss less important. When I lost Beau to cancer, holding him in my arms as they injected the drug, I lost my best friend. I did not get out of bed for three days after that. I feel his loss to this day. I also remember the joy, love and pride he brought into my life.

The loss of a pet is a family loss. Making a scrapbook of the dog's life can be a nice way to reaffirm all your feelings for the pet. Get together as a family and encourage discussion about the death. Having children draw pictures and write stories and poems can help them articulate their feelings. This way you all can remember your pet anytime you wish by opening the book.

People ask me "How will I know when it is time?" and I always tell them: "Love them, care for them, and when the pain is greater than the comfort, you'll know. Trust yourself, you'll know." You will, if you can keep the animal the priority. With Beau, I knew the cancer had spread. He was such a dignified dog. I could not stand him suffering or the loss of dignity his rapid physical decline guaranteed. When I found out he was ill, I took a month off from work. For two weeks we played on the beach, for two more weeks we roamed through the mountains. These were his two favorite places. And at the end of those weeks, I took him to die.

It is hard to let go sometimes. You can carry the pet in and out, medicate him several times a day, but at a certain point, his quality of life will be gone. Once his life is more pain than pleasure, it is time to go.

Your vet will help you through it. You can be in with the dog or not. Choose what makes you feel most comfortable. It's no good being there if you're going to get very upset before the fact. Do not let your dog's last feelings be of worry and concern. Support him to the last. Praise him as the needle slips in. Weep when it is over.

The actual drug takes only seconds to work. It is painless and quick. When Fawnie went, she bobbed her head once like a sleepy child, then slowly lay down on the table. Afterward there can be body twitches, reflexive gasping for breath, and tremors. These are the body letting go; the dog feels nothing at that point, he is dead.

It has taken me years to really be ready for another dog. Some of you will want another pet right away, some of you will not want one for a while, and some of you may never want one again. All these reactions are normal. Don't let other people tell you how to grieve. Respect your own way. It is right for you.

My beloved Beau. Strange, I don't have many pictures of him. I wish I did. Do yourself a favor, shoot a few rolls today. You will enjoy them in years to come.

Special Training for the Special Dog

I've worked with all kinds of dogs, including some very special ones: dogs with disabilities. These animals, owned always by extraordinary people willing to go the extra mile, can be trained, given a few tailored techniques.

Deafness

Deaf dogs are not all that uncommon. I see several a year, usually Dalmatians. One sure sign of a hearing problem is a dog that doesn't greet you at the door when you come home. If he gets excited when he sees you but isn't at the door, he's got a hearing problem. If you suspect a hearing problem, have the dog checked by your vet. Sometimes there are things you can do.

Regardless of how well-behaved your deaf dog becomes, he can *never* be let off lead unless it is in a fenced area. If these dogs get distracted, and they can, they can disappear out of sight in a few seconds.

Teaching these dogs basic commands involves two things: using hand signals and getting their attention. Because they are deaf, they tend to be visually sensitive—meaning they are distracted by everything that moves—so start training in an area with few distractions, where you are the most exciting thing happening.

Using the hand signals taught in the earlier chapters, teach the commands in exactly the same way: signal, placement, petting. Use grand gestures, arms open wide, clapping to show your pleasure. I shake my finger at the dog to signal disapproval. Since deaf dogs have a difficult time focusing, food reward is a must at first. Then, as he improves, wean him off of treats.

Indoors, I have used stamping my foot as a recall signal. The deaf dog can feel the vibration and learn to look for you when he does. You will need to develop a signal for "OK." Choose one and stick to it, he'll learn it quickly.

Some dogs look like they might have special needs but don't. Miss Slick is a Chinese Crested, they are not supposed to have any hair.

Blindness

Blind dogs are considerably easier to work with than deaf. They tend to want to stick close to their owners, and respond well to verbal instructions. Obviously, skip the hand signals for these dogs. The biggest challenge your blind dog has is getting around. If you are not a neat and tidy person by nature, become one for your dog. It is frightening for them to run into things that weren't there yesterday—like your briefcase. Also, don't shift the furniture around. Using a mildly scented spray, like a deodorant, and *lightly* spraying the sides of the doorways, legs of the furniture, and steps can give your dog a path to follow in the house. Keep in mind that your dog's nose is much more sensitive than yours. Use a mild spray. Use it as lightly as possible. If you can barely smell it, your dog can smell it from two rooms away. Go easy.

When teaching "Let's go," you will have to be absolutely consistent about your footwork and where you expect this dog to be. You will also have to be thoughtful about where you are walking. Pause and tell him "Stairs" when you come to some, "Curb" when you come to one; he'll quickly learn what you mean. The more you let him know what's coming, the more he will trust you and follow you willingly.

Amputees

Dogs that are missing a leg require no special techniques other than a healthy dose of common sense. Leg stumps can be sensitive, so place him gently on to a soft surface when you start the "Down." Don't be led to believe that he is slow or clumsy because of his loss. If he can chase a squirrel, he can keep up with you in "Let's go." If he can sit on a dime for a treat, he can do so with equal speed without one. Watch him as he moves freely about the house, then judge his responsiveness against that. Keep up the praise. Dogs compensate for this kind of injury amazingly well.

Frequently Asked Questions

My dog gets up on the furniture when I leave the house. Can I stop this?

Successfully stopping this is difficult because furniture is comfortable, it smells like you, and your dog likes both those qualities. The only way to get him off and keep him off your furniture is to make the furniture unpleasant to be on. Here's a couple of things you can try: Blow up a balloon and pop it in his face. Do this without apology or comment. This is supposed to be unpleasant! Then blow up several and tape them to the furniture he gets up on. If the balloon

A young Piper enjoys an afternoon nap on the living room couch. Sighthounds enjoy their comfort, climbing up onto the soft spots shamelessly. We got him a comfortable bed, then taught him to stay off our furniture.

doesn't impress him, put a layer of newspaper over the seat. Then slip a few old-fashioned snap-type mouse traps under the newspaper and tape down the paper. The traps will go off like little land mines when he climbs up, but because they are under the paper, he won't get pinched.

All of a sudden my dog doesn't want to get in the elevator. Why?

If your dog has gotten a toenail or foot pinched in the space between the car and the floor or his tail caught in the door, he'll get frightened of the elevator. Unfortunately, if he's an apartment dog, this is not optional for him. Be nice and happy. When the elevator doors open, tell him "Let's go" in a confident manner and go. If you hesitate, he surely will. It's largely a matter of physics.

My dog barks nonstop at anyone with a cane or crutch. It's so embarrassing; help!

It's embarrassing but understandable. Dogs bark at things that are unfamiliar to them. Get hold of a cane and use it around the house. Let your dog sniff it. For one week only play games with him when you pick up the crutch. That will quickly change his opinion.

Teaching him the "Say hello" command will help. It gives you a clear way to signal him that all is well.

When we're in the car, my dog tries to attack the people at the tollbooths. I try to get through as fast as I can, but how can I control this?

Put him on lead in back, with the lead running up front; down him when you come to a tollbooth. Tell him "Stop it" if he continues to bark, and give a lead correction if you need to. Use lots of praise when he settles. A quick shake of a shake can works to quiet some dogs.

When my husband and I hug, my dog tries to get between us. At first we thought it was cute, now it's obnoxious. Why does he do this and what can we do to stop it?

This is not a good sign. Leave a lead on him and tell him "Off" when he jumps on you; correct him if you need to. Praise him moderately when he complies, then ignore him. Set up the situation by hugging a lot. A dirty job, but somebody has to do it!

My dog loves to unpot the houseplants. Is there any way I can stop this?

Use a thick coating of ground black pepper on top of the soil to deter investigations. Bitter Apple makes a product just for plants. You can also blow up a balloon, pop it right in your dog's face, then tape a few balloons on the pot and the plant itself.

Thanks for Joining Me

I want to thank you for spending your time reading my book. I hope it helps your understanding of your dog's actions and gives you helpful ideas about how to direct your dog's behavior. Dogs are incredibly adaptable. Once they know what you want, they are usually only too happy to oblige.

Dog training is my life. I have met my first wife, my fianceé, my best friends, and thousands of individuals, both canine and human, through my work. The people that seek out my help are caring people who want what is best for their pets. People with those qualities are a pleasure to work with and know.

I've worked everywhere— from villas in Rome to yachts in the Caribbean. No other profession could have given me the opportunities this one has offered. I am always learning something new about dogs and people and feel incredibly lucky to be living a life that gives me so much pleasure. It is never boring. A life of continued learning is a gift.

I know how much the dogs in my life have meant to me, so I can well imagine what yours mean to you. Enjoy them. Pay close attention; your dog will tell you more than I ever can about what he needs, likes and understands.

Happy training!

The End

Photo Credits

Many people volunteered themselves, their dogs, their precious photographs and their time to this book. To all of you, I thank you. Specifically, I thank: Mr. Jim Kalett, friend, client, photographer extraordinaire; Mr. Paul Kunkel, whose many hours and fine sense of timing added greatly to the photos in this book; Susan Hoke, for graciously lending us a wide range of photos; Chris Pellicano (aka Aunt Christine—dog-sitter and cat lover), for your generosity; Tim and Amy Berkowitz, our deep appreciation; Beverly Sholofsky, thanks, I know this made you nervous; Toni, Linda, Tamar, Marc and Diedre, you were all great and your help was invaluable; Chester, Beau, Caras, Tri, Ruby, Piper, Matisse, Porterhouse, Topaz, Chutney, Dakota, Tina, Lawrence, Libby, Julia, Deacon, Flynn, Max, Kesl, Sasha, Rose, Sirius, Duncan, Zach, Jim, Ike, Casey, Jake, Eclair, Muffy, Jessie, Lacy, Cajun, Chelsea, Molly, Dudley, Blackie, Scooter, Lady and the many other wonderful dogs who modeled for this book.

Index